ALL

SHIPS

FOLLOW

ME

ALL SHIPS FOLLOW ME

A FAMILY MEMOIR OF
WAR ACROSS THREE CONTINENTS

MIEKE EERKENS

PICADOR   NEW YORK

This book is based on many interviews with the people who survived these events, as well as research in various archives, diaries, articles, letters, and other material. Memory and history are subjective, and any work of literary nonfiction has an element of subjectivity as well. I have done my best to adhere to the truth as I and my sources believe it to be throughout this book, based on the information I have. However, there may be details others might interpret or have experienced differently. In addition, in places I have filled in minor sensory details of scenes, grounded in the historical material available to me, in the service of narrative interest.

picadorusa.com • instagram.com/picador
twitter.com/picadorusa • facebook.com/picadorusa

Picador® is a U.S. registered trademark and is used by Macmillan Publishing Group, LLC, under license from Pan Books Limited.

For book club information, please visit facebook.com/picadorbookclub or email marketing@picadorusa.com.

Designed by Devan Norman

The Library of Congress Cataloging-in-Publication Data is available upon request.

ISBN 978-1-250-11779-3 (hardcover)
ISBN 978-1-250-11781-6 (ebook)

Our books may be purchased in bulk for promotional, educational, or business use. Please contact your local bookseller or the Macmillan Corporate and Premium Sales Department at 1-800-221-7945, extension 5442, or by email at MacmillanSpecialMarkets@macmillan.com.

First Edition: April 2019

10 9 8 7 6 5 4 3 2 1

For my parents, Jeff and Else; the survivors of war;

and all the ships that follow them.

The past is never where you think you left it.

—KATHERINE ANNE PORTER

CONTENTS

PART I: FATHER

PART II: MOTHER

PART III: COMING TOGETHER

A BRIEF WORLD WAR II TIME LINE RELEVANT TO THE NETHERLANDS AND THE DUTCH EAST INDIES

May 10-14, 1940: Germany, under Adolf Hitler's Nazi regime, invades the Netherlands with a blitzkrieg that destroys the Rotterdam city center. The Dutch royal family flees to the U.K.

May 15, 1940: The Netherlands surrenders to Germany, and falls under German occupation. Only the Dutch NSB (Nationaal-Socialistische Beweging: the national socialist party), headed by Anton Mussert, is allowed to stay active as long as the party allies itself with the Nazi regime.

1941-1945: Mass deportation of Dutch Jews to Nazi death camps, most via Camp Westerbork in the Netherlands. Out of approximately 140,000 members of the Netherlands' Jewish population, over 100,000 are killed in the Holocaust.

December 7, 1941: Japan attacks Pearl Harbor, Hawaii, in a preemptive strike to prevent the American fleet from interfering with its invasion of American, British, and Dutch territories in the Pacific including the Philippines, Guam, Singapore, Malaya, and Hong Kong. Their plans to conquer the Dutch East Indies are made clear, so the Netherlands declares war on Japan preemptively and begins to prepare. As Japan successfully invades each neighboring country, the people of the Dutch East Indies know they are one step closer to being invaded. With the Allied forces occupied in Europe fighting the Nazis, there is very little defense.

February 27, 1942: Japan begins its assault on the Dutch East Indies with the Battle of the Java Sea. This battle lasts only a few days, with the Royal Dutch Indies Army going into the battle assured of their own defeat.

March 8, 1942: The Dutch surrender to Japan in the Dutch East Indies. Dutch, European, and other Western civilians (including some British and Australian residents) are rounded up, registered, and sent to hundreds of internment camps throughout the islands, where they remain for the remainder of the war. Indonesian civilians are allowed to remain free. An estimated 30 percent of the POWs die in the camps, due mainly to starvation, with untreated bacterial diseases and officer brutality also contributing factors.

September 5, 1944: Mad Tuesday in the Netherlands. As the Allied forces move up from the south after D-day, the Dutch people erroneously believe they are about to be liberated, and begin celebrating. Many Nazi collaborators flee to Germany. Operation Market Garden, an attempt by the Allied forces to control the bridges and end the occupation of the Netherlands, fails disastrously, and the war continues.

November 1944–May 1945: The Dutch Hunger Winter. The Germans cut off food and supplies to the northern part of the country during one of the coldest winters on record. Over 4 million Dutch people are affected, and 18,000 citizens starve to death.

May 8, 1945: Germany surrenders, bringing World War II to an end in the Netherlands. Immediately, Hatchet Day, a period during which vigilante justice is carried out on collaborators, begins. Collaborators, members of the NSB party, and girls who have had relationships with German soldiers are rounded up and sent to internment camps to await trial for treason.

July 26, 1945: In the Potsdam Declaration, the United States, the U.K., and China demand that Japan surrender immediately or face "prompt and utter destruction." This declaration is ignored by Japan.

August 6, 1945: The United States drops an atomic bomb on Hiroshima, Japan. President Harry S. Truman threatens Japan with "a rain of ruin from the air, the like of which has never been seen on this earth" if they do not surrender.

August 9, 1945: The United States drops a second atomic bomb on Nagasaki, Japan, again demanding Japan's immediate surrender.

August 15, 1945: Japan announces that it will surrender. In the Dutch East Indies, the Red Cross drops leaflets into the camps, announcing the end of the war. However, prisoners are advised to stay in their camps, as Japan's notice of impending capitulation has triggered the uprising of an Indonesian independence movement. Indonesian rebels immediately begin fighting to prevent the country from reverting to Dutch colonial government control.

August 17, 1945: Indonesian nationalist groups, led by Sukarno, proclaim independence from the Netherlands. Dutch military forces turn from fighting the Japanese to fighting the Indonesian nationalists. Ironically, the Japanese soldiers who are awaiting official surrender in the Dutch East Indies are now enlisted to protect Dutch citizens and their own camp prisoners from rebel attacks by the Indonesian nationalist fighters. Still, many Dutch prisoners who have survived the Japanese internment camps, unaware of the dangerous political situation, do not get protection in time and leave their camps, only to be murdered by Indonesian rebels. Likewise, thousands of mixed-race Indos who have spent the war outside the camps are killed during this Bersiap period.

September 2, 1945: The Japanese officially sign a capitulation declaration, ending World War II. With the danger from the volatile war for independence in Indonesia, Dutch citizens there are immediately put on Red Cross ships and sent to various repatriation camps in places like Australia and Ceylon (Sri Lanka) to await further travel to the Netherlands. Most of these people never return to Indonesia.

December 27, 1949: After years of fighting in which many Indonesian people are killed, the Dutch government officially recognizes Indonesia as an independent country, and the Dutch East Indies as a colony of the Netherlands formally ceases to exist.

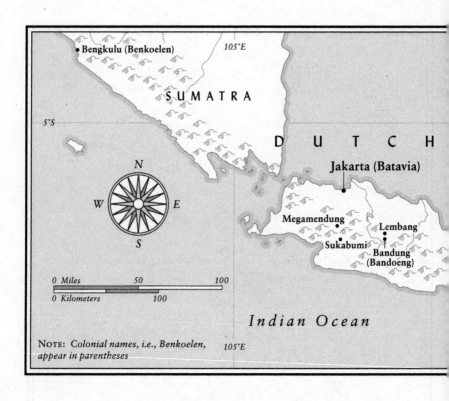

NOTE: *Colonial names, i.e., Benkoelen,*
appear in parentheses

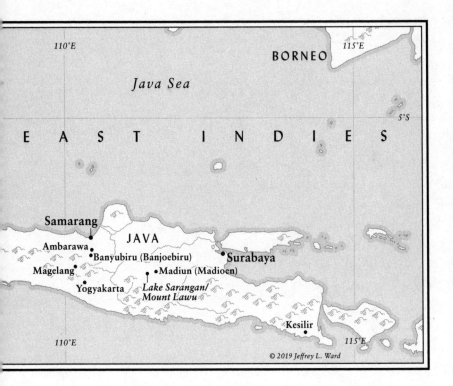

© 2019 Jeffrey L. Ward

PREFACE

My father was in a Japanese internment camp as a child. My mother's parents were arrested as suspected Nazi collaborators. These are facts. Also facts: My father was part of an oppressive colonial system. My mother was put in an orphanage, and her parents were tortured.

Growing up in the United States with the authoritative voice of history books and media, I absorbed an interpretation of war that adhered to a bifurcated world of absolutes. On one side, a medal pinned to the chest of a proud soldier. On the other, an officer in handcuffs. I learned about winners and losers, justice and evil, glory and shame. I learned that there are victims who have a right to their victimhood and others who have not earned the right to complain. It's a stringent voice of judgment to reckon with. But the more I hear my parents' stories and see how their war experiences influenced the people they became and how I was raised, the more I understand that war injures without prejudice. It injures participants and bystanders and all the people who come after them. Inherited trauma. Like a pileup on a foggy freeway, each car slamming into the car in front of it, war injures generations down the line who haven't a clue what started the chain reaction in that fog behind them but feel the impact and find themselves skidding off the road too.

World War II is an ever-present specter in my family. Beneath everything, there exists a silent backstory that my father has seen some kind of hell that I will never be able to tenant sufficiently to understand him. I know he was in a Japanese concentration camp in the Dutch East Indies, but what does that mean to me as I try to navigate a relationship with this difficult man sitting before me? When I was growing up, whenever my father did something strange or infuriating, my mother muttered, "That's his camp syndrome." For years I didn't know exactly what that meant, but we accepted it and understood that he was entitled to his character quirks and flaws.

My Nazi-allied maternal grandfather crept more silently in the family. I didn't even know he was there for many years, though I sensed a presence I couldn't explain and a sadness in my mother that couldn't be comforted. We always knew about my father's war trauma, but we never talked about my mother's experiences as a little girl in the Nazi-occupied Netherlands. I was a teenager when I learned that my mother's parents had been arrested after the war and that my mother had spent time in a children's home. But it wasn't until I was an adult that I learned about the conditions there, and about the struggles of her family as they attempted to reconstruct their lives as the subjects of seething cultural hatred. My mother felt she didn't deserve to claim her pain about the war the way my father was permitted his "camp syndrome." It was always something to keep secret because I think at her core, she believed maybe she deserved it.

I want to know why she lost her own sense of self-esteem and right to take up space in the world. I believe the reasons are connected to the war. But now, as I uncover more facts, how do I process them? Raised watching Holocaust films, visiting the Anne Frank museum, listening to my friend's grandmother talk to my elementary school class, the crude black numbers tattooed on her aging skin held up as an edict, what do I do now with the growing knowledge that all of that wickedness is also partly my heritage?

In a strange twist of irony, the more our parents bury their own trauma, their own grief over a lost childhood and a fragmented family, the more it bubbles up in me, my sister, and my brother—their offspring. But we can't name it. Unlike them, we have no tangible anchor for our sense of loss. Groping in the dark for memories we don't have, we can't quite explain why we have increasing difficulty parting with old magazines or T-shirts with yellow stains, what makes us withdraw from or cling to love neurotically, why we lie awake with anxiety as we run through an endless list of all the things that could possibly go wrong tomorrow and all the things we might lose. We can't tell you why we imbue food with a power beyond its purpose and starve ourselves or binge compulsively. But we learned some of these behaviors from our parents, and they learned them somewhere to protect themselves. Some of us can ignore our questions, quelled by all-encompassing explanations like "camp syndrome" and "survivor's guilt." And some of us, driven to give those terms a more comprehensive definition, hoping to fill in the blanks of our own gaping heritage, go looking for the past.

PART I

FATHER

In the midst of winter,
I found there was,
within me,
an invincible summer.

—ALBERT CAMUS

1

SELAMAT DATANG DI INDONESIA

Java Sea, Indonesia, December 2014

Humming above the warm equatorial waters of the Java Sea, a small commuter plane approaches the island of Java, Indonesia. Inside the plane, my eighty-three-year-old father hunches over the O of his window as the misted island comes into view after thirty hours of travel. He has grown quiet, his aging eyes focused on the world below as the plane drops altitude and the palm trees rise through the steam to meet us. I crane my neck to look over his shoulder while the Central Java city of Semarang fills the window. We have come here together, a journey of return for him, a journey of discovery for me.

Nearly seven decades earlier, my father stood on that soil below us, a skeletal fourteen-year-old kid in a loincloth who hadn't seen his parents in years, watching an Allied military plane appear in a halo of sun to announce that the war was over and he would live. He had spent two years in a men's forced-labor camp by that time, separated from his parents and siblings. In the country of his birth below, my father helped carry his friends out of that internment camp in bamboo coffins. He hallucinated during malarial fevers, and chewed banana leaves to settle the effects of dysentery. He tried to sleep on his stomach as the blood from a whip's lashes formed into itchy scabs on his back. Sixty-nine years earlier, in that place below, my father was a kid who had nothing left, watching the news fall from that plane in a shower of tiny papers, like so many butterflies descending from the sky: *To All Allied Prisoners of War: The Japanese Forces Have Surrendered Unconditionally and the War Is Over. Stay in your camp until you get further orders from us.* Deus ex machina. He was saved. Over a third of his camp's approximately fifteen hundred inhabitants had died of starvation and disease by that point. Standing in the center yard of his camp, my father raised his arms to his rescuers and lived to bring me into the world three decades later. And now he and I will stand together on that same ground.

The country we are approaching is my father's memory, but it has been my mythology. On the other side of the planet, in a suburb of Los Angeles, my siblings and I grew up with muddled identities as the children of Dutch immigrants. We returned to Holland every summer to stay connected to our roots, and lived in hyphenation as Dutch-Americans. Yet there was always a third cultural layer complicating our heritage, one that we had less access to. Like a relative who had mysteriously died prior to my birth and was never spoken of, the ghost of Indonesia silently filled our home with inherited relics: carved furniture and batik pillows, Bahasa words mixed into our English and Dutch, *nasi* and *bami goreng* fragrant with Indonesian spices on the dinner table.

Despite its significant presence in my life, I have never set foot in Indonesia until now. I've spent months planning this visit with my parents, mapping out a trajectory that will take us to the sites of my father's childhood.

We approach our starting point. We secure our tray tables. Flight attendants strap themselves in. Wheels touch asphalt. I look at my father, his hair an unkempt cloud of white, his hands spotted with age. He's stronger and more persistent in life than men with half his years, a scientist who still works diligently toward a breakthrough in his laser isotope separation process for hours every day in the hopes of revolutionizing the world with safer and more efficient carbon-free energy. But there's no denying that he's moving into the twilight of his life. This may be his first and last visit to his home country. It's a moment that takes hold of me in its poignancy. My heart rises into my throat. As the flight attendants take their places at the exit, we gather our belongings and prepare to disembark for a two-week journey through my father's past. I hope to find answers. I hope to connect to my father's war, and to better understand his wounds. I hope to find images to fill the empty spaces in my history.

Selamat datang di Semarang. Thank you for flying with us. Welcome to Java. Enjoy your stay.

In the arrivals terminal, my father's duct-taped suitcase appears between the sleek spinner bags on the conveyer belt, and we pull its frayed heft from the belt in a team effort. It's an unwieldy 1980s suitcase without wheels that he insists is still "perfectly good," crammed full of sweaters and jeans that he won't be able to use in this heat but brings along "just in case." He also has two pairs of busted shoes he has brought along because he heard that they can be resoled inexpensively here. My mind momentarily flashes on a vision of the 1940s suitcase that my father took when leaving this country after the war, packed with the relative lightness of all of his worldly possessions at that time. I eye my dad's double plastic bag, aka his carry-on luggage. "Maybe we can get you a duffel bag for that stuff while we're here, Pop." He grumbles, but the plastic handles have already ripped from the weight of everything he's crammed into the bag, so even he concedes to this necessity. I place my hand on his back. "Don't worry. It's a good thing. It will be much easier to carry."

A downpour begins as we emerge from the airport to meet our driver, Joko, with whom we have exchanged emails in the past months at the suggestion of my father's younger brother, who has also made this journey of nostalgia through Java. Joko is a fixer who has driven hundreds of former Dutch colonial residents and their children around the country. He speaks a bit of Dutch and English, and knows all the Dutch colonial sites of interest. Joko-from-the-internet is finally revealed to us outside the Semarang airport as a middle-aged, mustached man wearing a striped polo shirt, a pair of khaki pants, and sandals. Joko stands at the exit smoking a cigarette with another man. He holds a sign that displays our last name, ready to drive us through this most populated island of Indonesia for two weeks, all the way from the north of Central Java, through the interior of the island, to Western Java. It's a reverse journey of my father's youth here, starting with the last city where he lived as a prisoner of war, passing through the places he lived and spent time in as a child, and ending in the city of his birth, Jakarta.

We run through the hammering rain and ankle-high water to Joko's white van, and help him load the suitcases before ducking into the dry cab. After fifteen minutes, while we're still sitting in the heavy traffic leaving the airport, the shower clears to blue sky. This pattern repeats itself several times during the day as we nudge up against the beginning of the rainy season in Indonesia. Between these short explosions of heavy rain, the tropical sun beats down to steam us into sticky, flushed messes in the ninety-degree heat. Or at least, it does so to my mother and me. My father, having been raised here, is entirely unbothered by the heat. In fact, he seems to enjoy it as he downs bottles of cold mango nectar, a favorite childhood treat. While my mother and I mutter *Jesus, so hot* and fan our flushed faces uselessly, my dad, like Joko, literally doesn't break a sweat.

The locals seem to handle the erratic nature of the weather here with calm indifference. They haul their birdcages, bananas, puppets, or whatever wares they are selling to and from the side of the road multiple times a day, crank parasols up and down, and never complain. In a downpour, the throng of scooters in the road arches around deep puddles en masse, never ceasing its momentum. I watch from inside our van, relieved to surrender control to Joko, who navigates the swarming traffic with nonchalance. It's a beautiful dance for which everyone but I seems to know the choreography. Amazed, I witness a man beside us calmly maneuver his tiny scooter through heavy rain and flooded potholes. A clear plastic tarp contraption covers him, a baby sitting on his handlebars, the bag-laden wife sitting behind him, and a standing toddler sandwiched between them. They are like a monsoon circus act, performing death-defying feats as they fly through this chaos of an Indonesian city. My father is fixated on the scooters. "Wow! My God! Mieke, take a photo of all those scooters waiting at the traffic light!" he exclaims. "We never had this when I lived here! All of our roads weren't even paved yet back then."

By the time my father was born, the Dutch had already been in Indonesia for centuries, and an enormous amount of infrastructure had been built. The Dutch had maintained a foothold in the country since the late sixteenth century with the spice trade. They dominated the trade route via the United

East India Company, known in the Netherlands by its Dutch initials, VOC. The company—which imported nutmeg, pepper, cloves, and cinnamon, as well as coffee, tea, cocoa, sugar, and tobacco, from all over Asia, but particularly from Indonesia—was hugely profitable for the Netherlands. For that reason, the Dutch government granted the United East India Company the rights to protect their commercial interests by waging war, taking over territory, and creating massive stone fortresses in the areas of production to protect the stolen land. For two hundred years, Dutch people working for the VOC infiltrated the Indonesian archipelago, expanding operations onto more islands, establishing plantations. However, on December 31, 1799, the VOC dissolved, and the Dutch government, reluctant to cede the territory back to Indonesia, took control over these areas in Java, Sumatra, and a number of Indonesia's seventeen thousand smaller islands. More Dutch moved to Indonesia to start plantations and farms. The British seized control for five years, until the Dutch took the regions back in 1816. For decades, there was fighting with the British as the Netherlands conquered territory, including northern Bali and Lombok. Finally, around 1900, the entirety of Indonesia officially fell under Dutch colonial rule.

As the longest-held regions, Java and Sumatra had existed under colonial rule for 130 years by the time my father was born. Generations of Dutch families occupied sprawling plantation homes across the landscape, and Dutch society was firmly established within the colonial territory, with Dutch architecture, Dutch imports, and the Dutch language appearing alongside the Indonesian language on signs. Streets often had Dutch names, and the people even walked around in wooden shoes. This was mixed with Indonesian culture, with horse-drawn *dokars* and cycled *becaks* in the streets and Indonesian foods on every Dutch household's table. Into this culture, my father was born.

We waste no time immersing ourselves in my father's history. Jet-lagged and overwhelmed, we visit the Kalibanteng cemetery, maintained by the Dutch government for its war dead, on our very first day. This memorial cemetery is one of the last strips of land in postcolonial Indonesia that the Netherlands government still manages. Logically and emotionally, it may not be a great plan to visit it as a first destination. The visit constitutes a plunge into the smoldering remains of the war before we've even traced the buildup, similar to entering a theater during the final scene of *Hamlet*. This cemetery was created solely for civilian victims in the Semarang region during the war, and it is only one of many war cemeteries throughout the country, but even so, I am astonished by its size: thirty-one hundred people are buried here out of approximately thirty thousand Dutch civilian casualties, many of them women and children who died in the Japanese internment camps established for the Dutch in the area.

These dead were people who lived in this former colony of the Netherlands, some descended from hundreds of years of family history. These were not soldiers, who lay in other cemeteries. Nor were they all wealthy plantation owners, as one may imagine colonial inhabitants. These colonists were teachers and bus drivers and chefs. They were musicians and clockmakers and housepainters. They were twelve and they were seventy and they were twenty-five. They danced the Charleston and took their kids fishing on the weekend. They rode the train and did math homework and read bedtime stories. What they all had in common, from teacher to bank owner, was being herded into internment camps in the spring of 1942 by the Japanese forces that occupied the country during World War II.

Joko rings the buzzer at the huge wrought-iron gate spanned across the entrance, then drives down a short driveway. Joko is familiar with this place. He drives many Dutch people to these same monuments each year, former inhabitants or, more often lately, their surviving kin, on a similar mission of finding the past. Inside the cemetery gates, we are met by kind Indonesian employees with bottles of cold water. They invite us to sit down on the shaded patio, where we sign the guest log under the syrupy diplomatic smiles of the Dutch royal family, who look out at the cemetery from inside a frame hanging on the wall.

The clipped grass, a brilliant, unmarred green, stretches as far as I can see, dotted with white crosses. The cemetery employees give us parasols to protect us from the dogged sun. One of them is assigned to escort us through the cemetery. He looks up the number of my father's "aunt" in a massive book, and walks us down a long path to her grave marker. "Aunt Lien," one of my grandmother's best friends, died in the camps two months before the end of the war, and in her final days, she asked my grandmother to take care of her two children. I have read the account my grandmother wrote about this death in her secret camp journal, comprised of letters to her husband that were saved until their reunion at the end of the war:

*It is Sunday today. I just visited Lien. She is very ill.
It looks like she is ready to give up the fight. My sister
Ko is looking after her children, as I was recently quite*

ill myself and not so strong anymore . . . If only some food and medicine would come!

April 13, 1945. *Lien passed away in the night, at 11:30. I visited and sat by her bed in the afternoon. She was short of breath but eating and drinking a little better than the day before. At 11 p.m. in the night I was called. Lien was already unconscious and died quietly a little later. Her troubles are all over now. But she was so young. I cannot write much more about it.*

We stand quietly, staring down at the white cross that now represents Aunt Lien, just one in a row among hundreds of rows, neatly hammered into the shorn green grass. What is there to say now? We gather awkwardly around her grave, perhaps the only people who have ever done so. I'm not even sure if her bones are under there. I presume they were exhumed along with all the other bones in the camp graves when the war ended and moved here in a massive unidentified jumble. But were they? I realize that I don't know where Aunt Lien's body actually lies. There may be only dirt in this grave.

Our cemetery escort waits for us at a distance, and I walk past the rows, reading the names of the deceased. The separate area of smaller crosses for the children who died in the camps moves me the most, followed by the sole Jewish star, which catches my eye amid the acres of crosses. The irony of a Dutch Jew escaping the Holocaust by living in Indonesia, only to be interned in a camp and killed by the Japanese, sends chills up the back of my neck. There is also a section of Islamic tablets marking the graves of Indonesian-Dutch Muslims, those whose families merged with the Dutch families over centuries of colonialist communities, those who allied themselves with the Dutch. I had not expected to see these tablets, carved to resemble the tops of mosques. It complicates the narrative of colonialism and history. I appreciate that it muddles conceptions.

My mother has brought the ashes of a friend's recently deceased husband, Jongk, whose mother's grave happens to be in this cemetery. Jongk's mother died one day before the liberation of the camps. He was a young boy at the time, and had been in Holland on vacation when the Japanese invaded Indonesia; he never saw his mother again. Escorted by the man with the big book, we find his mother's grave. My mother produces a ziplock bag, carried from California inside a sock in her luggage, and sprinkles Jongk's ashes over his mother's grave while I videotape so Jongk's wife can see that he finally made it back to his mother. This too feels anticlimactic. It's breathlessly still in the moments that follow, and we wander quietly back to the path under the cover of our parasols.

I recognize in that moment what is so disquieting about this place, besides the obvious presence of the war and the specter of death. Ironically, it's that there's no sign of life in this cemetery. In cemeteries in Holland or the United States, people stroll the pathways, lay flowers, visit the graves of those they love. Car tires roll slowly over gravel. Lawn mowers buzz. There is movement, the signs of involvement, people engaged in the pursuit of remembering. Here, the stagnation is palpable. In the yawning green vastness of this meticulously groomed memorial cemetery, under the spotlight of the sun, we are the only visitors.

We walk to the end of the cemetery to see the monuments. There, I am surprised to find the original bronze statue of a miniature replica that sits on the mantel in my parents' house in California. It is called *The Patjoler*, named after the boys who went into the fields to do farmwork for the Japanese officers every day. The life-size statue depicts an emaciated boy in a loincloth with a hoe (*patjol*) over his shoulder. The plaque dedicates the statue to the boys imprisoned in my father's camp, all of them *patjolers*. My mother and I swallow our tears, but my father is stoic. "Pop, did you know this was here?" I ask him. "Oh sure," he says. This fits with the father I have always known, the father who responded to family deaths with quiet contemplation and pragmatism, who responded to every sobbing tragedy I had growing up with "It will get better, sweetheart; you just have to keep trying" and a pat on the back, regardless of the circumstances. Still, I don't believe he isn't moved. I know emotion is threatening just below the surface. I suspect he learned during the war to shut down his feelings. This man was once a boy who watched a friend die from grief in the internment camp, who learned that the boys who cried were punished by the Japanese officers, who had strict beliefs about men and emotion. I make my father stand next to the statue and take his photograph as he smiles uncomfortably.

My emotion is enough for us both. Walking back to the car past row after row of white crosses in this deserted place, I am moved in a way I haven't been before when hearing stories about the war or reading statistics back in the United States. Seeing markers for the dead here is overwhelming and makes the war real to me. Mothers, fathers, children, aunts, uncles. Their graves are still here in Indonesia, reduced to rows of white sticks in the middle of an oblivious city that has moved on, out of context in a place that doesn't exist anymore, thousands of miles from their families.

—

Bengkulu, Sumatra, Dutch East Indies, 1933

"Doctor Eerkens!" Two men my grandfather recognizes from the village hurry up the banana tree–lined drive to his grand colonial home. A hornbill in a tree is startled by the men and takes wing with a shriek. The peacocks in the garden fan their tails and high-step toward the visitors. My grandfather, Dr. Jozef Eerkens, stands on the porch in his linen suit, squinting, wondering what the trouble might be this time.

Having studied in the Netherlands during the 1920s, my grandfather has been assigned as the doctor to the Bengkulu area during his period of service to the Dutch military to work off his medical school costs, just as his father did before him in the Dutch East Indies. Now he is back in the country of his birth, stationed in this coastal jungle region of Sumatra, to service the health needs of the province. It has become quite clear to my grandfather by this point that to many of the rural inhabitants, "doctor" is a catchall term. The garden features adopted geese and peacocks that were left on his doorstep. A few weeks earlier, an orphaned sun bear cub had been brought to him after its mother was killed in a hunting expedition. Reluctantly, my grandfather took the cub in, and my grandmother began to bottle-feed it. Now, as the men rush up the driveway, the bear cub sleeps in my father Sjeffie's playpen on the porch.

Jozef Jr., or Sjeffie, pronounced "Sheffie," is a two-year-old archetypal Dutch boy with white-blond hair and blue eyes, dressed in a nautical bobby suit typical of the era. He is carried onto the porch by his *babu*, who is curious about the commotion. The nanny sets my father down in his play-pen with the bear cub, which wakes and ambles over. It begins climbing on my father, who laughs in delight at his playmate's antics. The men reach the porch and hold out a bundle of blankets to my grandfather. "Doctor Eerkens, you must help it." A mewling can be heard from within. My grandfather unwraps the bundle. Inside is a Sumatran tiger. A tiny version, to be sure, but yes, it is definitely a tiger. "No, no. I am not an animal doctor," he tells the men, but it's of no use.

The relief has already settled into their faces. They explain that the cub's mother killed two people in the village, so they shot her because a tiger with a taste of human blood will keep returning to kill again. They noticed afterward that the mother was nursing, and have brought her cub to my grandfather to raise, just like the bear cub. My grandmother, a plump and pleasant schoolteacher, emerges onto the veranda. She takes the tiger cub in her arms. Hungry and frightened, it cries. She sets it down in the playpen as she goes inside for a bottle, and my father is beside himself with glee at this development. Months later, my father will run through the garden with this same tiger, now grown to the size of a small dog. When the tiger grows too large to live safely with the family, it is sent to a zoo in the Netherlands, a sort of reverse colonization, but it dies from stress in a crate on a ship somewhere in the middle of the journey on the roiling sea.

My father and his siblings are doted on in this culture, and their early childhood is as idyllic and privileged as a childhood can get, the most colonial of colonial stereotypes. In old black-and-white family films, my father rides around in a cart being pulled by a goat, his face lit up with laughter.

A house staff member dressed in a white Nehru jacket leads the goat around the tropical garden. Later in the film, this man serves the children drinks from a tray.

Every family in the Dutch East Indies has many household employees, and my father's family is no different. At the head of the staff is the *djongos*, the house manager, who oversees all the other staff. He lives at the house with the family, in the servants' quarters. There are also two babus who live there, the head babu and the assistant babu, who do the washing and cleaning and watch the children. The rest of the servants have their own homes and come in to work. The *kokkie*, or cook, prepares the evening meals. To manage the lush, flowered grounds, there is a *kebon*, or gardener, and his assistant. Some of the staff become close with the family. For example, Suwardjo, their djongos, chooses to move with them each time my grandfather is relocated to a new city. Yet despite the appearance of harmony in this whole system, there are undercurrents of tension between the staff and their employers. When my father plays in the garden, the teenage assistant to the gardener sometimes is tasked with watching him, and corners him under the trumpet flower trees. "You better behave, *totok*," he hisses. Totok is the word for "white person," and it's clear to Sjeffie that the gardener's assistant doesn't mean it in a friendly way. "I might just have to kill your mother if you don't mind me." Sjeffie avoids the assistant kebon as much as he can thereafter, racing for the safety of the house or hiding behind the babu's skirts when he sees the boy approach. But he doesn't tell the adults.

My grandfather has a stately car, a sleek black Terraplane, and the *tjoper*, or chauffeur, drives him to make house calls, sometimes hours into the jungle. On short holidays, the family piles into the backseat and ventures into the jungles of Sumatra, where orangutans climb onto the hood and examine the intruders curiously through the windshield. On one occasion, they come to a river they must cross to continue, and travel across on a raft built out of logs, a makeshift ferry service designed by Indonesian men in the village nearby. For a fee, the Indonesian men swim the Dutch man's car across the river on the raft, their heads bobbing just above the waterline.

Like many colonial families, my grandparents often spend weekends at "the Soce," short for the Sociëteit, a social club for the upper classes in the tropics. Every city in colonial Dutch East Indies has a Soce. The members are mainly Dutch, but there are prominent Indonesians and other upper-class immigrants to Indonesia who can afford the monthly dues and are regulars at the Soce as well. They play tennis, have bridge nights, and drink *jenever*, special gin imported from the Netherlands. Sometimes they dance to the swing bands that perform there. The children usually stay home with the babus, except when they have afternoon roller-skating tournaments and puppet shows at the Soce. The women form knitting circles and gossip, and the men discuss the politics of the global depression and the rise of the Nazi party and Hitler in Germany. These people feel connected to the Netherlands, but they don't feel solely Dutch. Rather, they feel specifically Dutch-Indonesian, a different brand of Dutch, because they also talk about the treks through the jungle and hunting and coffee plantations that are part of their lives at the equator.

In 1932 and 1935, my father's sisters, Doortje and Fieneke, are born in Bengkulu, and my father revels in his new role as big brother and sole son. In the province around Bengkulu, the capital, his father is the senior government doctor. He's required to go on tours of small villages in the jungle or to Enggano, an island off the coast of Sumatra, where he holds clinics for the rural population, and he often brings little Sjeffie along.

These trips sometimes include visits to the jail in Bengkulu, and my father waits in the backseat of the car reading picture books and eating licorice while his father sees a prisoner patient. One afternoon, a warden walks by the car and sees Sjeffie. The warden raps on the roof of the car. "Little boy, why are you here? Have you been naughty? Are they putting you in jail?" He pokes his fat head in the open window of the Terraplane and chuckles from under a thick mustache, exchanging an amused glance with the tjoper, who leans against the driver's-side door, fanning himself. My father's five-year-old eyes widen. His lower lip trembles. "No, sir. My daddy's the doctor and he's going to see sick prisoners and then he's coming right back." "Is that so? Well, are you sure you're a good boy? If you aren't a good boy, we might just have to put you in jail." The warden's eyes twinkle with amusement, but the joke is lost on my father. He starts to cry. And he refuses to accompany his father to the jail ever again.

Every four years, medical doctors working for the colonial Dutch government are given six months of paid furlough between appointments that take them to different communities in the Dutch East Indies, so in 1936, when my father is almost five, the family uses my grandfather's furlough to visit the Netherlands. They sail for a month on a huge passenger ship via the Suez Canal to the "old country," the motherland. My father is introduced to many relatives, including his grandparents, for the first time. His grandparents moved to the Netherlands from the Dutch East Indies before my father's birth, and they are thrilled to meet their grandchildren.

The family spends four months in the Netherlands. In the

fall, as my five-year-old father witnesses his first red hues of fall and feels the first crisp breeze ever on his bronzed skin, the family journeys back to the perpetual summer of the tropical Dutch East Indies, where my grandfather is transferred to the city of Semarang, on the island of Java. He is appointed co-director of a large hospital there, and the family moves into a spacious house next to the hospital. Sjeffie thrills at the news that he'll finally get to go to school. "I'll learn how to do my numbers and letters now," he announces proudly. "I'm going to learn how to read."

—

Semarang, Indonesia, 2014

Joko points to an old colonial building as we pass it. Its art deco architecture stands out, and at my request, he pulls over near the former colonial center of the city so we can walk around. I have particularly been badgering him about finding the "Hotel Jansen," which I have seen referenced in the diaries of boys interned in my father's former prison camp at the Netherlands Institute for War Documentation in Amsterdam, where I read their words, sifting through dozens of folders and boxes. The boys write of how it's a thrill to be taken with an officer out of the camp to the stately hotel on errands. I have searched online for old photographs of Hotel Jansen. Joko says he thinks it was torn down a few years ago, but I can't believe that the grand hotel, a spectacular example of colonial architecture and an important landmark of Semarang, would simply be demolished. Joko's lack of enthusiasm about the destination of the "Old Town" I've been so excited to check out also doesn't register with me, initially. After months of looking at antique photographs of pristine colonial city centers, with their wide roads and breathtaking buildings, each more ornate than the last, I naively expect to find Old Town Semarang's architecture preserved as it was.

I read about *tempo doeloe* everywhere on Indonesian websites, and even see restaurants with this name, specifically referencing the colonial era in a nostalgic way as "the olden times." I expect the colonial buildings to have new functions in a modern, postcolonial Indonesia. I imagine they will be preserved as historically significant. I'm shocked to discover that this is not so at all, and that most Indonesian people I meet display little knowledge of the colonial era, especially the younger generation. At landmark after landmark, when people ask why we are taking photos and I explain the colonial history of a specific place, many of them express surprise.

As we navigate through what is left of the Old Town, a decidedly conflicted relationship with *tempo doeloe* becomes evident in what appears to be the complete abandonment of Semarang's former center of colonial life. There is not even a sidewalk, so we are forced to walk in the street, scooters and cars spitting exhaust in our faces as they rush past, just inches from us. I discover that with the exception of the spectacular railway station, still in use, and a couple of landmarks, most of the historic colonial buildings have not been preserved at all.

Some buildings still feature the faint imprints of their former colonial names, and their former grandeur is evident in their arched windows, tall double doors, and art deco embellishments, but they've almost all fallen into disrepair in Old Town Semarang. Plaster chips off their facades, and ivy creeps its leafy tentacles over everything, emerging from cracked windows. Roofs are caved in, red clay tiles dangling from the holes. Graffiti is scrawled across the art nouveau tiles lining doorways, and the pungent scent of urine emanates from the buildings. I have the unsettling feeling that I am perilously close to being colonialist myself in my thoughts about the neglect of these relics of my ancestry. It's a feeling I won't be able to shake for the rest of our trip. A feeling I know intellectually is problematic but that persists. A disappointment. A loss. A willful discarding of generations of heritage. Oddly, my father seems pragmatic in his response to seeing his heritage become a decaying ghost town. "It's a shame, because these are well-built buildings, but I guess they just can't afford the upkeep," he says, missing the point, or perhaps wanting to miss the point. "The modern world takes over. This is how life is." The immediacy of his acceptance of circumstance is remarkable. It's a big difference between my father and me. My father is endlessly adaptable, focused on utility over sentimentality, relentlessly forward-looking, while I cannot stop looking back.

In the afternoon, Joko takes us to my father's old neighborhood, and we search for his former house. What was once a village-like neighborhood is now filled in with concrete buildings, so my father does not recognize anything. "These were all fields," he says, "and the homes all had huge gardens." Now the neighborhood around the hospital is packed tightly with apartment buildings and small homes. Here and there, we find colonial homes, but they have little gardens, and it appears they've been subdivided multiple times for urban infill. The hospital too has expanded—right over my father's former house, which no longer exists.

While most of the hospital consists of newer architecture, the old hospital still stands as a separate wing, its colonial shutters and red clay roof tiles a distinctive feature. My father remembers visiting his father here, and I attempt to film him talking about his memories in the lobby of the old wing, but almost immediately, an armed guard in a military-like uniform appears and places his hand over my camera. "No photo," he says, scowling. I try to explain the purpose of our visit, ask what his concern is, but he just repeats, "No photo," wagging his finger at me. We leave the building, and he follows us out, hand resting on the butt of his machine gun, watching until we have left the parking lot.

The church my father attended as a boy still exists, adjacent to the hospital. While the hill it sits on is no longer covered in *alang-alang* grass, the church itself is unchanged. I try to envision this hill as it was, but I struggle to reconcile the image with this urban environment. We hike up the church's driveway and walk the perimeter, which is now covered in asphalt. The tall wooden doors are locked, and there doesn't seem to be anyone around. We are about to leave when a man appears from around a corner—the pastor. He shakes our hands and invites us inside, considerably more friendly than the hospital employees next door. The wooden pews are the same as they were in my father's day. He would have sat on these benches as a small boy, bored and fidgeting, thinking of the snakes he was going to trap later that afternoon. The thought is somewhat surreal, as though this structure was stuck in a time warp while the city around it grew and my father aged and built a life thousands of miles away.

"*Ayah . . . hampir . . . ummmm . . . dibakar . . . di sini,*" I attempt lamely, using the English-Bahasa word translator I've loaded on my computer tablet to attempt to communicate in Indonesian. The pastor looks puzzled. "Dad almost burned here," I've just told him. He shakes his head. I give up and switch to English. "Hello. My father almost burned this church down."

—

Semarang, Dutch East Indies, 1937

The tall grass flows like water, in gentle waves across the field. It is hot, very hot, the humid kind of heat that pricks your scalp and gets underneath your clothes until the stickiness itches under your arms, behind your knees, in the crease of your neck. It's especially bad if you are a fair-skinned Euro, a colonial white boy, a *totok*. Sjeffie stands on the hill above his house in khaki Bermuda shorts, his blond hair and crisp white socks contrasting with his tanned skin in the tropical sun. He's now six years old, curious and determined. The German neighbor boy, Friedl, stands beside him, swishing a bamboo rod back and forth through the grass. Friedl looks more like the local Indonesian kids than my father does. His mother is black, a Dutch woman from the South American colony Suriname. She works as a doctor in the hospital with Sjeffie's father. Friedl's white German father is an accountant. The crickets hum, and the boys are bored. They've caught and released *chichaks* for hours but have now grown tired of trapping the small geckos. Friedl's eyes light up. "Hey, Sjeffie, let's play cowboy and Indian." The boys have read about cowboys and Indians in their comic books. They know that in America, there are cowboys and Indians everywhere you look. "OK! I get to be the Indian!" my father says enthusiastically. But Friedl wants to be the Indian too, so soon they are just playing Indians. My father says, "OK, but listen, if we're Indians, we have to make a campfire for smoke signals." Everybody knows that Indians are constantly making smoke signals.

Friedl gathers twigs and grass and makes a pile. The boys crouch in the Indo sword grass, the alang-alang that towers and sways over their heads and blocks out the searing sun. My father lights the pile with matches he's swiped from the kitchen. The twigs catch, and the fire crackles. The boys dance and whoop around the fire. But the grasses dip down in the breeze, and the fire licks at their edges. Soon the flames move up their blades. Blade to blade, the fire grows, moving outward. My father stamps at it, but it is spreading too fast. Friedl gets scared and runs home to his parents, but my father stays, stamping furiously as he watches the fire march farther up the hill toward the church at the top. In a panic, he sees that he cannot stop it. He is too little. He is just one boy, helpless against the advancing flames.

Thankfully, the fire department is already on its way. The firemen spray the flames with water and save the church, though it's blackened on one side wall. Sjeffie is overcome with gratitude for his rescue. But when he comes home, the mood is decidedly different. There is no gratitude; my father is grounded for many weeks by his father. Bungawati, his babu, scolds him in both Dutch and Bahasa Indonesian. He's a naughty boy! How could he be so careless? "*Stout*, Sjeffie. *Anak bandel!*"

Luckily, Sjeffie is now six and is going to school, where he can't burn anything down. He has to sit on a chair and listen to the teacher. In school, my father learns to read and write letters and numbers. He goes to the Bible school, so the students have to sing and pray to Jesus at the beginning of each day. The school is integrated with Indonesians, Dutch, and Indos, the mixed Dutch and Indonesian kids.

My grandmother, meanwhile, has been growing round again. She lets my father and his two little sisters put their hands on her taut belly. "Your baby brother or sister is in there," she says. "Are you children ready for that?" They nod enthusiastically. When baby Kees is born a few weeks later, my father is ecstatic that he is no longer the only boy in the family. As Sjeffie sits on the carved wood settee in the family room, his mother lifts Kees from his bassinet and places him on Sjeffie's lap. "Hold on to him," she says, and she and the babu smile as my father grips his little brother nervously, kissing his downy head. *"Ati-ati,"* says the babu. "Careful with the baby."

When baby Kees is two and my father is in the second grade, my grandfather is transferred to a new hospital and given the position of director. Tearfully, the family says good-bye to the neighbors, and to the household staff who won't be coming with them. They pack up the house and move five hours south, from coastal Semarang to the center of Java and a city called Madiun. There they settle beneath the massive volcano Mount Lawu, which rises green and lush from the landscape, its crown disappearing ten thousand feet into the clouds.

2

INFAMY AND INVASION

Sarangan, Indonesia, 2014

Hot magma from the earth's core forces Mount Lawu perpetually higher into the Javan skyline. Joko winds his white van up the slope of its base, lime-green rice terraces flanking the road. As we move from sea level into the sky, the thick heat dissipates into expansive, cooler air. We've been sweating for days in the city's humidity, and I understand why my father's family vacationed here in his youth. It's a welcome respite. Joko has promised to take us to an old colonial hotel overlooking the lake, the same hotel where my father's family took their meals when he was a child. We've all been looking forward to this stop as a highlight of the trip. My father recalls childhood days of swimming, rowing on the lake, family walks.

"Black panthers here," says Joko, waving his hand toward the dense foliage.

"Really?" I ask, scanning the tops of the trees for yellow eyes. But a Google search reveals the critically endangered status of the animal. A relic of an era long past. As is their historical nature, humans have hunted them and taken their habitat for themselves. It's not likely that many people will see a wild black panther on Java before these animals are declared extinct. Still, my eyes flit from branch to branch as we pass the forest. I continue to look for something I know isn't there.

The hotel, much hyped by Joko on the drive as a colonial beauty, is utterly depressing to me. It immediately becomes clear that it hasn't been maintained at all. Joko pulls up and greets the owners warmly. They smile and clap their hands to one another's shoulders, offer one another cigarettes. Joko leaves us in the lobby and vanishes into the night to visit friends in the village; he will reemerge in the morning as he usually does. The grand salon, once the center of colonial social life in this area, is vast and empty, with cracked and torn mismatched couches, folding card tables with plastic patio chairs in the dining area. I imagine it as it once must have been, upscale and filled with people eating at teak tables, a chandelier overhead perhaps, a piano in the corner, then almost immediately I feel ashamed of my romanticization of the colonial era. The owners of this hotel don't have the money to replicate such opulence. I'm being a snob. But then my sense of aesthetics is again triggered and I lament that the good bones of the building are being neglected. I flop onto a couch in the cavernous lobby, irritated with battling internal voices, all of which feel patronizing and ugly, no matter what side they argue. *Ugh. I'm a colonist.* The only other guests in the hotel appear to be a French couple holding their cell phones in the air on the couch opposite, who immediately tell me there is no hot water and the Wi-Fi doesn't work. "Forget it. No signal in this place," says the man, standing and walking to different positions in the room with his phone outstretched before him. I get the key and walk to my room. A gray industrial rug repaired with duct tape at its frayed edges covers a cracked tile floor. There is no shower curtain in my bathroom, and the mirror has a crack down the middle. *Stop judging. Good bones.* I step out onto the veranda, which looks down over the lake. That's nice. I imagine that in the summer, families sat on these verandas drinking coffee and reading the paper. My parents emerge from their adjacent room and we decide to walk down to the lake, since that's what we are here for.

When he sees the lake, my father's face reveals a disappointment that gnaws at my conscience. My father misses the country of his youth. This is not a condition unique to him, certainly, but I have brought him here on a journey of nostalgia. Now his memories are being overwritten as he sees firsthand that the Indonesia he once called home, that he still thinks of as a fixed part of his identity, no longer exists. This is true for anyone who returns to a place they call home decades later, but there are many more layers to my father's experience, layers that include being raised in a colonial system and ultimately ejected by force from the only home he knew, from a country of people who considered him and his family intruders. Colonial Indonesia doesn't exist anymore, and there is no going back for people like my father. As his aunt Jo, interned in a camp near Jakarta during the war, wrote bluntly in a letter to her sister during the Indonesian War of Independence, before their repatriation to the Netherlands, "Pep wrote that you are disillusioned . . . I keep thinking about that. Had you expected gratitude from the Indonesians? . . . An uncomplicated, easy life like we had in the past here we won't have again, but that's not what you meant, is it, that you had expected that and now no longer expect it?" I think the war for independence shocked many of the Dutch in Indonesia. The loss was not only of their home but also of their illusion of harmony.

Along the lakefront, where once there was only sand and grass, dozens of vendors now line the concrete shore, appealing to us as we walk. Costume jewelry, T-shirts, ball caps, bubble gum, yo-yos, pork rinds are on offer. *Good price.* There is a photo of my grandfather in a rowboat on this lake during the 1930s. He wears a conical thatched paddy hat, Bermuda shorts, and shoes with dress socks pulled up over his calves. He smiles broadly. My father and his siblings hang off the sides of the boat, likewise grinning. It's the "before" photo of my father's World War II. I don't see this carefree joy on their faces in any postwar photos.

Sarangan Lake is supposed to be the highlight of our trip. But as we sit at the card tables in the dining hall of the hotel that evening, eating a pile of underseasoned bami, it just feels entirely depressing. I question everything about this trip and feel a mixture of grief over the loss of something I never got to see, confusion about the scars of colonialism that run as an undercurrent during our entire trip, and guilt for thinking that returning to the sites of his childhood would be an amazing experience for my father rather than highlight his lack of home. When I read my father's travel notes later, however, I find the neutral tone remarkable, the disappointment I had seen on his face at the lake completely absent from his account. "We arrived at the hotel, which has a beautiful veranda that looks out over the lake," he wrote. "However, this former superior hotel appeared somewhat poorly maintained since its heyday, and we decided not to stay there longer than for one night. The next morning we left for nearby Madiun, where Mieke reserved two nights at the modern Colton Hotel." I'm consistently awed by my father's persistence in looking forward and not dwelling on circumstances. While I've inherited several of my father's characteristics, this forward-thinking agathism is a trait I haven't mastered. I dwell. I marinate in pain and try to understand it better. My father gets on with living in the present, and perhaps this is something one learns directly only through life-or-death survival, through actually having weathered a traumatic experience firsthand and putting it behind you.

—

Madiun, Dutch East Indies, 1938–1941

In 1938, Sjeffie is seven years old. His father works in the hospital on the Van Ingenluyfflaan, the broad road where the family's house stands at number 49, surrounded by a shaded garden with tropical flowers and mango trees. Papa runs the hospital with Dr. Sajidiman, the Indonesian doctor with the tall walled villa at the end of the road. Sjeffie plays with Dr. Sajidiman's boys, Dermawan and Suwarno. He loves to stand in the aviary in their garden, watching colorful birds flit from branch to branch while the parrots squawk and crack nuts with their black curved beaks. Sjeffie gets along well with Suwarno but less well with Dermawan. After playing in the garden until they are sticky with grime, the boys are told by Mrs. Sajidiman to wash up for supper, and they pour cool water from the basin over their hands with the pitcher in the *mandi kamer*, the tiled washroom. They scrub under their armpits with washcloths. Dermawan enters the mandi room with a grin and his hands behind his back. "Sjeffie!" he calls out. Sjeffie turns, and as he does so, a brown missile is propelled at his bare chest. It bounces off him and falls to the floor. A turd. Dermawan laughs hysterically and runs from the mandi. Repulsed, Sjeffie scrubs at his chest with soap and water and holds back his tears. "You'll be in trouble with Father!" Suwarno yells after Dermawan. Sjeffie towels off and sniffs. "I'm going home," he says, swallowing hard. "So go home, totok!" Dermawan yells. *Totok*. White boy.

Sjeffie is excited to start "real" school again in Madiun. Time to learn big-boy things. In the fall, he enters second grade, where he will get to practice writing and learn the way that numbers stack up and order the world around him, a thing he will love religiously for the rest of his life. An *ayam* lays one egg per day. How many eggs does it lay in a week if there are seven days in one week? There are twenty *mangas* on a manga tree. If you pick two mangas every day, how many days until the tree has no more mangas? This math is a beautiful thing underlying everything. The school is only a couple of blocks from his house, and he is allowed to ride his bicycle there. Like every proper Dutch child, he has mastered the art of cycling by the age of five, and now he pedals his little legs, still rounded with baby fat, to and from the First Government School, where most of the Dutch and mixed-race Indo children go to school. Indonesian children who speak Dutch also attend the First Government School, as the lessons are taught in Dutch. Next door is the Second Government School, where the same lessons are taught to Indonesian kids in Malay, otherwise known as Bahasa Indonesian.

In his true forward-thinking character, Sjeffie thinks it is about time to find himself a girlfriend. There are two contenders. The first is Ingrid, a pale, serious girl with long black hair and dark, intense eyes, and the other is Dieneke, the blond, wholesome daughter of the local pastor. Ingrid quickly knocks Dieneke out of the running when she tells Sjeffie that she is actually a Russian princess whose parents fled to

Indonesia via China to escape the Bolsheviks during the revolution. This may or may not be true, but either way, she's more interesting than Dieneke to Sjeffie.

When he gets older, Sjeffie sometimes bikes across town with Piet Kreijger, his classmate, to Piet's home near the sugar plantation. Piet's father works for the sugar plantation, so they get to live in one of the small wooden bungalows across the street from the giant processing factory where the sugarcane is transformed into crystal, to be stirred into the tea and coffee that originally brought the Dutch to Indonesia four hundred years earlier via the United East India Company. Sjeffie and Piet and the other boys whose parents work for the sugar plantation play hide-and-seek in the tall sugarcane. They break off stalks and chew the sweet ends into a pulp as they crouch down amid the cicada hum, waiting to be found.

—

Madiun, Indonesia, 2014

Joko pulls over in front of the sugarcane fields at the edge of Madiun, still there after all these years, growing with the seasons as they've grown since the seventeenth century, impervious to their boys becoming men, to war, to the papers that indicate who owns or no longer owns them. My father and I walk to the edge of the fields. "When the sugarcane got higher than it is now, it towered over our heads, and nobody could see us. You could get lost inside a sugarcane field," he says. I think this is the impulse of all young boys around the world, seeking out the spaces beyond reach, building their forts, the places they can hide from the eyes of others.

Madiun is a playground to my father in the 1930s. The spaces are open, and there are trees to climb.

My father and I walk toward the former sugar refinery. It is now abandoned, but the old mill is still in the open clearing of the factory, and I take a photo of the massive machine. Seeming to appear from nowhere, two men in uniforms materialize. They wag their fingers, speak sharply to me in Bahasa. I lower my camera. Joko, who has been leaning against his van and smoking, wanders over with a frown on his face and begins to speak with them, becoming increasingly loud. They yell at one another using words I cannot understand. My parents and I hurry to the van and get in. Eventually, Joko storms back to the car, calling things back to the men over his shoulder. We drive on. Joko stares straight ahead without speaking as I take photos of the small cottages where the sugar mill workers lived. I don't dare to get out of the car again, so I take photos through the open window.

"What did you say to those men back there?" I finally ask Joko, a little afraid of the response.

"I told them they are stupid," he says angrily. "You are trying to see this part of your father's home. You just want to take a picture. So stupid, these men." He waves his hand in their direction, shaking his head with irritation. But I know there is more.

I have been afraid of encountering anti-Dutch attitudes, and everywhere we go, I feel the anxiety of representing the face of hundreds of years of colonial ancestors to an entire population of Indonesians. I don't know how to negotiate this history that was never my choice, never my father's choice as someone born into it. While I understand the anger and resentment, I am grateful for the generous attitudes of Indonesians like Joko, who seem to make up the vast majority of the people we meet. To be shut out of one's nostalgia so deliberately seems terribly sad, though my father says nothing about it. I wonder how much of my sensitivity to this inherent tension is generational, though. I'm not even sure if my father understands the roots of these little conflicts we encounter, if he can inhabit a space where he understands why a totok is sometimes still resented or can feel himself to be an interloper. I am not even sure I want him to, given how he loved this place and how much he's already lost. He doesn't have the required emotional distance to take on the recalibration of his own history, the idea that perhaps the people he thought were his friends and neighbors didn't love his being there the way he loved being there as a little boy. Maybe that's my job as the next generation.

Joko pulls to the side of the road when my father says, "Piet lived in one of these two houses." Through the open window, I quickly snap photos of both cottages, the paint flaking off their sides, photos that will be sent to my father's childhood friend, who has never returned to Indonesia himself.

While Joko navigates us through the streets of Madiun, my father clicks back into his childhood momentarily as we near his old house and he suddenly recalls the route to school on his bicycle. Despite the vast changes to the neighborhood and its concrete makeover, he remembers each turn perfectly, instructing Joko and leaning forward to peer through the windshield excitedly. "Right here. Yes, left at that next cross street. Down this little road." Memory, even when it has slipped into the darkest corners of the mind, imprints and emerges, unfolding like a map. Each street is seamlessly connected by the senses. We pull up in front of a low pale green building.

"Yes! This is it! The First Government School. It's the same as it was!" We climb out of the van and walk along the fence in front of the school. Children in uniforms are in the yard. They spot us and wave. "Hello! Hello!" they call, all smiles. A man sitting on a motorbike in the front scowls at us pointedly. The younger generation inside the school are surprised and excited to see our faces in their city, one rarely visited by Western tourists. They clamor at the fence, calling to us in the words they've learned from English class. They beckon us in, and we walk to the entrance, where school staff members emerge from the front office with bottles of water for us. They smile and chatter in Bahasa Indonesian while my father, whose Bahasa returns more and more each day, responds with broken sentences. The English teacher is summoned. The whole school is now gathered outside the office, curious students giggling and waving at our odd group. We awkwardly wave back, sipping our water. The principal arrives with the English teacher. It turns out the English teacher doesn't speak English very well, but we manage to convey that my father went to school here as a young boy, and she translates this to the principal. He shakes my father's hand vigorously and beckons us to follow him to his office. There, my father is asked to sign a guestbook, and as if by magic, the entire faculty has appeared with cameras. The principal poses in photo after photo, waving away faculty members who want to get into the picture. Only when he has finished do the other faculty members get photos with us. The English teacher brings forward her star pupils, who converse in their best English with us one by one. I am mortified by this attention and make lame jokes to cover my discomfort. My father accepts it graciously, posing with each person. He is taken to his former classroom. He folds his eighty-three-year-old body

into the little wooden desk there, grinning at me as the children
crowd around him.

—

Madiun, Dutch East Indies, 1940

The news from the motherland is not good. At the Soce,
Sjeffie's parents huddle with other adults over a card table,
drinking jenever. They pause their games of bridge to lean
across the table and speak in low tones about the blitzkriegs
over Rotterdam, offering their opinions on the Nazi occupation. *Surely the Germans will be pushed back by the Allied
soldiers from Great Britain and Canada. Surely this kind of
inhumanity cannot stand.* But the news arrives first as rumor and then officially. After only five days of fighting, the
Dutch army surrenders to the Nazis. *The queen has vanished, I heard. No, the royal family has fled. Yes, the royal
family has fled to London, in fear for their lives. Confirmed.
Heard it on the wire. I raise. Can I get another jenever over
here? And some peanuts for the table?*

Questions swirl for weeks. Was the royal family right to
flee? Did they abandon their citizens? Was it the only way to
save their lives? Rotterdam is in flames. The charred bodies
of nine hundred people bombed in their homes, pulled from
the piles of brick, are all that is left of the inner city. Those
people didn't get a chance to flee. Those who have family in
Rotterdam worry constantly. Are their loved ones in the rubble? Late at night, the Dutch in the colonies turn the knobs
on their radios and hang on the scratchy words of the radio
announcers. News comes by boat from loved ones back in
the Netherlands, so slowly that their lives may be entirely different lives before their words even reach the Indies. Houses

may have fallen in the interim as the letters crossed the sea, doors kicked in, people pulled from their beds in the night. In the thick midafternoon drone of the tropics, with its motionless geckos pressed against the walls to keep their bodies cool, the pregnant hours of silence eat at one's nerves.

On December 7, 1941, more shocking news comes. Sjeffie sits on the floor of the living room while his parents hunch over the giant wooden radio. The reporter announces that the Japanese have bombed Pearl Harbor in Hawaii. The United States has not been involved in the war to that point, though it has cut off its oil, steel, and iron supply to Japan in an attempt to thwart Japan's intentions to invade countries in the Pacific. Japan has already run through China with a fury, and has made a pact with Germany and Italy as an Axis power for a "new world order." The ambush attack on the United States is intended to destroy most of the U.S. naval fleet in the Pacific preemptively so that Japan can carry out its plan to take over Southeast Asia. To this end, at the same time that Japan attacks the United States, it attacks strategic military targets in Hong Kong, Singapore, Thailand, and the Philippines.

The next day, December 8, the American president, Franklin D. Roosevelt, declares war on Japan. *A date which will live in infamy.* Sjeffie hears the words come through the radio and they send chills through him, though he doesn't understand what they mean. The gravity of Roosevelt's voice says it all. *Suddenly and deliberately attacked by naval and air forces of the Empire of Japan . . . American ships torpedoed . . . severe damage.* But even before the United States' own declaration, the Netherlands declares war on Japan, knowing what is coming. They have to gather what little military power they have in the Pacific, and they have to do it fast.

The Dutch East Indies readies itself to fight the Japanese. My grandfather is sent to the military base in Surabaya. As a military doctor, he was issued a gun when he enlisted, but as a physician, he barely knows how to shoot it. All military personnel, regardless of function, are now called back to base for a crash course in combat.

My grandmother does her part as well. She and other women take weekend courses to learn how to drive trucks, climbing up into the cabs in their skirts and heels. They try to ignore the implication of the need for them to take on these nontraditional jobs as their husbands attend emergency combat training. At the Soce, members deposit all of their metal items in a collection box to be melted down for the war effort.

While the adults have a period of adjustment and anticipation, Sjeffie, now ten years old, continues to go to school each day. No doubt the adults shield him and the other children from the fear that seizes them.

By now my grandmother's sisters, Jo and Ko, have both come to live in the Dutch East Indies. Aunt Jo has adjusted to the Dutch East Indies very well. She has begun a religious school with her friend, an Indonesian woman named Soeretna whom the family knows as "Aunt Soer." Unlike Ko, Jo doesn't live close to the family, though the family often spends holidays swimming in the pool near Aunt Jo's mountain cottage near Sukabumi, a lush area abutting a coffee plantation. In a remarkable stroke of bad timing, Ko has moved from Bolivia with her husband, Jan, just before the war. Jan is immediately drafted and sent to the front lines on Java. My grandmother's brother still lives in Bolivia, and has sent his eleven-year-old son to live with Aunt Ko and Uncle Jan in Java and get an education in a Dutch school like his cousins, since the war with Germany in the Netherlands has removed the option of his studying there. So Sjeffie's cousin Kees has joined Sjeffie at the Dutch school in Madiun, arriving just three months before the bombing of Pearl Harbor.

Parents are understandably anxious about sending their children to school during this period of waiting for the other shoe to drop, scanning the skies nervously, startling at every sound of a motor. What will happen to them? How can they protect their children from bombs? Sjeffie and his peers are sent to school with pots, colanders, and soup tureen helmets tied upside down on their heads with ribbons and shoelaces, some brandishing pan handles like horns, a feeble but courageous army against the Japanese. My grandfather, home for the weekend before returning to the base in Surabaya, gives Sjeffie a rare military gas mask, something that fills my father with pride. He wears it to school, blinking at his classmates from inside it like a goldfish in a bowl.

At school, workmen furiously dig three long trenches in front of the building to serve as bomb shelters. The teacher tells the students that they will practice air raid drills as soon as the shelters are completed, lining up and climbing into the trenches. So when the air sirens go off one afternoon, Sjeffie assumes it is their first drill. But as they crouch in the shelter with their pot and pan helmets clanging against one another, the situation becomes clear. The sound is distant but unmistakable: airplanes. It's not a drill. Sjeffie and his classmates hunker down. The teacher shouts, "Heads down, children! Stay down!" Then the first Japanese bombers fly over them with a swelling, all-encompassing roar that fills every space, their black widow undersides marked with the red dot of the Japanese flag. The children look up as the shadows pass over their faces. The planes strafe the airfield nearby, killing the military fathers of several of Sjeffie's schoolmates while they crouch beside him in the trench in front of the school, listening to the thundering rage of war and their teacher crying.

It is the end of something, or it is the beginning of something. This is the liminal moment between before and after for these children and my father, who haven't known to feel fear before now. Their worlds begin to tilt.

For a month, a battle rages between the Allied forces and the Japanese, mainly in Surabaya and naval battles off the coast. My grandfather and Ko's husband, Jan, are at the front near the base in Surabaya, and the rest of the family waits tensely for updates. My grandmother turns on the radio every night to get the news, transmitted by the Nederlands-Indische Radio Omroep Maatschappij, NIROM (Netherlands-Indies Radio News Agency). They hear about the tremendous battle in the Java Sea, the last line of defense for the Allied forces in holding back the Japanese troops. The Japanese forces have twenty-eight well-equipped ships to the Allies' fourteen cobbled together from Dutch, U.S., U.K., and Australian navy forces. The British, Australian, and American navies have suffered losses in other battles and are reluctant to call in more forces. The Japanese have jammed the radio frequencies, and because of stormy weather, nighttime air assaults on their ships aren't possible. The Dutch navy must decide whether to move forward with such a small fleet. They know the Japanese are unbeatable. But to do nothing means an assured invasion of Java. Thousands of Dutch and Indonesian citizens wait on the mainland, bellies knotted with fear, hoping for a miracle as news of the battle reaches them. During my research, I come across an interview with Theo Doorman, son of the Dutch naval commander, Karel Doorman, whose name is still on street signs and memorial plaques in the Netherlands. Theo Doorman recalls his father putting him and his mother on an evacuation plane headed for Australia right before the historic battle.

"Did your father know how bad it was? Did he know he would die?" the interviewer asks.

"Yes. I think he knew he would never see us again," says the son.

The crackling last words of naval commander Karel Doorman are announced through the radio on February 27, 1942, as my father, whose youthful faith in heroes is strong, listens. Doorman's words to his men, transmitted as his ship heads out to meet the Japanese fleet, have gone down in Dutch history as some of the most noted because they represent persistence and unwavering bravery even in unwinnable circumstances: "All ships follow me." They are brave and stupidly perseverant words spoken in the face of terrible odds, words that are repeated in the homes of thousands, including the home of a little boy who desperately wants his home to stay safe and needs a hero.

When my father tells me this story back in the United States, to my shock, he begins to weep, breaking down at Doorman's famous words, "All ships follow me." I can count the times I have seen my father cry on one hand. He does not cry while standing in his former concentration camp. He does not cry while describing his friends dying or being beaten by the Japanese soldiers. But my father cannot speak Karel Doorman's final words without his voice cracking, even after several tellings. It happens again at Thanksgiving dinner as he tells the story to my sister's husband. He can't get that sentence out, and clears his throat repeatedly, drinking water and shaking his head. This famous line, which represents absolute commitment and stubborn determination to many, makes my usually stoic father emotional because he has internalized it as part of his character, perhaps as a result of this moment of hope that Doorman provided to a terrified child and nation.

I finally ask my dad, who isn't comfortable talking about his feelings, why this Karel Doorman story and those last words, "All ships follow me," make him so emotional. "Doorman was willing to keep fighting for what he believed was right," he says. "He sacrificed his life to defend us. Same with the soldiers who tried to liberate us and lost their lives in the process. I believe in fighting for what's right, even if the odds are against you, even if you can't imagine how you'll overcome the obstacles. You fight until the death."

"Do you think Doorman affected your own character?" I ask. "Did you try to be like that yourself in life?"

"Well, yes, I tried. If I believe in something, I believe you keep going. You never give up."

On a symbolic level, Doorman is who my father forced himself to be for the rest of his life, the spirit animal that got a little boy through the war to adulthood. My father never admits defeat. He won't admit when things are broken or impossible, ramming square pegs into round holes with remarkable determination. It can be maddening. But when I hear about Doorman, I also understand why my father feels like he has to be that man.

I read the rest of the story about his hero. After seven hours of battle, the Allies lost six of their ships. Admiral Karel Doorman's ship was struck by a Japanese torpedo and heavily damaged, with many casualties. Heavy fire from Japanese Zeroes prevented any possibility for rescue. Despite being initially uninjured in the attack, Doorman stayed on board with his injured and dying men for the full hour and a half that it took for the vessel to sink, choosing to die be-side the other twenty-three hundred men who lost their lives in the battle. A few days later, Japanese troops stormed the beaches on the island of Java.

—

Java, Dutch East Indies, March 1942

Like ants descending on a dying bird, the soldiers stream out of boats and planes into the cities and villages of Java between February 28 and March 1, 1942. Occupation, inva-sion. They ride on bicycles, pedaling in formation, row after row, rifles and bayonets angled across their backs, some with guns strapped to the handles of their bicycles like mini tur-rets. Behind the bicycles are tanks and jeeps and trucks, flowing over the landscape in every direction.

The fighting is furious and bloody, but short-lived. The KNIL (Koninklijk Nederlands Indisch Leger, the Royal Dutch Indies Army) is vastly outnumbered and lacks the weaponry of the Japanese. Back in Madiun, Aunt Ko paces the floor, knowing that her husband, Jan, who has no mili-tary experience outside of his few days of training, has been sent to the front to fight. The following day, a message ar-rives: *We regret to inform you.* Jan was mowed down in gun-fire on the front lines almost immediately as the Japanese came ashore. Ko is inconsolable. Cousin Kees and Sjeffie and his younger siblings watch with wide eyes as she sobs with wild animal sounds into my grandmother's neck. The im-mensity of this is almost too much for the children to take in.

Back at the military airfield in Surabaya, the Dutch Indies Army takes heavy fire. My grandfather, as a doctor, is charged with establishing medical relief in the hangar, which has been set up as a makeshift hospital. He hears the fighting from the hangar, where he receives dead and wounded bodies, organizing triage. As he and another doctor watch, a Dutch plane comes in for a landing, and the Japanese Zeroes chase it. The plane, on fire and skidding down the runway, billows smoke as the Japanese fighters pull up and turn to come back for another strafing run. The top of the Dutch plane pops open, and a bleeding airman emerges into the smoke. He climbs clumsily out of the cockpit, falling to the runway below.

The Japanese fighters are now heading back, low. The Dutch pilot tries to get to his feet, but he is injured, and he falls back down. Like a target, he lies there, grasping at the air with his hands. The Zeroes are getting close. My grandfather and the other doctor look at each other. Then they run. Dragging the pilot by the arms, they pull him into the hangar as the bullets hit the tarmac around them and the Japanese fighters turn for a third run, the Dutch plane now completely engulfed in flames. After the war, my grandfather will receive the Bronze Cross for this act.

The Dutch East Indies surrenders ten days later, on March 9. Those left standing hurry home to their families as quickly as they can, before the handover of power to the Japanese forces takes place. Over everyone's head hangs the question: How will the Japanese govern them?

In Surabaya, my grandfather arrives at the train station, desperate to return to his family. The Japanese have ordered the trains to be halted so they can use them for their troops, and this is the last passenger train to Madiun before the transfer of power. The trip to Madiun takes hours. My grandfather insists he be allowed on board, persisting until they open the doors to him. He arrives in Madiun exhausted but relieved to be able to take his family in his arms. Uncle Jan doesn't have that option anymore, something they all are aware of as Aunt Ko sobs into my grandfather's embrace.

In a matter of a few days, like many of their colonial neighbors, the family goes from a life of very little worry, with a nanny and a chef making sure they are clothed and fed each day, to being invaded by hostile forces.

Sjeffie, ten years old, watches from behind glass as the Japanese soldiers move into Madiun on their bicycles. He has been ordered to stay inside by his parents, and is playing in the living room when he sees the soldiers begin to pass the house, their faces stern and unmoving as their legs pump beneath them. He calls out, "Mama! Mama! The Japanese are here! On bicycles! They have guns!" His mother rushes into the room. The windows rattle as a tank follows the soldiers, a Japanese gunner's head prairie-dogged out of the top.

In the center of Madiun, there are sounds of gunfire. Sjeffie sneaks out onto the road in front of the house, and in the *slokan*, the gutter running down the side of the road for the monsoon rains, he suddenly sees a number of cans bobbing along. He fishes them out. Soup, beans, condensed milk. In the center, some people have looted the stores in the chaos of invasion. When they saw two Indonesian men hanged by the Japanese troops in a square and realized that people were being searched for stolen goods, they dropped their cans into the gutters, where the rainwater now carries them to Sjeffie. The Japanese army has quickly established order and control. There will be no more resistance.

Meanwhile, Sjeffie's father rushes to his bedroom, opens his closet, and pulls his military uniform from a hanger. The boy loves seeing his father put on the uniform, with its shiny brass buttons and starched shoulders. He feels proud. His father opens a box on the bureau with a key and takes out his pistol. Sjeffie watches wide-eyed. He's never seen his father with a gun before. His father puts the gun on the uniform and rolls it all up in a ball. "Papa, what are you doing?" Sjeffie asks. His father stops and sits on the edge of the bed. "Listen carefully. If the Japanese ask, I am not in the military, OK?" The boy nods, his breath stuck in his chest. He follows his father out into the garden. His father walks quickly to the well. He dumps the whole bundle into the hole. There is a pause, then a loud splash that echoes up from the pit. His father turns and goes back to the house. Sjeffie grips the edge of the well and stares down into the black. He cannot see anything. His father's uniform and gun have vanished into the underworld.

It doesn't help. The Japanese take over government offices and have access to military records. A few weeks later, a truck rumbles up the driveway and several Japanese soldiers emerge from it. They bang loudly on the door, and then they are taking my grandfather away in a truck to a military prison. Sjeffie watches the truck growing smaller as it moves down the driveway, dust kicking up in its wake. His mother is given orders by the Japanese to vacate the house. The staff are told they no longer have jobs. My grandmother gives them some of the money she has, but the Japanese officers tell the nannies and chauffeur and cook they must move out of the house as well. It's uncertain where they will go. The djongos, Suwardjo, says he will stay near the family, though he has no work now, no income to support himself. The servants are being displaced too. Days later, Sjeffie and his remaining family, including Aunt Ko and Cousin Kees, move into a small cottage down the road with another Dutch woman and her children, while the Japanese officers are living in Sjeffie's home, eating at his table, sleeping in his bed. He wonders if they've found his secret hiding place in the attic yet, if they've discovered the trick to the loose door handle in the bathroom upstairs, if they climb his tree.

Europeans are placed under house arrest by the Japanese. Sjeffie is no longer allowed to go to his beloved school, and in Batavia (known later as Jakarta), the heads of European schools are arrested.

War doesn't mean just physical control. It means psychological control, and psychological control means the control of communication. Political conversation is banned. The Dutch residents still get some news on the radio from the NIROM station, but this lasts only a short time. On March 8, the day the Dutch surrender, the announcer ends the program with "We now end our broadcasts. Farewell until better times. Long live the queen." However, for a week thereafter, three defiant radio employees continue sending short broadcasts that end with the "Wilhelmus," the Dutch national anthem. When the Japanese discover this, they behead the employees, and thereafter, any European caught listening to a radio is executed.

In Bandung, Dutch government officials are executed and their offices taken over by the Japanese. Throughout the country, the official calendar changes overnight from the year 1942 to 2602. Japanese characters replace roman numerals. All newspapers, Dutch and Indonesian, are taken over by the Japanese authorities and begin to churn out propaganda in Bahasa. The newspaper *Asia Raya* now fills the newsstands, praising the brave and powerful Japanese soldiers fighting against the weak, indecisive Allied forces. Dutch as an official language is banned. The printing or sending of any literature is halted, punishable by death.

By April 1942, the Kempeitai—Japanese military police— have begun to spread into the villages. There are executions

for people breaking the rules. All people over seventeen in
Java must register, and pay a registration fee, as well as sign
a document pledging loyalty to Japan. Europeans are charged
exponentially more than the native Indonesian population.
The Dutch are told they must pay 150 guilders (valued at
around $1,000 in today's currency) for men, 100 for women,
in exchange for "protection" for their cooperation, the implication being that others would possibly come to harm for
not paying the fee. The registration is only a means to get
the names and addresses of the residents, however, as there
is no sign of any unique protection if one pays the registration fee. Ultimately, the police begin making deals with un-
registered people so they can register for 1 guilder, just to get
their names and addresses down on paper.

Next door to the cottage where my father moves is an
abandoned school to which the city tows cars, perfect cars
that have been intentionally destroyed and abandoned on the
roads by their owners: long white Pierce-Arrows and convert-
ible Willys-Knights with rounded tops and shining leather upholstery. They are ridiculously gorgeous cars. There are
photographs of my grandfather sitting in one of these grand
autos, like something out of *The Great Gatsby*. In the days
before the Japanese make landfall, when the Battle of the Java
Sea is lost, family tjopers watch these fine machines they've
driven for years retreat down the palm-lined roads, carrying
their jobs with them. Then the Dutch men work together to
remove the tires, cut the gas lines, and smash the headlights
and windshields of their own cars. They know the autos will
be confiscated, and they don't want to give the Japanese any
more vehicles with which to wage war. They may be conquered, but they will not aid the Japanese war effort.

Sjeffie and the other kids in the neighborhood sneak into
the schoolyard and scavenge any remaining parts of the cars.

They open the hoods and discover remnants of gasoline in the glass reservoirs, which they siphon through a bamboo shoot into coffee cans. They decide to make a fire with it, dousing auto upholstery and gathering sticks. They pour the gasoline over the pile, then set it on fire. Still boys, even in war. It explodes into flames, larger and more ferocious than they had anticipated. They turn and run home to their mothers.

The Japanese are perplexed and angered by the behavior of Dutch children like Sjeffie, still playing outside after the invasion. They have strict codes of respect, and these children do not seem to understand this. The Japanese insist that the Europeans should "behave more like conquered people." A formal decree is drawn up and posted. No more roller-skating, to begin with.

ANNOUNCEMENT 20 APRIL 1942

The mayor of Batavia informs you: Due to complaints received from the Nippon authorities about the annoyance caused by roller-skaters, the mayor of Batavia must forbid any roller-skating traffic in the vicinity of buildings where the Japanese authorities live and on public roads. If there is no halt to the roller-skating traffic, more severe controls will be enforced.

Other rules are printed and distributed as well.

ANNOUNCEMENT

On orders from the Nippon government to all Europeans, It is expected of all European residents that as members of a conquered group, you will show respect to Dai Nippon, especially the Nippon military.

The following rules should be observed:

- *Don't come outside unless you have no other choice.*
- *Rules must be followed if you do find yourself in public. Specifically, in restaurants, cafes, and other public spaces loudness is not permitted and you may not cause a disturbance.*
- *Anywhere outside, at any time of day, you must display to Nippon military—regardless of their rank—a display of respect by bowing.*
- *To avoid severe disciplinary measures, the Nippon authorities expect a strict adherence to above-named rules.*
- *European women are expected to dress themselves decently. Clothing such as long pants, which is an imitation of men's clothing, may no longer be worn, given that this is in opposition to Eastern mores.*

I find this ban on roller-skating and the Japanese regime's insistence on respect from the losing side illuminating about the particular harshness of life under Japanese military occupation in the years that follow, because it speaks to an underlying philosophy about roles. Knowing one's place seems to matter a lot to the occupying forces. The social roles of conquerors and the conquered are self-explanatory and obvious to them, so they are baffled when they encounter a culture where adherence to the rules is not second nature. In this way, the dynamic of an invading force conquering a colonial population that is itself an occupying force and used to being in a power position creates an extra layer of hostility from both sides.

Sjeffie doesn't live in the cottage very long—two months. Then the Japanese officers come to take the women and children away, like the men before them. Before they arrive, my grandmother gives her most important possessions to the Indonesian Dr. Sajidiman for safekeeping, a foresight that means our family has photographs and films of the family's life before the war, unlike so many other families who leave everything behind with the naive belief that they'll be returning to untouched homes after this bit of trouble blows over. My grandmother does keep a few special family photos and her jewelry, sewing it inside her clothing. She brings cans of sugar and coffee too. But most of the family's belongings must be left behind. Each of them can bring one suitcase with them. Taking a deep breath and hoping she's taken the right things, she closes the clasps and walks out of the little cottage. The officers have arrived, shouting commands. The women and children, along with hundreds of Dutch people from the region, are taken on flatbed trucks to the train station, where they are loaded onto waiting steam trains.

"I actually thought it was kind of an adventure," my dad says now about the transport. "There were a lot of families at the train station. We didn't know where they were going to take us. We had no idea it was going to be bad. But one thing I knew pretty quickly was that I didn't like the Japs very much." He always uses the term *Japs*, the term they all used then, and I always feel uncomfortable because I know this is a slur. But I don't correct him anymore because he doesn't stop. I've read how the Japanese officers would beat the prisoners if they heard them refer to the officers as *the Japs* in the camp. Yet people still did it and risked a beating, a small demonstration of defiance and disrespect toward captors who insisted on respect. I know this is stuck in my father's psyche, this term he uses solely for the Japanese forces that captured him rather than a catchall term for Japanese people. In the camps, it became the internees' way of fighting back against their own subjugation. I am not sure how possible it would be for me to uncouple the slur "Jap" and the Japanese military forces in his mind, or to insist on political correctness from my father when he is referring to the officers who insisted on his obedience in this regard. "The Japs were already swinging their whips at the train station. I made sure to stay out of their way," he says.

My father's train is going to Semarang, in Central Java. They travel all day, watching the lush green rice paddies and banana trees flow past, disappearing behind them. When they arrive in Semarang, they are loaded into trucks that take them from the station to the gates of their new home, which is surrounded by fencing and, in some places, loops of barbed wire. The gates open, and the trucks pass under the arches. Across the top is written "Lampersari." Camp Lampersari. Outside the camp, guards patrol the perimeter. The gates shut behind the new camp residents and two Japanese officers stand in front of them. The detainees are now officially prisoners of war.

3

POWs

Semarang, Indonesia, 2014

I have booked us into a hotel in the green hills above Semarang that was described as a magnificent example of a colonial hotel, thinking it would trigger some nostalgia in my father. But it becomes clear upon arrival that while the skeleton of the hotel betrays a certain former status, its flesh has wasted away over the years. Our rooms, once made grand by their high ceilings, now feel cavernous with a single dim lightbulb hanging high above our heads, dingy walls, blinds too small for their windows, and beds dwarfed by a dearth of other furniture. The following day, I book us into a skyscraping hotel in the city, with modern amenities. The tallest building in Central Java, it has a rooftop infinity pool and spectacular views across Semarang. In the evening, we go for a swim and have dinner at the elaborate gourmet buffet, overseen by three chefs.

The next morning, Joko picks us up to take us to the site of the former internment camp Lampersari, where my father was first brought with his mother and siblings. He drives two blocks, then pulls his van over. "What's wrong?" we ask. "Nothing wrong. This is Lampersari," he says. Our hotel is still in view, towering over this neighborhood. We could have walked here.

It looks like a working-class neighborhood now. Very little remains the same, outside of the narrow pedestrian lanes and slokans running down the side of them. The lanes branching off the main roads are named the same, but numbered: The Main Manggaweg and Manggaweg 1, 2, 3, 4, 5, 6; The Blimbingweg and its four offshoots. My father stands before a tiny stucco house with a tile roof on the spot of the house he once shared with several other families. These were *kampong* houses, shacks with thatched roofs, when he was here. We walk down the narrow lanes as I videotape. We find one leaning, abandoned shack that appears to be original. "This is close to how it was," my father says. Residents stare at us as we pass. A woman emerges from her house and asks why we are filming. We explain that this entire neighborhood was once a prison camp for nearly eight thousand women and children, surrounded by a fence. "Really?" she asks. She has not heard anything about it before. She shakes my father's hand.

The homes that stand in this neighborhood today are filled with people who have no knowledge of their neighborhood's dark past. It seems difficult to believe that people could not know that their homes were part of an internment camp during World War II. However, it also makes sense that the Indonesians, who fought for and won their independence from the Dutch, failed to memorialize the wartime experiences of the Dutch colonials. Everywhere we look in Indonesia, there are memorials to the Indonesian independence fighters. But aside from the memorial cemetery maintained by the Dutch government and a tiny plaque installed by Dutch visitors in one or two places, the Dutch have been erased from the war landscape entirely, as though they were never there for it at all. In some ways, for the local Indonesians, they weren't. The Japanese erected *gedek*, which literally means "coverage," to shield the Dutch prisoners from view of the Indonesian locals during the duration of the war. It was made of woven mats attached to the fencing, so the Indonesians outside the camps couldn't witness their conditions and no longer interact with the colonial Dutch who had been among them before the Japanese invasion.

The Japanese used the conflicted feelings native Indonesians had about the colonial power structure to try to gain their trust and foment solidarity with the Japanese forces. *Asia for the Asians*, they chanted. They hung posters in the shops: "Japan—Asia's Light, Asia's Protector, Asia's Leader." "Fight to rebuild Grand Asia! Be willing to suffer together with Japan!" They stoked the anti-Dutch sentiment and encouraged the indigenous Indonesian population to help them in their cause, appointing Indonesians to local governmental positions. If they could appeal to a sense of racial loyalty as Asians, they would be seen as liberators rather than invaders, at least initially. As a result, the Indos, people with mixed Dutch and Indonesian blood who were made to choose with which side they identified, often had it harder when they chose to stay outside of the camps than they did inside the camps, as anti-white rhetoric was spread and encouraged by the Japanese regime, and these people with white blood were labeled as tainted. The racism now came at mixed-family Indonesians from both sides.

—

Camp Lampersari, Semarang, Dutch East Indies, December 28, 1942

Authority in Lampersari is established immediately. As they enter the camp, some women are pulled from the line and their suitcases opened to be searched for contraband: money, Dutch or English printed material, radios, and more. Sjeffie, now eleven years old, watches wide-eyed as the Japanese officers hit mothers with their batons to make them move when they get off the trucks. They shout orders in a language none of the prisoners understand, and when these orders aren't followed, the flat ends of their sabers come down hard on whomever they happen to reach, sometime splitting flesh and drawing blood. It's a new violence for most of these children, and a cacophony of cries adds to the chaos. Luckily, Sjeffie's mother is toward the back of the group of arriving prisoners and escapes injury, though later in the year she will not be so lucky, and her children will have to watch her being beaten to the ground because she doesn't notice an officer approaching and therefore fails to bow to him in time.

In the camp, the internees cannot avoid the constant bowing to officers. Crouched in front of the houses next to tubs, arms deep in water to try to wash some of the dirt out of their few items of clothing, they must drop what they are doing and stand. As the officer passes, they must shout, "*Kiotske!*" Then they shout, "*Kere!*" and they fold at the waist to ninety degrees, hands to knees. Standing straight again, they shout, "*Naore!*" Only when the officer has passed can they go back to what they were doing.

Sjeffie and his mother and little sisters and brother are assigned to a small house on the Hoofd Manggaweg, the Main Mango Road. There are already three families living in the

two-bedroom house when they arrive, and they shrink themselves into the corners, hanging a sheet up for privacy. Soon
more women and children arrive, truckload after truckload,
and Sjeffie and his family contract their spaces repeatedly,
compressing more tightly with each new family until there
are thirty people living in the house, crammed into every
square inch. Children sleep in drawers, on and under tables,
piled in sweaty heaps in the tropical heat. Snoring bodies lie
shoulder to shoulder on mats on the floor. One toilet without running water serves all thirty of them in the house, and
it soon overflows with human waste. They try to fend off
malaria by hanging up *klamboes* over their sleeping bodies,
a necessity in the Indonesian tropics, so that the house at
night fills with ethereal clouds of hazy mosquito netting from
wall to wall. My grandmother keeps a secret diary in the
camp, penciled onto onionskin paper hidden in the pages
of her Bible. She addresses her entries to my grandfather
throughout her internment:

> I am sleeping with the boys in what was once a
> kitchen . . . The children are very sweet. Sjeffie seeks
> me out more than he used to and offers to help, though
> he sometimes falls back into old bad behavior . . . On
> February 2 the first group arrived [of the 2,000 new
> internees] . . . 860 people. Until this point, they had
> been housed in nice, large homes where they had taken
> care of themselves. There was a lot of hustling and the
> empty places streamed full. They had no sleeping rolls
> with them. Still, some of them managed to find a bed
> or sleeping roll. They have a lot of adjusting to do . . .
> Exactly a week later, the second group came. There
> were a lot of German women in that group. We got
> two kind women and five children in with us. We were

able to lend them a few things . . . It was a lot of work for the officers and very difficult to find everyone a spot. In the chapel, it is very full. Tomorrow we'll get another 250 from Soerabaya.

Like many children, Sjeffie is remarkable in his adaptability. As a fearless eleven-year-old who wants to know everything about everything, he sees this all as a great adventure. Like a hamster in a new cage, he immediately scurries around the maze of the camp to discover the parameters of his environment while his mother busies herself with practical matters, foremost being how to bathe and feed her children and maintain some sort of daily structure for them. Sjeffie's engineering proclivity is already evident, and in the first few days, while exploring his new quarters, he discovers some tubes protruding from the kitchen wall: gas lines where stoves must once have stood. He pulls off the end caps and looks into the black depth of the tubes, smells them. There is a faint whiff of gas. He sucks on the ends of the tubes, just as he had done to siphon gasoline out of cars back in Madiun. Suddenly, he gets a mouthful of gritty old water, which he spits on the floor. Water runs from the tube for a moment and then . . . a hissing sound. Natural gas. The Japanese haven't shut off the gas valves that run into the houses, they've simply filled them with water, as the main gas line also feeds their officers' quarters up the hill. Sjeffie lets out a yelp and plugs his finger in the tube to stop the gas flow. "Mama! Mamaaaa! Gas! There's gas!" The house's thirty residents crowd around. "*Verrekt!* The kid's found gas!" The implications aren't lost on them. It means they can sterilize water, cook rice and any food they find or catch, make tea and coffee. Sjeffie finds the connection hose of the stove in a cabinet and reconnects it quickly. Word spreads through the camp quickly: *A boy in the house at Manggaweg 50 knows how to hook up the gas!* Other internees begin to knock on the door and ask for Sjeffie. He sets up a little business, trading tablespoons of sugar, coffee, or tea for setting up gas service in other houses. My father. Always finding the way forward in a situation where most see only a dead end.

This survival instinct seems innate in his family. Almost immediately after they arrive in Lampersari, Aunt Ko begins covertly teaching Sjeffie, his siblings, and other boys and girls in the camp from contraband Dutch language textbooks she has smuggled in. Every day, she sets up a little schoolroom in the tiny kampong house while the others clear out and stand watch in case an officer passes and hears them. Sjeffie gets to practice his numbers again. He gets to read, sucking up the words, reading the same books again and again. In one of the houses across the road, he and some other boys have set up a little hidden library under the thatched roof, where they collect their books—Jules Verne's *Twenty Thousand Leagues Under the Sea* and *Around the World in Eighty Days*, Chris van Abkoude's *The Adventures of Pietje Bell*, Hector Malot's *Nobody's Boy*, Cervantes's *Don Quixote*, and other books with wide appeal to young boys. Most of the children or their parents have brought pencils and notepads, but very quickly they realize how scarce these things are. "Sjeffie, make sure you write small. Save room on your paper," Aunt Ko says sternly during class. Aunt Ko is very strict. She's a religious woman who does not approve of waste or idleness. Sometimes she draws on the dirt floor with a stick so she doesn't have to waste paper or pencil.

Meals during the first month in the camp are meager but sufficient. The prisoners get small portions, mostly of rice but also of some vegetables and meat in the beginning. The meat lasts only a short time. The vegetables last longer, but they too dwindle after several months. After that, all meals consist of a cup of rice or tapioca porridge twice a day, sometimes once a day. Sjeffie lines up with his mother and siblings with all the other prisoners, holding their tin cups. When they get to the front of the line, their cups are filled from giant pots that the kitchen workers have cooked the rice or porridge in. One measured portion per person. Being assigned to work in the kitchen is a coveted job because there are chances to tuck food under one's shirt, swipe a finger inside the rim of the pot when the officers look away, or sneak a second helping. But the job is dangerous; the rice or porridge is cooked over open fires in massive cauldrons, and more than once, a woman trips and is badly burned. They also have to carry the cauldrons two by two suspended on bamboo rods. One misstep and the boiling mush will sear skin clean off.

Most of the women are sent to work in the fields or to feed and care for the livestock that the Japanese are raising for themselves. A half hour's walk from the camp, at the foot of the Tjandi Hills, there are pigsties and fields that the women sow full of Japanese eggplant, broccoli, cucumbers, and tomatoes while the officers watch them. Lampersari is one of the first camps in Indonesia to be targeted for the infamous "comfort women," the women specifically selected to be raped by the Japanese officers. A recruiter is sent to Lampersari for this task. However, the women hear the rumor about what is about to happen and gather en masse to fight back. They block access and fight fiercely to protect the young mothers and teenage daughters that the Japanese officers prey upon, forcing the Japanese to abandon Lampersari as a suitable source for comfort women, not worth the trouble after repeated violent beatings only seem to strengthen the prisoners' resolve to fight back. The Japanese have set up two hundred internment camps throughout the Dutch East Indies, and prisoners at these smaller camps are easier to overpower. In Java, Lampersari and three other camps are the only ones where the prisoners fight back.

Sjeffie's inherent perseverance is his best asset in the camp. When the meals begin to dwindle and the prisoners' bellies begin to learn the gnawing twist that will become their daily reality, he patrols the narrow paths of the camp, looking for snakes, lizards, rats, or bird's nests with eggs or baby birds. Despite the lack of food, everyone drinks coffee, still rather plentiful in the Dutch East Indies. The caffeine keeps them awake as their bodies, drained of nutrients, rapidly shrink with their forced labor in the sun.

My grandmother continues to write my grandfather letters in her secret diary throughout their internment, but the worry creeps into her language as her optimism begins to wane:

Sept. 12, 1943

It has been so long since I have heard anything from you. I am going to try to write you every day . . . We all long so much to live together with you again. I'm writing this on my bed, the only place where you can be alone here.

Sept. 21, 1943

This week we've had to do roll call twice a day . . . Turned in all our books, besides Bibles . . . This is especially unfortunate for the children, especially now that the school is closed. Now they play in their fort the whole day; make masks, "bow and arrows," etc. and have scavenger hunts . . . The newspaper doesn't appear anymore since 10+/- days ago and the radio has been taken away. Now we are completely deprived of news. No news is good news, we have to believe.

A day comes when the Japanese post a notice on the bulletin board in the camp. All males over ten years old will be moved into separate barracks up the hill nearer the officers' quarters, on the other side of the Blimbing Road. The mothers furrow their brows. Why are their sons being separated from them? They aren't given a choice. After a year in the camp, Sjeffie is now twelve years old. He has to go. The boys pack their few items into their suitcases and are marched up the hill to their new quarters. Every day, Sjeffie and the other boys count off for the officers in charge of them. *Ichi, ni, san, shi, go. Roku, shichi, hachi, ku, juu.* They learn the drill quickly, because if they don't say it properly, they are whacked with a stick by John the Whacker.

The officers who guard them inside the camp quickly get Dutch nicknames. In addition to John the Whacker, the officers include Little Ko; Hockey Stick; Pretty Karl; the Bloodhound; the Easter Egg; Bucket Man; Chubby Baby; and Dick and Jane, who patrol together.

Seikon Kimura, the man known as John the Whacker, is arguably the most sadistic. He earns his nickname for the way he seems to enjoy striking internees indiscriminately, without warning. When he discovers that a woman in the camp has been hiding money, he confiscates it and punches her in the face. He kicks her in the back until she is unable to stand while her children scream. He has her carried to the center of the camp, where he makes her lay injured in the equatorial sun from morning until evening without water. After the war, the Allied war crimes tribunal will sentence him to death for his human rights violations during the war. He is convicted of "carrying out a systematic reign of terror," with witnesses at his trial describing his beating of a woman with a piece of wood until her arms broke in several places for sitting down during her work, causing a woman to go permanently deaf after being beaten for thirty minutes for smuggling cigarettes, forcing prisoners to stand in stress positions, withholding water and food, and whipping children until their flesh was in tatters, among other atrocities.

Hockey Stick earns his name from the wooden hockey stick he carries with him throughout the camp and uses to take the legs out from under a prisoner. Then he makes them stand up so he can do it again, over and over, laughing every time. The Bloodhound is more selective, but he is capable of beating people into a coma when he does lose his temper.

Sjeffie still comes down the hill for his daily lessons from Aunt Ko, during which he gets to see his mother and siblings, but when the sun sets, he has to say goodbye and return to the barracks for the older boys. One morning, he notices a boy whispering with another boy and gets curious. "What are you whispering about?" he asks. They tell him they've discovered a crack in the wall of the storage room where the Japanese officers store the bags of rice. After dark, they stick a sharpened bamboo shoot through the crack to pierce the bag leaning against that wall and siphon the rice. During the day, the boys smuggle it off the hill when they go to see their mothers, who cook it in tin cans. "You can come with us," they tell Sjeffie, "but you can't tell anyone, or we'll get in trouble."

At first, Sjeffie doesn't dare. But after he has seen the boys get away with it a couple of nights, his hunger wins out and he decides to risk it. Three other boys also learn about the secret and start siphoning rice through the hole in the wall.

Emboldened, they return to the crack repeatedly over the course of a couple of days, taking a bit more each time. The laws of physics catch up to the boys, and as they drain it, the bag starts to slump over. That's when the Japanese officers discover it.

John the Whacker and another officer enter the barracks unexpectedly, holding whips. One of them demands that the rice thieves step forward. Sjeffie's heart rises into his throat. The blood in his veins curdles. His breath freezes in his lungs. He has seen what these men do to human bodies. When nobody steps forward, John the Whacker says if nobody confesses, they are going to beat all of the boys in the barracks. The other boys start murmuring, "Confess! Don't make us all get beaten!" One of the thieves steps forward. And then, shaking, so does Sjeffie. He turns to look at the other thieves, waiting for them to step forward too. But they don't move. They know what comes next, and two sacrificial lambs seem to satisfy the officers. John the Whacker steps in front of Sjeffie, who trembles uncontrollably. He puts his face in Sjeffie's face and shouts in Japanese as the other officer translates into Bahasa. "Take your shirt off! Turn around and face the group!" Sjeffie pulls his shirt off and faces the other boys. The officer steps back. Then he begins unleashing blows on Sjeffie's back with audible cracks. Tears run down Sjeffie's face. He can feel warm blood begin to run down his back. The officer stops, and Sjeffie thinks it's over, but it isn't. The officer turns him around and whips his chest until he bleeds. Then he pushes Sjeffie back toward the other boys. The other boy is bloodied too, and the boys encircle them both.

As soon as the officers leave, Sjeffie runs. Scared, he can think of only one thing: Mama. He arrives at the Manggaweg house covered in welts and blood. But Mama isn't there. Aunt Ko is there. In ragged bursts, he tells her what happened.

But instead of comfort, he finds her Calvinistic anger. "You shouldn't have stolen! Stealing is a sin!" she scolds. "You could have been killed." As punishment for stealing, she sends him outside with a can. "Dig holes in the ground as penance," she says, not able to think of anything else. So he does. He digs holes while his blood dries in the sun, then runs again with sweat. When Sjeffie's mother returns, she finds him there, on his hands and knees, digging, and asks him what's happened. Aunt Ko appears in the doorway and explains that she's punished him for being a thief. My grandmother says, "You shouldn't have stolen. Don't do it again. But you've dug enough holes now."

This could be the gravest trauma my father suffered in the camps. Not the beating, not the starvation, but the moment he realized that when he was injured and needed to be soothed, there was no mother to take him in her arms, and he was truly all alone. In every boy's diary I read at the Netherlands Institute for War Documentation, there is a forced hardening, a pivot from describing the overwhelming homesickness for Mother to describing the practical things the boys do to survive. Mentions of parents in these diaries become less prevalent as the war continues. It's a palpable resignation. It breaks my heart more than anything else my father endured, more than the abuse or malnutrition. Loss of tribe. Every man for himself.

In September 1944, the Japanese officers announce that the boys on the hill will be transferred out of Lampersari and tell the mothers to say goodbye to their sons, those scab-kneed, lizard-catching children now considered mature enough to do hard labor in a separate camp. The phrase the Japanese use is "men over ten." As in, "All of the men over ten are hereby reassigned to new camps." And so with a change of one word, with a relabeling, they justify the transfer.

The women clutch at their sons and weep. They whisper words into their ears as they hug them goodbye, hasty insufficient summaries of all the things that they would have taught them in the remaining years of childhoods that now have to be condensed into a few minutes. Sjeffie's mother tries to remember things to tell him. *Wash whenever you can, check for lice and ticks, find a buddy and work as a team, don't fight, keep practicing your equations, whatever you do just don't do anything to anger the officers, that's very important, OK, you have to promise me, can you promise me that?*

Aunt Ko says, "Say your prayers every day." Sjeffie's little sister Doortje hugs him and gives him some coffee. Fien, his youngest sister, hugs his legs, and my father kisses the top of his baby brother Kees's head. Through the agitated buzz of the Dutch mothers, camp officers shout angry words in Japanese, words like *iikagennishiro* and *teiryuu* and *shuutai* and *hikihanasu*, words that tumble into one another and mean nothing to the women until the guards start whacking them with their batons and whips, pulling son from mother and mother from son like starfish from wet rock.

The boys are marched out of Camp Lampersari as their mothers wail and their younger siblings watch wide-eyed. The cries of *Mammie, Mammie* rise repeatedly from their midst as they pass through the camp gates, heads swiveling for their last looks back.

The newly branded "men" march with their little suitcases banging against their knobby knees for what Sjeffie believes is many hours, along the banana trees and the *warungs* and the *kopi* carts. A rumor spreads in low tones through the group as they walk.

"I heard they're taking us to Bangkok."

"Yep, they definitely said they're taking us to Bangkok. I heard the Jap say it."

"*Psst*, hey, word is we're going to Bangkok."

"Bangkok! That's not even in the Indies! I won't ever see my family again!"

"Well, that's where we're going. Bangkok."

Within what is in all likelihood less than one hour, they arrive at the front gate of a convent, and the officers leading them stop. This is Camp Bangkong, their new home.

4

MEN OVER TEN

Camp Bangkong, Dutch East Indies, September 1944

Camp Bangkong is a former Catholic convent with an attached school. When my father arrives with the other boys from Lampersari, the classrooms have been cleared of their desks and chairs and the chapel has been cleared of its pews, to be turned into housing for prisoners. Inside, there are hundreds of men, old and young. As the boys arrive, female prisoners leave the camp through the back gate. They are headed to Lampersari or Camp Halmaheira, swapped for the new "men over ten." The only women left in the camp are a handful of nuns whom the Japanese keep to work as nurses for them. Sjeffie recognizes the same officers from Lampersari, who rotate between the camps. John the Whacker, Hockey Stick, Little Ko. His pulse quickens as he passes the officers who beat him for the rice incident. The boys haven't managed to leave these officers behind.

Sjeffie's friend Peter is not doing well with the transfer. A few weeks earlier, his mother had died in Lampersari, and his teenage sister had taken over caring for him. Peter was still in mourning, sobbing daily, when he was ordered to leave for Bangkong. Whereas some of the boys are mature for their age, he is a young eleven. His sister and the other women had begged the officers to let him stay with them in Lampersari, given his recent loss. The officers refused, shouted that he had to get in line with the other men over ten. As Peter stood there, tears running down his cheeks, his sister ran to him again to tell him to be brave. A conscripted Korean *heiho*, or camp guard, watching this immediately stormed up to them and hit the girl in the lower back with the blunt end of his bayonet-tipped rifle. As he did so, the bayonet end caught Peter's thigh, causing a gash. So this is how they parted, the sister knocked to the ground, her little brother limping and bleeding out of the camp while sobbing and looking over his shoulder until he could not see her anymore.

As he left his sister behind, something in Peter cracked, and all the children saw it. On the walk to the new camp, he stared ahead, expressionless. "Peter, it's going to be OK," Sjeffie whispered, but Peter didn't look at him. He limped with his injured leg, struggling to keep up, falling back to the end of the line. Like a zombie, he plodded on, silent, dragging his injured leg.

When the boys arrived in Camp Bangkong, they were told to get in formation and say their names, to count off. But Peter didn't say his name or count off. Catatonic, he stared straight ahead. The officer in charge interpreted this as insolence and decided to make Peter an example for the others. He motioned two other officers over. They dragged Peter out in front of the rows of boys. Sjeffie's heart drilled against his chest. He willed his friend to speak. "Name! Count!" Peter did not answer. The officer in charge pulled out a bamboo rod and brought it down on Peter's shoulder. He stumbled but didn't speak. "Name! Count!" He was beaten to the

ground with a rod each time he failed to respond, then pulled
back onto his feet by the other two officers for another round.
"Name! Count!" "Name! Count!" Despite Sjeffie's silent
pleading, Peter did not open his mouth. Bleeding from open
cuts on his face and back, he didn't cry, and he didn't talk.
This seemed only to make the officer more angry, and he beat
him harder. Ultimately, when Peter couldn't stand on his feet
anymore, two officers carried his bloody body to the sick bay.

There he lies, staring straight ahead. He refuses to drink
water or eat rice. The nuns are at a loss. One of them asks
around and learns that Sjeffie is his friend. She asks Sjeffie
to come talk to him; he has to drink and eat. Sjeffie stands
by his bed and says, "Come on, Peter. This is a terrible situation, but you have to snap out of it to get better. I'll help you.
We have to get through it." Peter finally speaks. *Mammie.* It's
the only word he repeats every time anyone pleads with him.
The nurses give Peter's untouched portion of rice to Sjeffie,
who swallows it down gladly, despite the flies that have been
sitting on it for a few hours. Then they send him out.

Sjeffie learns of Peter's death when the nuns give him his
friend's suitcase a few days later. Unlike Sjeffie's suitcase,
which is filled with clothes and practical items, Peter's
suitcase contains mainly toys, including an erector set. It's a
special treat for the boys, something to play with. Anything
to distract them.

—

My father concedes that watching his friend die of a broken
heart at a young age affected him in a profound way. I articulate it for him and he nods. *Feel too much, and you could
die.* Yes, maybe that's true. It's something understood implic-

itly in the camps. The boys in the camp don't show their soft underbellies when they can help it. They go into the latrines to shed their tears if they feel them come during the day, and as soon as the sun sets and their sleeping quarters go dark, echoing back from the walls and ceiling are the sounds of anonymous phlegmy sniffles and muffled sobs. The dark also masks older men, who hunch over the more vulnerable boys in the black night. My father observes all this, the tangible consequences of weakness, and he carries the knowledge with him for the rest of his life.

The first month at Bangkong is very difficult for the boys. One boy with diabetes dies within a week because there is no insulin in the camp. When I begin to research the camps, I find dozens of journals kept by POWs, including boys in my father's camp, donated to the archives of the Netherlands Institute of War Documentation. The entries in the beginning of these journals reveal profound heartache and loneliness, children missing their mothers. But even for these children, more immediate physical discomforts quickly take the place of these soul pains. Initially, Sjeffie sleeps in the chapel at the center of the camp. The boys sleep on two-by-four-foot *kesilirs*, thin mats on the floor. At night, bedbugs crawl over their bodies, the camp being completely infested with them, and many of the boys' journals describe the stench of the bedbugs that hangs perpetually in the air. The welts pepper their skin. But the boys' bodies are exhausted, and eventually, despite the biting bugs, they sleep the sleep of the fatigued, having come home from a day in the patjol field to one cup of rice or half of a three-inch square of rubbery tapioca. Everyone in the camp, approximately fifteen hundred men and boys, washes themselves under two primitive cold water showers or at an elevated concrete mandi basin containing buckets of water. Each person tries to bathe once or twice a week.

Like the men in the camp, each boy gets a white armband with a Japanese number written on it that corresponds to his *han,* his living quarters. The boys learn the alert signals for roll call, air strikes, meals, and lights-out. Sjeffie moves into the end room on the top floor in the north wing of the cloister, with thirty boys per room. Three rooms form a han, which is headed by a *hancho*, or section head, and an assistant head, called a *komicho*. The European hanchos and komichos are selected from the older male POWs in the camp and assigned to watch over the boys. Every night, on a rotating basis, two boys have to walk back and forth in front of the han, to make sure order is kept. If a Japanese officer approaches, the boys must repeat the words they have been taught. My father recites them for me: *"Dai go han, fushinban, fuku mudju, ijo arimasen."* He says this means, "This is Han Five, I am the night watch, there is nothing unusual to report." They never learn the words to say if there is something unusual to report.

This becomes clear when one night, a boy they've nicknamed Penkie goes missing. Penkie is in Han Five with Sjeffie. Like a few other children of internees, Penkie is an Indo boy, half Dutch, half Indonesian. This means that unlike the blond, blue-eyed boys in the camp, he can slip undetected into the Indonesian population outside the fence, something he figures out how to do. In the dark, Penkie sneaks out of the camp when the officers are distracted, and goes to the nearby kampongs. The Indonesians give him a chicken and fruit, and Penkie smuggles the food back into the camp. He does this for several nights, until one night his luck runs out. He's captured by a patrolling officer, and the camp sirens wail through the halls at 3:00 a.m. The boys and men have five minutes to file into the center of the camp. Eyes blinking with sleep, hearts pounding, they rush down the stairs and get in formation for roll call.

In the black of night, a Japanese officer walks down the rows. He stops in front of each hancho, asking for a head count and the number of sick in the han, as is customary at roll call. The officer stops in front of the hancho for Sjeffie's han, an older man from Luxembourg. The man states the number of boys in the han, to the best of his knowledge, having been woken only moments earlier. The officer asks him to repeat the number, then asks him again. The hancho falters, confused. The number comes out as a question the third time. Sjeffie's breath catches in his throat. What is going on? Suddenly, the officer removes his belt and begins to beat the hancho in the head with the buckle end, until the hancho falls, covering himself. "Lies! How dare you lie to me!" the officer yells as the blows fall. Stunned and bleeding from the cut in his head, the hancho looks up, confused. The officer calls out and some officers lead a handcuffed Penkie into the clearing. The officer shines a flashlight into Penkie's bloody, swollen face. He's held up by the officers, unable to stand. "Who was on night watch when this boy escaped?!" the officer demands. Two terrified boys are produced from within the rows. These boys are also beaten. Then the whole camp is subjected to an hour-long rant in Japanese, translated into Indonesian, about the severe consequences of attempted escapes. There will be zero tolerance. Finally, they are allowed to return to their sleeping quarters, except for Penkie, who is locked into a storage room with bars over the open windows so everyone can see him as an example.

Penkie stays locked up for three days, guarded by a camp

officer with a bayonet. He is under orders not to receive food or water, but by the second day, one of the Korean officers begins to take pity as the boy becomes dehydrated, and looks the other way as someone slips him a can of water through the bars, saving his life. But the Japanese officers haven't finished making Penkie an example for the others. After three days, two Kempeitai officers arrive, just as the patjolers return from the fields. They sit at a table in the center of the camp, and Penkie is brought before them. They sentence him to a water torture, which is carried out immediately in front of hundreds of horrified boys and men. Penkie is tied, writhing and screaming, to a *baleh-baleh*, a bamboo cot. A hose is inserted into his mouth and turned on while they hold his nose shut. His belly swells. The officers turn the baleh-baleh upside down, then begin to beat his distended belly with a rod until he vomits the water out. The twelve-year-old Penkie survives the torture, but nobody dares attempt an escape after that.

The officers and Kempeitai are not the only enemies inside the camp. The older prisoners can be just as bad. Power corrupts, even when power comes in the form of a prisoner given the task of watching over a group of children weaker than he is. The komicho of Sjeffie's han has a mosquito net over his kesilir, unlike most of the prisoners. He sleeps with Sjeffie on one side of him and an eleven-year-old boy named Hans on the other side. Sjeffie hears the komicho whisper to Hans in the dark, "Come under my mosquito net so you won't be stung." Sjeffie, while naive, knows something isn't right with this. In the night, he hears Hans sobbing from under the mosquito net and the komicho whispering angrily for him to stay quiet, covering his mouth. Sjeffie thinks about telling someone, but he keeps quiet, afraid the komicho will turn to his other side in the night and reach for him instead. One night, Hans becomes very ill with a sudden fever, moaning softly on his mat. In the morning, his body is cold and stiffening, just feet away from Sjeffie. This memory still gnaws at my father, who wonders if the komicho had anything to do with Hans's death. He knows that he himself dodged something very bad, and he feels guilt for having done so.

I read other vague references to molestation by the older prisoners in some of the diaries of the boys in my father's camp and realize again how the threat of this possibility shapes life philosophies in young, formative minds: self-preservation at all costs, even if it means sacrificing someone else. As with food, where survival depends on each boy getting as much as he can for himself and not helping out his neighbor, the sexual abuse forces each of them into an impossible role of betrayer. If they speak up about what they see, they may become targets. So they keep quiet but feel enormous guilt about their decision: *I'm glad it's him, because otherwise it would be me.*

In the camp, there is a makeshift medical facility and a pharmacy, run by prisoners who were doctors. There isn't enough medicine, however, so the pharmacist is left to improvise, grinding up papaya leaves as a cure-all for any number of ailments. With the lack of proper nutrition and oral hygiene, the boys' teeth start to develop abscesses. Sjeffie too develops a tooth abscess. There is no dentist in the camp. He goes to the medical room and the doctor pulls the tooth without anesthetic, then sends him to the pharmacy for some ground-up papaya leaves. When the pharmacist sees Sjeffie's last name, he asks, "Do you happen to be Dr. Eerkens's son? I worked with him in the hospital here in Semarang, before your family moved to Madiun." And so Sjeffie lands a coveted job as the pharmacist's assistant, and no longer has to work in the fields every day with the other patjolers. Instead, he spends his days in the tiny pharmacist's room grinding papaya leaves with a stone mortar and pestle, something that causes an enormous amount of jealousy in the other boys.

Amoebic dysentery spreads through the camp because of unsterile water, and soon the latrines, open toilets with a curtain separating each cubicle, are filled with boys who feel their bowels turned inside out, and those waiting cannot hold it. The ground in front of the latrines and the stairs to the latrines are covered in diarrhea each morning, to be cleaned up by the boys with that unfortunate duty, and the disease spreads further. Many succumb, and there are more dead bodies than usual those weeks. Themes of mortality and survival replace the theme of homesickness in the boys' diaries by this point in their internment.

Sjeffie has thought about where he can hide if the Japanese begin to shoot them. These are the thoughts of a thirteen-year-old boy, based on rumors murmured through the camp. Initially, he thinks the latrines are his only option. Once those become a sea of feces, however, he begins to look for other options. He roams the hallways, scanning the buildings for possibilities. When he notices a place on the upper floor with a ceiling access panel that can be reached via a railing, he decides that this is where he will hide when they begin to shoot.

But the daily misery in the camp also amplifies the smallest joys. Just as there is a daily reminder of the human capacity for cruelty, so too is there evidence of the human drive to connect and find points of light. Sjeffie and the boys find moments of levity, along with moments of human kindness in the Japanese and Korean officers. I read in a journal of a boy crying in a corner of the camp and an officer who, unexpectedly, sits beside him and confesses that he misses his family too, patting the boy on the shoulder. I hold on to these rare moments in the relentless and depressing succession of stories, not only as a writer trying to find some variation and movement in a dark narrative, but as a human being who imagines her father and these scared boys all alone in horrendous circumstances. I wish for them the promise of a kinder world than they live in.

Little Ko is one of the Korean officers. He is rumored to be homosexual by many of the boys because of his soft demeanor and his mannerisms, but he never behaves inappropriately with the young men. He doesn't beat the boys for sport like some of the other officers, and he actually smiles at them from time to time. Little Ko loves music. He often hums when the other guards aren't looking. On Christmas Eve, he is left behind to oversee the camp while the other officers go into the city for their own event. Swearing the camp prisoners to secrecy, Little Ko disappears into the officers' quarters, asking two men to come with him. Amazingly, they emerge from the officers' quarters rolling an upright piano, which they place in the center of the camp. Sjeffie and the boys crowd around. Little Ko asks for a volunteer, and a boy who is very good at playing the piano steps forward. He begins to play, ragtime and jazz and Dutch Christmas songs. Little Ko beams, delighted by the boys' happiness. He gestures to the boys. *Sing! Sing!* They sing and dance the jitterbug with each other. One boy starts a soft-shoe tap dance. They haven't heard music or been allowed to dance in years. It's the best Christmas party most of them have ever had, simply for the sheer surprise of it. The boy playing the piano looks at Little Ko, who is dancing and smiling. He takes a calculated risk. He begins playing the "Wilhelmus," the Dutch national anthem, and the other boys sing along, though the anthem is explicitly banned by the Japanese. Little Ko doesn't know the anthem, and he sways along obliviously, beaming. After a couple of hours, Little Ko drags the piano back into the officers' quarters, before the other officers can return to discover what he's done. Unfortunately, somebody appears to have snitched, because a few days later, Little Ko is taken away, and never returns to their camp. But my father still remembers this night, and his face lights up with the memory. He wonders how harshly Little Ko was punished, and whether he knew how significant his act of kindness was. "He was not a bad guy. He disappeared. They said that the Kempeitai got after him and put him in jail for it. He was not supposed to fraternize with the enemy, which is what they considered us to be," my father says.

The cruelty of the Japanese forces during World War II is well documented, and yet it is difficult to understand the reasoning behind the officers' cruelty toward my father and the other boys. Most of the officers were enlisted in the military involuntarily, so it isn't clear why they felt it necessary to be harsh toward their prisoners, especially when those prisoners were children. Little Ko brought some happiness into the lives of the prisoners he was charged with watching. It made them more agreeable. He could have been an example, but instead he was punished and removed as an officer. I think about this a lot. Perhaps it comes back to the human defense mechanism of compartmentalization. For many of the officers, I imagine, it would be impossible for them to do their jobs and imprison other human beings if they did not vilify them. West vs. East. White vs. Asian. Dehumanizing the prisoners was integral to maintaining the rules and order. Little Ko had to be punished for his act of compassion.

Sjeffie still has contraband copies of *Don Quixote* and *Twenty Thousand Leagues Under the Sea* that he snuck into the camp and hid in a spot under the rafters. He uses them to curry favor with the other boys, promising some tempo-

rary distraction after their days of silently plowing and planting rows of Japanese eggplant, spinach, and cucumbers in
the heat. The boys gather around and read out loud, savor-
ing the words. Words are a desired commodity in the camp,
far more valuable than they ever had been outside of the
barbed wire. The imagination-inflaming adventures of sea
monsters and Spanish wanderers are a reminder of when they
were boys, or a reminder with each giggle and whisper as
they huddle around the pages that perhaps they are still boys,
and only pretending to be men.

These moments of levity last until the day the Japanese
officers announce that any remaining papers that hold or
might hold Western words will be collected in an offer of temporary amnesty, and thereafter any prisoner found with reading material will be severely punished. My father is given the
job, along with another boy, of pushing a handcart through
the camp to collect the books, and *Don Quixote* is among the
first to go onto the bed of the cart. The books are heaped in
piles and taken to the officers for burning. The boys stand
solemnly along the path, watching *Don Quixote* make his
way past them and out of sight on his way to the fire.

Without their books, distraction becomes more and more
important, because after many months of dwindling food,
the prisoners are fading. They will do anything to stop thinking about the twisting in their guts. Sjeffie looks at his ribs
slash across his skin like zebra stripes. He thinks only of
food. When my sister asks him what they did, what they felt,
how they got through the days, he says, "We were hungry. We
couldn't think about anything else but food." That is reflected
in the camp diaries I read. What is remarkable about them
is how reliably every one of them becomes less and less about
missing family or feeling lonely or the fear of being shot
and more and more about the diary writer's starving body,

until that is almost without fail the dominant topic on every page.

With the sanitation problem in the camp come a lot of flies. The officers' way of dealing with this is to exploit the boys' hunger. They promise a spoonful of sugar for every two hundred flies the boys can kill. The boys bring the belly-up insects to the officers' quarters to be counted. A spoonful of sugar is extremely valuable. It has calories. You can eat it or trade it. When the boys are given some coffee brought in from the plantations, they mix it with the sugar to take away their hunger pains. They call this "doef-daf," for the sound it made when they beat the mixture in their cups. I read about their fly counts in their diaries, the ledgers of flies and spoonfuls of sugar as meticulously recorded as tax documents.

It's an epiphany when I read this, as a strange behavioral tic of my father's falls into place. When I was a child, my father always went into an all-out assault on any flying insect that deigned to enter our house. We had a flyswatter hanging in every room. My father seemed to relish inordinately the act of killing flies, dancing wildly across the room as if possessed, smacking the swatter onto objects until he exclaimed, "Got him! Ha-haaaa! Bastard!" It was a running joke to my siblings and me. "Oh, Dad and his flies." When I moved into a new apartment as an adult, my father was there to help me. He called a time-out in the middle of unloading the U-Haul to drive to the hardware store down the road, and returned with not one but three flyswatters, because he had spotted a fly in my new apartment. He embarked on his usual flyswatting dance immediately. I always viewed my father's weird obsession with flies as amusing and quirky, but I never understood its source until I read those diaries and asked him about this dead-fly reward system in the camp. The next Christmas, I bought him an electric flyswatter called "the Executioner." I've never seen him more pleased with a gift.

In the last six months of their internment, the internees barely get anything to eat, outside of a two-by-three-inch cube of starch paste mixed with sawdust, which they are instructed to break in half and consume for breakfast and dinner, as well as half a cup of rice. Only an occasional bit of protein from the patjol fields, where creatures scurry, now supplements their diets. The *kepitings*, small crabs that occasionally crawl into the fields, are a particularly rare treat to catch. The boys call the skinniest kids in the camp "birdcage," teasing them for their rows of ribs. In one diary, I read of a boy who was so emaciated that the diary writer had mocked, "Whoo-hoo, look at you, birdcage!" "Hey, I'm not that bad," the boy responded. "I'm not a birdcage yet!" But in the morning, he didn't wake up. Some of the boys' stomachs grow round, distended from the protein deficiency kwashiorkor. Many of them see their feet and legs swell with edema from the vitamin B deficiency beriberi. Malnutrition can make people go mad, and the boys become aware of this as they start to feel their minds fade along with their bodies. Every day now, a cold corpse remains on its mat in the morning when the others rise for roll call. Boys carry their friends out on stretchers made of bamboo, covered with thatched grass. "Shlepping corpses" is the least-desired job in the camp to be tapped for. Sjeffie tries to look busy in the pharmacy when he sees a body brought into the storage shed, but he too is tapped a few times to carry bodies out. In the tropical heat, the stretchers drip bodily fluids onto the boys' feet as they struggle to carry the dead across the camp and out through the front gate, where they are placed onto a cart to be brought to mass graves. Shlepping corpses gives boys the willies, but they don't dare admit it. They have to use these crude words and make light of what is becoming abundantly clear—the fact that they are starving to death—because if they look it in the eye and acknowledge it, they may lose their sanity altogether. "Damn. I got tapped by the Bloodhound to shlep a corpse tomorrow," they say, yawning. Acknowledging weakness is like opening the door to their own mortality. So they scoff and deny and pretend they are superhuman, unaffected.

There are two infamous brothers in the camp, the Schuyer brothers. As they lose weight, they begin to lose their minds too. With a bit of wire, they meticulously cut their grains of rice into three or four pieces, spending an hour or more hunched over this task every day. Then they eat each rice piece one by one to make the meal last longer. They inspire a new insult in the camp: "Schuyering," a verb that means to show cracks in one's sanity with obsessive-compulsive behavior. "Stop Schuyering" is a common taunt heard in the camp whenever a boy begins measuring or counting his food.

—

Some days, the women from Lampersari are brought to work in an adjacent field to the patjolers, and while they aren't allowed to speak, the mothers can scan the boys for their sons or the sons of others, and vice versa. These days are a psychological lifeline for the boys, and in diary after diary I saw the excited announcement, "I saw Mama today! She's alive and she waved to me." When Sjeffie hears that the women have been in the patjol fields for several days in a row, he asks another boy to switch places with him in the pharmacy, and he joins his cousin Kees and the patjolers for a day. Sure enough, he looks across the field and in the distance, he sees his own thin mother, shovel in hand, staring across the field back at him under the stern watch of an officer, her message unspoken but understood: *Stay strong. I love you.*

In her diary during this period, my grandmother writes to her absent husband:

> This paper has been in my Bible for more than a year now. Life is getting increasingly difficult. The boys have been in Camp Bangkong since September 13. Last Wednesday I went to pull weeds in the fields, and saw both of them; wasn't allowed to speak to them. Thankfully, they looked OK. There are more and more people dying in our group, and over there as well. If this lasts much longer, the hatred will only grow stronger. I long and pray so hard that I will get to see you again. To be able to begin again and recover together. But God's will be done . . . I hope so much to be able to give you this letter in person, as a diary. But if that doesn't come to pass, I am grateful for everything I experienced in this life. Don't be bitter. The children are in God's hand.

Her loneliness is palpable. She makes a tiny brooch out of some embroidery thread and photos of my grandfather, my father, and her nephew Kees, the men who have been sent away to other camps. She pins their images inside her clothing to keep them close to her.

Tension and irritability increase on the part of all parties in the camps. The months plod on relentlessly with no sign of the situation ending. Hope begins to dwindle. The hanchos become more like their captors every day, drunk with their power. Two of the hanchos in Camp Bangkong are especially sadistic: the Dernier brothers. Increasingly, they beat up the younger boys, one losing his cool and taking it out on their charges in a rage, until the other brother steps in to pull his sibling away, afraid the victim will die. Not only the prisoners show signs of mental decline. Hockey Stick, one of the more dreaded officers, has a complete breakdown one day, according to one diary. He has found a puppy in the street outside the camp, and ties the animal to a rope to walk it around the camp as his new pet. Initially, this amuses the boys, of course, though at that stage of starvation they would just as soon have made a meal of the puppy to save their lives. According to the diary, the puppy, being just a puppy, will not walk next to Hockey Stick obediently. He demands that the puppy sit, pushing its bottom down. But the puppy pops back up and pulls at its leash. Hockey Stick barks orders at it in Japanese. Then he suddenly flies into a rage, swinging the puppy like a tetherball in a circle around his head violently, snapping its neck. He immediately collapses and begins weeping when he realizes that he's killed it, talking to the dead puppy and trying to get its lifeless body to stand again. The boys also get in trouble more and more often as mental stability begins to break down in the camp. They are beaten and told to stand in the sun as punishment for increasingly minor infractions. This entails standing under the clock for many hours with a bare torso, turning so the hot sun is always at one's blistered back as it moves across the sky. The Japanese post some news about the world outside the camp and the war, though it is always filtered through their propaganda machine. They announce glorious victories for the Nippon Empire, but the prisoners notice that these victorious battles with the Allies are happening closer and closer to Indonesia, implying a decided Allied advance. Communication, or the prevention of communication, becomes a major theme in the camps.

Until I began to research the camps, language was something I never thought of in relation to war, the way that it was withheld to keep people deaf, mute, and powerless. I see now how words were weapons and their theft a tool of war. I see how words became precious in their scarcity in the same way that things like food and medicine and shoes did. What is more central to the human drive than communication? The Japanese cut this instinct off at every turn in the camp as a form of psychological warfare. They make the prisoners speak Bahasa, and ban their native Dutch. They make them learn Japanese. They install the isolating gedek so they cannot communicate with the Indonesians outside the fence except in faceless whispers. They confiscate their books. Pens, pencils, and paper in the camps are guarded and hoarded as obsessively as food.

In the Bangkong boys' diaries, this becomes clear. While reading them at the Netherlands Institute for War Documentation in Amsterdam, I marvel at the delicate creased onion-skin paper of the letters and diaries, just like that of my grandmother's, the minuscule letters inscribed on every available centimeter, getting even smaller as words swarm toward the end of the paper with each page. Eventually, I have to ask at the desk if they have a magnifying glass I can borrow. "Of course we do," the man there says, because many of the documents in the archives were written on the backs of wrappers and cigarette papers, he tells me; whatever a prisoner could get his hands on and hide from the authorities. It's surprising to me that as a writer, I haven't registered this particular hardship of war before. I suppose it's because I take words for granted. I have never once had to worry about having access to the tools of expression whenever I wanted to use them. I open my laptop and type, I use full sheets of thick white paper and write in big letters. Sometimes I cross things out in frustration, crumple the paper. Sometimes I crumple several pieces of paper. I complain about not getting the words right. I start over. I cut and paste. I shake my pen when it runs out of ink and drop it in the trash, then reach for another.

This privilege comes into sharp relief as I sit hunched over a table in Amsterdam squinting at Lilliputian script through a magnifying glass, noticing the economy of the tiny penciled attempts of one thirteen-year-old boy to document himself in abbreviations: *8 Sept. D Spitz died. 13 Sept. Boys fr Lampersari arrived. 19 Sept. J Kramer died. 28 Sept. Won't lend my pencil anymore. Getting too nubby. 1 Oct. Can't think straight. Have the runs. 29 Oct. Earned 1 spoon sugar catching 200 flies for officer. Have malaria. Pencil just nub now. Problem w/ b-bugs. 28 Feb. Miss my mother. Air raid. Is it Unkle Sams?*

As their own words are progressively taken away, new words are put into the prisoners' mouths, words they do not choose. They are encouraged to send postcards to their families abroad, something that initially causes surprise and excitement, but that excitement quickly sours. The postcards are white, two by five inches, and a prisoner's message can consist only of three sentences chosen from among of a list of approved pre-printed sentences and copied word for word onto the postcard. "I have dysentery and am starving to death, and over a third of the people in my camp have died" is not one of the included sentences. The approved sentences are: "We internees are permitted to write home by the generous government of Nippon." "My health is excellent." "Our camp is well equipped, and the accommodations are comfortable. Our daily life is very pleasant." "We have plenty of food and much recreation." "The Japanese treat us well, so don't worry about me and never feel uneasy." "We are permitted to grow vegetables and flowers which we like and enjoy working in the open air." "This is a land of perpetual summer, full of natural beauty, with plenty of bananas, pineapples, mangistano, and coconuts. Love, _____." Of course, the cards are a ridiculous farce, but sending them at least allows a prisoner to communicate to loved ones that he is still alive.

The reality of the prisoners' conditions is in such stark contrast to their postcards that the Red Cross determines that the prisoners are in crisis and delivers aid packages with food and medical supplies to the camps. On May 2, 1945, Bangkong receives a delivery, which is initially withheld from the prisoners, and then delivered with great ceremony on May 16, after the Japanese government receives international pressure for withholding humanitarian aid, and relents. The Japanese officers post a long screed in the center of the camp, and a translator reads it to the prisoners in Dutch. The speech is titled "Are Our Enemies Human?" It begins with the lines "During the course of the Pacific War, the Anglo-Americans . . . have time and again been guilty of numerous instances totally opposed to the dictates of humanity." The announcement then details a long list of specific military strikes against Japan by the Allied forces. "In retaliation, the Japanese Government would be perfectly justified in withholding distribution of the relief supplies . . . nor would the Allies be in a position to lodge a protest against such action . . . To confiscate supplies destined for [POWs] would be an easy matter, as easy as twisting a child's hand. But the Japanese know that these internees and prisoners of war are not and should not be held responsible for the treachery of their governments . . . His Majesty has directed that these relief goods be distributed among captive enemy nationals as originally planned, and this Imperial order will be faithfully carried out." The prisoners are jubilant. The one hundred aid packages are to be shared by around thirteen hundred men and boys in the camp; there is food they haven't seen in years.

There are two types of packages, American and British, with slightly different contents, including canned corned beef, Prem and Spam, canned pudding, canned butter, condensed milk, chocolate, raisins, chewing gum, sugar, and processed cheese, among other items. It's a feast for the starved prisoners, even if thirteen people have to share a package. In the corner, the Schuyer brothers segment their share of the food, counting and recounting. Sjeffie inhales his Spam and goes for the chocolate. To hell with rationing. He's hungry right now.

—

Camp Bangkong, Semarang, Indonesia, 2014

After we visit Lampersari, Joko drives us to Camp Bangkong, the place of most significance for all of us. Both my father and I are astounded by how close to each other the two camps actually are. It could not have taken more than forty-five minutes to walk between the two. It's a stark reminder to me of how subjective memory is, how there is no such thing as a fixed account of history, and how "nonfiction," outside of dates and measurable facts, can only ever be one person's version of "the truth." "It really, truly felt like hours that we were walking," my father says, and he seems genuinely troubled by the clear evidence that his memory doesn't match up with the facts. For me, it's jarring as well, as I have always thought of the physical distance between my father and his mother as significant and now must adjust the story, which I have heard several times. But fact and truth are two different things. In the end, I think that regardless of how far the walk from Lampersari to Bangkong was in actual miles, to my father and those other boys who believed they were being taken to Bangkok and who would not speak to their families for years, it was a walk to the other side of the earth. That was and is their truth.

Today, Camp Bangkong is a private school. Children in uniforms have their classes in the former internees' hans. My father shows us the han where he slept upstairs. As I video-tape, children slip out of the class, the more extroverted ones giggling and performing for my camera. Their teacher comes out into the hall, and we try to explain why we are there, but she doesn't understand, though she allows my father to stick his head through the door of her classroom to see his old quarters. He laughs and waves at the children, a massive smile on his face. It's good to see the space now filled with learning and joy.

My father shows us the different parts of the camp, and I make him take me to where he was standing when the war ended so I can photograph him there. He shows us where the boys left via the back gate to work in the fields, where they stacked the bodies of campmates who died, where they carried them out. He shows me the "pharmacy" where he worked, now a locked utility closet. Meanwhile, it's the middle of a busy school day, with oblivious children and teachers walking through the halls in the twenty-first century. It adds to a surreal experience of being in the spaces as my father explains what the function of each one was.

We see another teacher near the chapel and again we explain what we are doing there. She seems aware of the school's past and begins nodding, then hurries off. There is a small plaque on the wall outside the chapel that acknowl-edges the people who lost their lives there. The school direc-tor appears with the teacher we've just spoken to and a log for us to sign. She tells us that many children of former prisoners of the camp have been there and signed the log-book, but in the past decade, my father is the only person she has met who was actually interned there himself and returned. She tells my father it is an honor to meet him and shakes his hand, which I can see makes him feel good.

Later that evening, after an emotional day, my father and I visit the buffet on the roof of our hotel, next to the infinity pool. My father cannot resist an all-you-can-eat buffet, often overfilling his plates on multiple trips. A chef stands at a station making stir-fry to order, satay and rice with peanut sauce are available at another station, and fresh fruit salad and different Indonesian desserts are displayed on another table. It's a beautiful evening, the sun just setting. There is a live band playing music, the tropical air has cooled to the perfect temperature, and the views are spectacular. We look out over the city to the Tjandi Hills. Suddenly, I realize that a building directly in our line of vision is unmistakably my father's former camp, the school we visited that day.

"Oh my God, Dad! That's your camp right there."

"Wow!" he says. "It looks so small from here."

For me it offers a moment of symbolic satisfaction, seeing my father next to this pool, seventy years later, looking down at the place where he nearly starved to death, with an all-you-can-eat plate of food.

—

Hiroshima, Japan, August 6, 1945

In the black of night, Little Boy passes over a sleeping Pacific, snug in the belly of the Enola Gay. A worse misnomer than "Little Boy" for such a destructive and powerful force could not exist. The atomic bomb, the first the world will know, is armed just before 8:00 a.m., just before Little Boy is released over the city of Hiroshima. The crew of the Enola Gay moves into place.

There is a moment when the bomb falls, suspended in air, a moment between what Little Boy was and what Little Boy becomes in the time line of history. In this liminal moment, innocent lives are being traded for other innocent lives, for as much as rightfully horrified minds have tried to reason that perhaps Japan would have surrendered on its own, the fact remains that it would not have been in time for my father or his family or most of the internees in their camps, who were months, if not weeks, from death by starvation on August 6, 1945. In some cases, it would prove too late and they would die in the days that followed. This second in time, in which the belly of the Enola Gay opens, determines that my father will live and others will not live. It allows me to be born and prevents others from existing at all. It ensures the war trauma of generations of Japanese families. For forty-three seconds, Little Boy plummets silently through the atmosphere. Then, in a flash, seventy thousand people and an entire city center are blown cleanly off the map. Three days later, "Fat Man" free-falls over Nagasaki, sweeping another forty thousand to seventy-five thousand lives from the earth. It saves my father's life.

—

Camp Bangkong, Semarang, Dutch East Indies, August 1945

He doesn't know it yet, of course. In the week following the bombing of Nagasaki, Sjeffie hears distant explosions rumbling throughout the city, and the prisoners see planes.

Smoke plumes rise into the sky, black and thick, only a few miles away. There are excited whispers throughout the camp. The prisoners don't know it, but what they are witnessing is the Allied fighters bombing the Semarang harbor. The Japanese officers are tense and quieter than usual. They patrol with their bayonets gripped tightly and don't bark the usual orders at the prisoners, keeping their eyes averted. They announce that the patjolers will not be going to work in the fields this week. This announcement increases the rumors, but still, the prisoners are unsure of what is going on. Some are afraid that the Japanese will kill them instead of surrender. Sjeffie practices climbing up to his secret hiding spot, preparing himself. Then a small plane flies over the camp, dropping slips of paper and rolling back and forth to "wave" its wings at them. These turn out to be Dutch pilots stationed in Balikpapan, the already-liberated seaport city on Borneo. Almost all of the slips flutter off into the wind, missing the camp, but one or two land inside. They say "*De redding is nabij*": "The rescue is near." The few who have caught slips hide them from the officers, afraid of being harmed. After many false alarms, they begin to hope that this could be the real thing. And it is. Sort of. The Japanese officially surrender on August 15, 1945, but this fact is not announced to the prisoners, and the officers stay at their posts, ordering the prisoners to remain in their barracks or in the yard. For another full week, the prisoners live in this limbo, unsure if the war has ended or if they are doomed to be imprisoned forever, or worse. A few succumb in this week, and the others carry the bodies out as usual.

On August 23, Sjeffie goes to his job in the pharmacy. While walking there, he hears shouting coming from behind the gedek. Making sure nobody is looking, he climbs a pillar behind the pharmacy from where he can look over the double fence. There, he sees Indonesians running through the streets. One man spots him and calls out, "Hey, boy! The war is over! It's over! Do you have clothing? Trade clothing for food!" Unbeknownst to him, the Indonesians on the outside of the camps, while still having access to food, have had no access to textiles throughout the war, and clothing has become a valuable commodity. In the camps, where close quarters mean lice and sweat and it's nearly impossible to keep a wardrobe clean, the boys and men haven't worn full clothing in years, and now wear only shorts or a *cawat*, a loincloth that they can easily rinse each day. The Indonesian man holds up a large bundle of bananas, and Sjeffie can't believe his luck. He still has a couple of untouched shirts in his suitcase in the han. "Wait here! Wait here! Don't go away!" He scrambles back down the pillar and runs as fast as he can to his han. He returns, out of breath, with a shirt, and scrambles back up the pillar. To his relief, the man is still there, holding the bananas. "Throw the bananas over first!" Sjeffie yells, afraid it is a hoax. The man pauses, considering, but there are more bananas, and he regards this skeletal child behind the fence. He throws the bananas, and they land with a thud a few feet from Sjeffie's pillar. Sjeffie quickly balls up and throws the shirt. The man catches it and smiles. Then Sjeffie scrambles down so nobody else can grab his bananas.

He wolfs one down immediately, then hides the rest of the bananas in a secret spot he has in the pharmacy where sometimes the nuns leave him extra food from the unused rations of patients who die. There is another boy who works in the pharmacy, Fons, and Sjeffie motions him over eagerly. He reveals the bananas, offering to share extra food as they usually do. But Fons frowns. "That's illegal. You can't talk to anyone outside the gedek. We'll get in trouble." "Fine," Sjeffie says. "You don't have to have any. But I am eating them."

An hour later, though, a hancho shows up. Sjeffie has been ratted out. The bananas are confiscated and Sjeffie is ordered to stand under the clock in the sun as punishment. Sjeffie watches his plump, beautiful bananas leave with the hancho and walks dejectedly to the clock. He stands there and stands there. Sweat trickles from his shorn head and down his face in the relentless sun.

But around him, the camp begins to stir. Others have gotten similar offers from the other side of the gedek. They start trading over the top of the fence too, and nothing happens. Sjeffie looks around and notices that the Japanese officers who have been guarding them vigilantly for years have suddenly evaporated. He takes a cautious step from his appointed spot. Nothing happens. No officer appears. No John the Whacker. No Bucket Man. No Hockey Stick. He takes another cautious step. No Pretty Karl. No Bloodhound. No Chubby Baby. They have all vanished. Nobody stops him. He takes a few more steps, looking around him. Nothing. And then he is running to the gedek, where the others are now furiously trading, throwing clothing over the fence as fruit, pastries, even meat come flying back over the top. Emboldened, some of the prisoners begin tearing down the gedek. Nobody stops them. They now climb through the hole and trade openly with the Indonesians.

And then a low rumbling begins, a rumbling that swells to fill the corners of the camp, the sound the prisoners have waited for every day of every week, every week of every month, every month of every year. Three years they have waited for it. They have imagined it as they laid on the floor in the dark every night while the bedbugs emerged from the cracks to swarm their bodies. They can hardly believe their ears now as the sound fills the air and vibrates through their bones. Sjeffie looks up and sees not the red circle but the stars, white on blue circles, painted on the wings of an Allied plane as it passes over the camp. Grins stretch across the prisoners' hollowed faces. They cheer and wave, two arms over their heads, waving and waving, all necks craned skyward, yelling, "We are here! We are here!" The plane circles back, flying low. My father shields his eyes, and he sees that the door of the plane is open. A soldier in an olive-green uniform and a half-globe helmet is standing in the doorway waving back at them, and there are thousands of tiny papers falling like snow from the plane. Sjeffie joins the crowd around a man holding one of the slips of paper. He strains to see. "What does it say?" The slip is printed in Japanese characters on one side, English on the other. The man reads aloud slowly, laboring over the English words.

To All Allied Prisoners of War:
The Japanese Forces Have Surrendered
Unconditionally and the War Is Over.

We will get supplies to you as soon as is humanly possible, and will make arrangements to get you out, but, owing to the distances involved, it may be some time before we can achieve this. You will help us and yourselves if you act as follows:

(1) Stay in your camp until you get further orders from us.
(2) Start preparing nominal rolls of personnel, giving fullest particulars.
(3) List your most urgent necessities.
(4) If you have been starved or underfed for long periods, DO NOT eat large quantities of solid food, fruits or vegetables at first. It is dangerous

> *for you to do so. Gifts of food from the local*
> *population should be cooked. We want to get*
> *you back home quickly, safe and sound, and we*
> *do not want to risk your chances from diarrhea,*
> *dysentery, and cholera at this last stage.*
>
> (5) *Local authorities and/or Allied officers will take*
>   *charge of your affairs in a very short time. Be*
>   *guided by their advice.*

Late in the afternoon of August 23, the Japanese officers reappear to erect a platform in the center of the camp. Sjeffie and the other prisoners are called to attention. They stand in rows before the podium. Then a grim-faced commander in full uniform mounts the platform and begins speaking in Japanese, while a translator translates.

He tells them that the Japanese government officially surrendered on August 15 after the United States dropped two massive bombs on Japan on August 6 and 9, and he has been ordered to release all POWs in this camp. Furthermore, he has been ordered to increase the food supply, including vegetables, and they are free to have as many servings of rice as they like. Sjeffie and his campmates cheer. The officer finishes by telling them that the Red Cross has ordered them to stay in the camp for further instructions. Then he quickly exits the stage, hurrying back to offices where documents are hastily being destroyed to get rid of evidence for the war crimes tribunal that the Japanese know will be coming. The patjol spades vanish, as does all other evidence of forced labor. And then the commander and officers retreat into the shadows, though they've been ordered to stay to keep the camp safe until the Red Cross arrives to take over.

In the camp clearing, Sjeffie and the others initially celebrate, cheering and dancing. From some hiding place, somebody produces a contraband Dutch flag, which is unfurled. They begin to sing the Dutch national anthem. But after they celebrate, they are left feeling stunned. They are free. Now what? They sit down to wait for the Red Cross as instructed.

Not Sjeffie. Sjeffie finds his cousin Kees.

"Hey, listen. I'm not staying in this place for one more minute. I'm going to walk back to Lampersari to find Mom. Are you coming?"

Kees is afraid. "Don't leave. We are supposed to wait for the Red Cross," he says. But as my father tells it now, he was sick of being told what to do; he no longer respected authority. He asks other boys in his han to join him. They also are too scared to leave. So ultimately, he leaves by himself. He gathers what possessions he has left, walks over the portion of the gedek that has been torn down, and emerges onto the streets of Semarang, where the people stare at this emaciated, barefoot totok. He asks Indonesians on the street directions to his mother's camp, though he vaguely remembers the way, walking in reverse from the march of what seems a lifetime earlier. Now that he is finally outside the gedek, he sees the effects of the war on the Indonesian people. While they were free from internment, the war had been difficult for the Indonesians as well, particularly for those of the lower classes who were not given positions in the Japanese-ruled society. People on the street wear tattered clothing, some even passing him in little more than burlap sacks. They too look thinner, and worn down.

He arrives at Lampersari to find that the gedek there has been torn down in places as well. He walks through a hole and follows the main road toward the kampong house where his mother lived when he left the camp. The little children point at him as he passes. "Mama! Look! A big boy!" they call. He is just fourteen. They have not seen a boy over ten years old in years. When my father walks into the barrack his mother is housed in, a woman's back is to him. The woman is hunched over a bucket washing her shirt, topless, and he sees the ladder of her vertebrae and her breasts hanging like empty skin from a concave chest. Horrified, he turns to leave just as the woman turns to face him. Her eyes fill with tears when they meet his. It takes moments before he registers with shock that this is in fact his own mother he is looking at.

When my father tells me this story during my interviews for this book, it is the second and only other time I have seen him cry. For several moments he cannot speak, shaking his head and clearing his throat. "My mother. She was so emaciated, I couldn't recognize her. That image, I'll never forget it." He covers his face, overcome with the memory. In the barrack that day, my grandmother takes him in her matchstick arms. His sisters and toddler brother come running in and gather around, hugging their brother. Sjeffie is back. Alive.

Across the island in Eastern Java, Sjeffie's father is freed from the camp in Bandung, but as a military doctor, he is immediately enlisted in the rescue effort by the Dutch government to tend to the nearly sixty thousand surviving civilian prisoners in the dozens of camps throughout the island of Java alone who are malnourished and suffering from a variety of illnesses such as malaria, dysentery, and beriberi and other vitamin-deficiency diseases. He writes increasingly panicked letters to my grandmother during this time, sent through the Red Cross.

Dear Bep,

I do not know if you received the two postcards I sent a few days ago. Although I've made every effort to reach you, I have heard nothing back so far, which

*makes me worry, especially as the rumors are that it
has been particularly bad in your camps in Central
Java. Thank God the misery has come to an end,
although there may be more difficulties ahead. Stay
for the time being in Semarang, where I hope to
come and get you. Where we are going is not
certain. I am doing OK. Have been ill during the
internment in Banjoebiroe, where we did not have it
easy. I've had influenza-like fevers a few times and
once a hunger edema that passed. As a doctor in the
camp, I always had something of a privileged position and got something extra in the worst hunger
periods. Kesilir was the best in comparison with
the other camps, Banjoebiroe bad, here moderate,
though we have had it pretty good lately. Yet there
have also been a lot of hunger edema and dysentery
deaths here . . . I long to see you again and will
praise the day that we are together again, I hope all
of us are still healthy. Goodbye, my dear, keep your
chin up. God bless you. Many kisses, also to the
children and Ko from your Pep.*

Dear Bep,

*This is the seventh letter I have written to you
since the capitulation, but I still have received no
answer. The news arriving here from Central Java is
very bad and I really am very worried about you.
I am trying to reach you through all possible chan-
nels. Are you trying it vice versa too? It would be a
great reassurance for me if I knew you were still
alive and healthy. I cannot leave here yet. Officially
we cannot leave the camp. In addition, I work in the
hospital and therefore cannot abandon my post. So*

I have to wait until an official arrangement has been
made. You stay in Semarang. I hope to find you
there. I am looking forward to seeing you all again.
I am doing fine. A bit older and thinner maybe, but
not bad.

Dear Bep,
    Just now I received a telegram from Pastor de
Quay for which I am extremely grateful. Thank
God that you are all still alive. The Red Cross has
just been here and I have asked them to send me to
Central Java. Five doctors have to go there and I will
very likely be one of them. Either we will be divided
among various camps, and then I will try to come to
Semarang, or we have to open a hospital in Magelang.
In any case, I will be closer to you and the connec-
tion easier. Mail still hasn't arrived from Central
Java and people are very worried about this. Batavia
has been allowed to write. Ruschtk is here with me
and asks how his wife is. Maastricht is also very
worried. Well, goodbye my dearest, I hope to see
you soon.

In the end, my father's family is one of the first families
to be fully reunited, as most internees are still waiting to be
evacuated from camps spread out across Java. However, there
have been losses that Sjeffie and his father only now hear
about. They learn about the death of Aunt Lien, one of my
grandmother's closest friends, leaving her two children to be
taken care of by my grandmother and Aunt Ko. After a week,
Cousin Kees arrives in Lampersari, having finally left Bangkong with the permission of the Red Cross. My grandfather
is permitted to send a Red Cross message to the family in

Bolivia and my grandmother's brother in The Hague that they are safe and alive.

Sjeffie's mother and sister Doortje are both extremely malnourished and close to death. My grandmother has developed beriberi. The lack of food in the last months of the war has been particularly bad in Lampersari, even worse than in Bangkong. Sjeffie's sister tells him that their mother, on one occasion, was so weak that she fell while carrying the family's rations back to their quarters, and the broth and rice spilled out on the ground. Sjeffie's father says that my grandmother and Doortje won't survive two more weeks without treatment, and he gives both injections and "liver pills" to reverse vitamin deficiencies that are destroying their organs. Food, plentiful now, is nonetheless introduced cautiously, as many discover their bodies can no longer digest anything more than rice and become extremely ill after their first meals of meat and vegetables. Flour and eggs come back into the camp, and Sjeffie is put in charge of making a fire to bake the bread in. He feels like a man.

One imagines that when prisoners are liberated, they immediately flee the confines of camps where they've been tortured and imprisoned to pick up their lives, but this is not the case. While conditions improve, the former internees still have no homes to go to, having lost everything when they were interned years earlier. The Red Cross rations arrive in the camps. The doctors' medical facilities are in the camps. The administrators who take down their details are in the camps. So in the camps they have to stay. In that respect, little changes. People are also still dying, their organs now too damaged from malnutrition to be saved, even with vitamin injections. Every day, my grandfather returns to his family with tears in his eyes as he tells them that an internee he fought valiantly to save succumbed anyway, surviving to see the end of the war but too broken by it to recover. I cannot help but think of how in the cities of Hiroshima and Nagasaki, similar scenes play out as lives flicker out on pillows, in burn wards, with family gathered around. The war is over on both sides, but it is not over for these victims still succumbing to starvation or dysentery, burns or radiation poisoning. For their loved ones, just as for those on the Allied side, the war is never over.

Close to the Lampersari camp, in the Tjandi Hills, there is a former Dutch school that the Red Cross commissions as a temporary orphanage and school for the children whose parents have died during their internment. They ask my grandfather to become the director of the school. Two widowed teachers are asked to become caretakers and teachers. A month after the war ends, Sjeffie's family, Aunt Ko, Aunt Lien's two children, and Cousin Kees all move into the Van Deventer School along with one hundred orphans, the two teachers, and several widowers who work in the kitchen and garden. Amazingly, they are brought there in Jeeps driven by Japanese soldiers, who are now under orders of the Red Cross and the Allied forces to help in the postwar recovery effort, because they have an administrative infrastructure in place, with essential vehicles and supplies. These Japanese soldiers bear little resemblance to the Japanese soldiers of a few months prior. These Japanese soldiers are courteous and polite. They don't strike anyone or make Sjeffie and his family bow to them and say *"Kere! Kiotske! Naore!"* whenever they pass. There are two houses and a dormitory at the Van Deventer School, and Sjeffie and his family move into one of the houses, near the front of the school along a circular drive. While caring for the orphans, my grandfather continues to work half days treating patients in the Lampersari camp, being picked up in the morning by a Japanese soldier in a military vehicle and brought back in the afternoon.

It seems that things are finally getting better. By the fall of 1945, the family has been living in the Van Deventer School for about two weeks, and the orphans have started their classes, along with Sjeffie and his siblings. All of them are quickly gaining weight, growing stronger each day. They know that the Indonesian leaders Sukarno and Hatta declared independence on August 17, two days after Japan's surrender, and that the Dutch government has not accepted the declaration, insisting on holding on to its prewar rule of the country. My grandparents know there is civil unrest, with freedom fighters protesting and rioting in some places near Batavia, but like most Dutch who have been isolated inside the camps for years, they naively believe that everything will go back to the way it was before the war and don't fully grasp how the flames of revolt are catching and building, moving quickly from village to village. The uprising feels far away. They receive mail back from my grandmother's brother in The Hague, addressed to "Sis" and "Pep," my grandparents, and the rest of the family:

> *How overjoyed we were with your short message that relieved our worry over your fate. What a nightmare you must have experienced. If only you survive the period of unrest that Java is currently in. Try to come to Holland as quickly as possible. It's safe here again, though not everything is ideal. Did my sister recover from the beriberi all right? It's impossible to explain in a short letter (I have to finish it quickly, because it will be taken with someone from the Red Cross) everything that we experienced here with the Germans. The*

main thing is that we survived. Even Mother and Father are doing OK, although they lost almost everything. They are living back in Arnhem. During the assault on Arnhem in Sept. '44 they fled on foot with only one suitcase. Unfortunately the evacuation was too much for Pa Eerkens. He had been operated on twice in the winter, and was very weak. In October 1944 he passed away in the emergency hospital in Nijkerk . . . Sad for you, Pep, that you won't be able to see your father again.

Although the family in Holland worries about them in an escalating revolution, my grandfather cannot just leave even if he wants to. He is still a doctor employed by the Dutch military, and is tasked with the care of the thousands of former POWs who are slowly recovering from malnutrition and diseases in the makeshift Red Cross hospitals. My grandparents don't feel it is too dangerous to stay.

But the working-class local Indonesians see their chance to upend a system that has kept them down economically while the Dutch colonialists, Sultans, Chinese merchants, and wealthy Indonesians in business with the colonial ruling class all prospered. They begin to attack these different groups with the rallying cry of independence. This happens within the relative chaos of the postwar recovery period. The Dutch civilians have not been present in Indonesian society for years at this point and are oblivious to the level of anger that has been growing in members of the community, who have been fed continuous anti-Western literature and films by the Japanese troops throughout the war. For years, the Indonesians have heard that Asia is for Asians and that the Dutch are using them. Now that the Dutch are emerging from the camps, many of the Indonesians aren't interested in a return to the way things were. Japan, meanwhile, had begun manipulating and mistreating the Indonesian people as well during the war, causing resentment against all occupiers, Dutch and Japanese. Things have not gotten better for the Indonesians under Japanese rule, as they had been promised, but have only gotten worse. The Indonesians are tired of being ruled by outsiders. When the British troops arrive to help restore order, to organize the rescue of the interned Dutch, the transport of Japanese soldiers back to Japan, and the arrest of Japanese officers, there is a vacuum of leadership. The British are there only temporarily and are solely focused on getting all subjects back to their respective homes. They don't know that when they tell Japanese soldiers to lay down their arms, many of them give their weapons to local Indonesian independence fighters, either voluntarily or under pressure. In short, there is a lot of naiveté, a lack of order, much suffering, and a lot of resentment—the perfect cocktail for an uprising.

The initial fighting is near the capital in Western Java, so it is peaceful in the school on the hill where Sjeffie has resumed his studies and play and meals around the table with his family. Until one day, it isn't. The Bersiap, the violent uprising that marks this early period of the Indonesian National Revolution, spreads and comes to Semarang. Civilian rebels, often with no organized command, begin to attack all non-Indonesians, conducting raids on households, where they drag the men out and murder them or kidnap them, demanding ransom. Mixed-blood Indos are also targeted, and those who have been allowed to live outside the Japanese internment camps because of their mixed heritage are now left without the same protection as the (re)interned Dutch-Indonesians inside the guarded camps. Thousands of men, women, and children, entire families living in villages all over

Java, are murdered by the *pelopors*, or rebels, in the name of restoring the country to the Indonesians.

When the pelopors begin to move through Semarang, it surprises my father's family completely. My grandfather leaves in the morning for the Lampersari camp hospital to take care of the internees. While he is gone, Sjeffie and the other children, sitting at their desks, begin to hear shooting, explosions. They've barely had a reprieve from this sound with the end of the war, so they know it well. The teachers suspend class and take the orphans into the dormitory to be safe. Sjeffie and his siblings hurry back to their house, where their mother is anxiously peering out the window. Then they hear a truck crunching gravel in the drive, coming to a halt just outside. Four Indonesian men get out, holding rifles. Pelopors, rebel fighters. Sjeffie's heart is pounding. The rebels shout, "Send out your men!" Sjeffie's mother turns to Sjeffie and Cousin Kees, shaking. The teenagers are both taller than she is. "Get under the bed, boys. Get under the bed, right now!" Sjeffie and Cousin Kees scramble to the bedroom and crawl on their bellies under the bed, terrified. The pelopors are at their front door now, pounding. "Send out your men!" My grandmother shouts back through the locked door, "There are no men here, only women and children!" The pelopors move to the other side of the school. They kick in a side door. They emerge with five male kitchen and garden workers, whom they load into their truck with guns at their backs. They yell, "We are coming back! You can't hide!" Then they drive off. The children are all crying. Sjeffie and Cousin Kees stay under the bed for a long time.

Once they are certain the truck is gone, Sjeffie and Cousin Kees are allowed to come out from under the bed. But my grandmother tells them to get down low in a back bedroom. She runs through the inside door to the dormitory to check on the orphans. The teachers order all the children to sit in a hallway while they stand guard at each end with an iron bar in their hands. From the top of the hill, Sjeffie can hear shooting and explosions throughout Semarang. The family sits together in the back bedroom, too terrified to come out. Finally, after the sun sets, they hear another truck come up the driveway. Sjeffie's mother pushes the boys back under the bed, holding her finger to her lips. Footsteps. Then voices.

Japanese voices! There is a knock at the door. My grandmother calls through and the voices say they are safe. She opens the door. There she is greeted by a Japanese officer, three Japanese soldiers, and her husband, who has been escorted back through the fighting from Lampersari, sick with worry for his family. The Japanese officer tells the family that he has been ordered to protect the orphanage against the pelopors with a detachment of Japanese soldiers. He quickly has his soldiers take up guard positions at the main corners of the grounds and asks permission to use one of the storage rooms in the school for sleeping quarters. Sjeffie cannot wrap his head around this development; the same troops that had been his enemies and captors a month prior are now his protectors and saviors.

Five or six Japanese soldiers stand guard day and night for weeks as a civil war for independence rages in the city below. The Allied forces are sending troops to handle the handover of power, but with the abrupt end to the war with Japan, it will take several weeks for them to arrive, so initially, the Japanese soldiers step into this new, unexpected role out of necessity. But in Semarang, they soon become committed to this new responsibility after a violent showdown with the pelopors. The rebels had driven to a Japanese garrison in Semarang and demanded that the soldiers stand at attention in the courtyard while the pelopors read a proclamation that the country was now under Indonesian control and the soldiers should put down their weapons. Approximately one hundred Japanese soldiers, trained to follow orders, put their weapons down. The pelopors gather the weapons and gun down the Japanese soldiers execution style. A few of the soldiers pretend to be dead and lie still under the corpses until the pelopors leave. Then the survivors crawl out from under the bodies, and race to the Japanese garrison in Semarang that has not yet been attacked, to warn them. The infuriated Japanese military commander of Semarang declares martial law. The rebels now have a new enemy. It takes the Japanese military three days to gain control of the city.

At the orphanage, despite the protection of the Japanese soldiers at their posts, the rebels make another attempt on the school. One afternoon, the children hear gunfire coming from a small kampong behind the school. They are immediately told to lay flat on the floor. Sjeffie lays on the floor as the new Japanese guard draws his revolver and slowly walks toward the kampong while his soldiers cover him. He looks up at the coconut trees from where the bullets came and aims his pistol. A pelopor jumps out of the tree and runs. They are not shot at again.

—

Van Deventer School, Semarang, Indonesia, 2014

These days the Van Deventer School is a trade school. The buildings are still the same, and as we pull in to the driveway, my father's face lights up. He recognizes the house attached to the school where he lived for a short period. We go into the school's office and introduce ourselves to the woman behind the desk, but she doesn't speak English, and my father's rudimentary Bahasa is not good enough to explain why we are here. She smiles and gestures for us to wait, then returns with a man who speaks some English. He explains to her that my father once lived here and that we'd like to take a look around. She smiles and joins the man in giving us a tour. In one hallway, my father stops us. "This is the hallway where the children were hiding from the rebels," he says. "This is the hallway." The man translates for the woman. It's hard to know what they think about the story. All over Indonesia, there are murals and plaques commemorating the men who liberated the country from Dutch colonialism. To the Indonesians, the pelopors are martyrs. They are freedom fighters and heroes.

5

INDEPENDENCE AND DISPLACEMENT

Semarang, Dutch East Indies, 1945

In October, British troops arrive in the Dutch East Indies. Because the atomic bombs have ended World War II so suddenly, the Allies struggle to move a sufficient number of their own forces quickly enough to replace the Japanese troops, who still occupy a large area of Southeast Asia. British general Louis Mountbatten, who commands the Allies' Southeast Asian forces, is tasked with retaking the Dutch East Indies from the Japanese forces, who have been attempting to maintain the peace in this new conflict of shifting alliances and obey the orders of the Allied forces to keep the Dutch and Indonesian citizens safe. The Netherlands, which has just been liberated from Hitler's devastating occupation, does not have enough time to reorganize and train a task force to relieve the Japanese in the Dutch East Indies. So the job falls to Mountbatten and his British troops. Even with seasoned troops under his command, however, it takes Mountbatten a few months to organize transports for his men from India and Burma to the Indonesian archipelago.

During this long interim, and in this relative vacuum of power, Sukarno and the Indonesian fighters gain momentum in their fight for independence. When Mountbatten's troops finally arrive in Semarang in October, rather than merely take over organization of the recovery effort as expected, they are thrown directly into this battle.

At the Van Deventer School, a thrilled Sjeffie watches the arrival of the British troops, many of whom are Indian Sikhs and Nepalese Ghurkas from Britain's own colonies. When these men get sick or injured, some of them show up at my grandfather's medical clinic at the orphanage, asking for treatment. One afternoon, Sjeffie walks into the living room to find a tall Sikh with an elaborate uniform and an impressive turban waiting for his father. Sjeffie's eyes widen when he sees the pineapple-shaped hand grenade hanging from the man's belt. Now fourteen years old and bolder than he once was, he asks, "Excuse me . . . is that a real grenade?" "Yes," says the Sikh. "Is it dangerous to carry that inside a house?" asks Sjeffie. "No, young man. See?" The soldier loosens the grenade from his belt and holds it in his hand with the explosion-timing release pin held down by his middle finger. At that moment, Sjeffie's mother enters the room and blanches. "Sir, please! Put that away!!" The man grins as he puts the grenade back on his belt and winks at my father.

General Mountbatten's troops quickly lift martial law and initially relax their focus on the pelopor movements while they help organize the Japanese soldiers to facilitate their transfer home to Japan. Lady Mountbatten, the general's wife, tours Java to survey the camps and their survivors. Her photos are some of the only ones that document the camps and the medical condition of the survivors immediately after the war. Viewing those photos on the internet, I scroll through images of emaciated ex–prisoners of war lying in hospital beds. It gives me some access that I can't get through my father's stories alone. Seeing these people's bodies makes his experiences there more palpable.

Within three weeks of the arrival of the British troops, a second insurrection by Sukarno's men takes place, and again they occupy large parts of Semarang. But this time they are more prepared and have better weapons. The Van Deventer School is now guarded by British soldiers instead of Japanese, and the Indonesian pelopors take up positions in the treed foothills behind the school that overlook Semarang. Many families are not as lucky as my father's family. They don't have soldiers guarding them. On the first night of the second uprising, the pelopors sweep through houses and murder Dutch and mixed Indo civilians who have made the mistake of returning to their old homes in the suburbs of Semarang. In response to this new uprising, the British position a battle-ship at the entrance of Semarang's harbor and start to bomb the hills behind Sjeffie's house at the Van Deventer School with cannon-fired heavy missiles. Sjeffie looks up to the sky and sees the missiles fly overhead, exploding with a thunder-ous noise in the trees behind the school. It quickly becomes very clear that the Dutch and Indo ex-internees are not safe and a plan needs to be formulated to get them out.

At this point, not all of the camps have been completely cleared of internees, many of whom no longer have homes, jobs, or money. In Semarang, the camps are protected by the British troops, but there are several additional camps inland that are much more rural, with several thousand Dutch intern-ees still in residence. They have very few guards. During this second uprising, the pelopors decide to overtake those camps and eliminate the occupants. Trucks with armed pelopors arrive at the gate of one such camp, Camp Ambarawa, de-manding to see the Dutch camp administrator, as the Japanese camp administrator has already been sent home by the British. The pelopors tell the approximately six hundred women and children still living in the Ambarawa camp to congregate immediately at the center of the camp for an important announcement. Then the pelopors yell *"Merdeka!"*—Freedom!—and throw hand grenades into the crowd.

At that moment, those left standing hear the indisputable sound of a tank crawling toward the gate. Armed British Sikhs jump out of a truck behind the tank and run toward the pelopors, shooting their guns into the air as a warning. The pelopors turn and run, with most of them managing to escape. However, they leave behind a bloody scene in the camp clearing. About fifty women and children have been killed or wounded by the hand grenades. Some of the British Sikhs try to do triage as others quickly call for backup. It's clear that the situation is out of control, and the former internees are not safe. All the Ambarawa survivors are evacuated, along with former internees at several other inland camps. But now there are hundreds of evacuated internees in trucks, and nowhere to bring them. About fifty of these Ambarawa survivors are brought to the Van Deventer School, where they sleep in the gymnasium. Choking up over the cups of tea held in their trembling hands, they tell Sjeffie and his family about the traumatic experience they've just been through, shell-shocked and grief-stricken over the loss of the family members and campmates they've just seen blown apart after surviving for years in the prison camps.

Sjeffie and his family don't stay in the Van Deventer School much longer. The British forces and Red Cross immediately begin evacuating European and Indo people on every military battleship and plane they can call to the Semarang harbor for an emergency rescue mission. As soon as they gain partial control over the city again, they begin to move women, children, and civilian males out of Java in trucks with military escorts. The ships take as many refugees as possible to Australia and Ceylon (Sri Lanka). In Eastern and Western Java, people are also evacuated from Java's two other main ports in Surabaya and Batavia.

Sjeffie and his family are among the last ex-internees to be evacuated from Semarang, as Sjeffie's father is under orders to stay at his station at the Van Deventer School until most civilians have been evacuated. Then Sjeffie says goodbye to his bedroom and the living room and the little house. He says goodbye to the Van Deventer School and climbs onto the bed of a military truck. As the truck moves toward the harbor, he says goodbye to the Tjandi Hills, goodbye to the jasmine and the orchids and the banana trees, goodbye to the chichaks and geckos, the sugarcane and coffee plantations, goodbye to Mount Ungaran in the distance. Snaking down past Camp Lampersari and Camp Bangkong in the distance, he says goodbye. And then he is boarding a huge ship in the harbor, and he says goodbye to Semarang as it slides from view, and then to Java, and then to the whole of Indonesia, the only home he has ever known, columns of smoke rising in scattered spots on the island, which recedes behind the churning water in a strip of shore and monkeys and mango trees that thin and flatten before becoming one with the horizon and vanishing entirely from view. It is December 25, Christmas Day.

—

Semarang, Indonesia, 2014

It's hard to calculate how many people died during the Bersiap, this violent period immediately following the war. Among the Indonesian rebel fighters, the estimate is anywhere between 20,000 and 100,000, depending on the source. The British and British-Indian relief forces lost around 650 troops, with a further 320 permanently missing. The Japanese army fighting the rebels lost 402 in this conflict, with 88 missing. The mixed Dutch-Indonesian victims of the Bersiap are estimated at around 20,000, with 3,500 confirmed dead and the rest kidnapped and presumed dead, their bodies never recovered, though mass graves were reportedly seen by soldiers at the time. The Chinese Indonesians outside the camps lost hundreds of lives as well.

In what is considered a shameful period of Dutch history in the Netherlands, after the Dutch were evacuated from Indonesia, the Dutch army returned to try to win back its lost colony. It fought for three more years during this war of independence, leading to enormous bloodshed and recently discovered atrocities on the part of the Dutch fighters against the Indonesian people. Ultimately, the Dutch government had to accept that the Dutch East Indies would be no more, and that after hundreds of years, Indonesia would never again be a colony of the Netherlands. In December 1949, the Dutch transferred sovereignty to the Republic of Indonesia. With the transfer, a huge wave of remaining mixed Indo-European people migrated to Europe, no longer feeling there was a place for them in the new republic, even if they had survived the targeted attacks during the Bersiap period. There are Indo people in Europe today who still feel an intense amount of pain over having been forced to abandon the heritage of their Indonesian parent. They speak of a sense of rejection and a schism in identity due to their mixed race and expulsion from Indonesia.

As Joko drives us out of Semarang from the Van Deventer School in the Tjandi Hills, we pass the church on the hill that my father almost burned down as a young boy. I imagine the fire surrounding him and chasing him from the hill, the unstoppable advancing force, and how this was a foreshadowing of years later when he would flee these same hills, escaping from rebel fighters.

We pass the memorial cemetery and the thousands of white crosses that represent the souls that rest there into eternity, those left behind. I feel an odd sense of abandonment myself as we pass them in Joko's van. When this trip is over, I will go back to the United States, where my friends and family wait. My father will go back to his couch and his favorite blanket and will push the numbers he loves around on his papers. These crosses will stand there then, with no visitors, or maybe only one or two visitors a month, in monsoon and glaring sun, in a grass plot in the middle of a city of people who forgot they were there.

—

Java Sea, Indonesia, Christmas 1945

Sjeffie stares out over the billowing waves of the Java Sea from the deck of the HMS *Princess Beatrix*, a former passenger ship that was converted into a Dutch troop transport ship during World War II. He is en route, but to what he is en route remains unclear. Everything has happened so quickly. Left behind in Indonesia are the remnants of the only life he's known, and once again Sjeffie finds himself in a liminal space, with no sense of where his place in the world is. The authorities call it *repatriation*, but that word feels wrong for people who never lived in the Netherlands. Repatriation of the great-great-great-great-grandchildren of the first colonists, perhaps.

It takes five days to travel to the Red Cross refugee camp in Ceylon. When the refugees disembark in Ceylon's main harbor, Colombo, they are taken by train to the inland city of Kandy, and from there by trucks to a nearby temporary displaced persons camp, formerly used by General Mountbatten for housing his troops. There are already thousands of Dutch refugees there, as several shiploads of people from Java have preceded them. With their arrival on the last ship, the total head count of Camp Kandy swells to around five thousand. Sjeffie's father, who is still officially employed as a military doctor, is appointed co-administrator and hospital director of the Kandy refugee camp by the Dutch government. Sjeffie thinks of all his friends from Lampersari and Bangkong who just happened to be loaded onto the evacuation ships headed to Australia. They never even got to say goodbye. At this point in his life, he knows better than to become attached to people, but it's still difficult for him to wrap his mind around the idea that he will never see them again.

The family is in Camp Kandy for about four months. Fourteen-year-old Sjeffie and his eldest sister, Doortje, now thirteen, attend an official government-licensed Dutch school run by ex-interned teachers, while their little sister, Fieneke, eleven, and brother, Kees, eight, attend elementary school. The elementary school is farther from the camp and a long way to walk for little legs, so some days the younger children get a ride on the backs of elephants trained by the local inhabitants. It is the first time in three years that the children attend school, and most of them have fallen far behind the standards for students their age. They now work hard to catch up, knowing that in the Netherlands, they will be tested and placed in grade levels according to the results. Sjeffie is determined not to be stuck in a class with younger children when he arrives there. Because of his sharp mind and Aunt Ko's secret lessons in the first part of their internment in Camp Lampersari, he is not as far behind as the others and manages to reach the equivalent of a second-year Dutch high school class during three months of schooling, right on par with his age level.

The routine of school and the freedom the family experiences at the refugee camp after the years of war are welcome gifts. On the weekends, Sjeffie and his parents and siblings hike from the camp through the surrounding mountains to a nearby lake. After watching a massive monitor lizard emerge from the bushes to plunge into the water on one of these excursions, Sjeffie becomes convinced that there are crocodiles in the lake and refuses to swim there despite his father's assurances, but he still enjoys sitting at the edge, picnicking with his family. His favorite thing about the camp is movie night, held every Sunday. He has never been to the cinema, and this is a spectacular development in his life. He and his friends are enthralled by the films of Ingrid Bergman and Humphrey Bogart playing out on the giant white screen. Sjeffie's favorite movie is *Can't Help Singing*, with Deanna Durbin, a musical that floods him with feelings. The former prisoners are listening to music and making art, as their senses reawaken to beauty and emotion they've had to repress for years just to survive. As a result, rather than the refugee camp being a place of darkness, it is a place of great joy, an intellectual and emotional renaissance for many. "I really enjoyed the refugee camp," my father says now, when I ask him about his experience there. "I got to join a Boy Scout troop for the camp, which was really fun. I remember how amazing it was that we could get free snacks in the recreation building. About thirty to forty of Mountbatten's soldiers ran the camp.

I was jealous of those soldiers, because all the girls hung around making eyes at them, and of course I wanted the girls to be interested in me. They really showed off, these British soldiers in their uniforms." He still seems a little sore about it.

After four months, in April 1946, the refugees are put on ships bound for Holland, the ultimate destination for all evacuees in Camp Kandy. My grandfather, as group leader and medical doctor of the refugees, is given an officer's cabin next to the captain on the SS *Willem Ruys*. He shares it with Sjeffie's mother and three younger siblings, but quarters are tight, and as a fourteen-year-old male, Sjeffie has to sleep in the troop hold of the ship with about two hundred men and boys fourteen years or older on canvas bunk cots stacked four high. Another converted cargo hold houses around six hundred women and younger children. Sjeffie and the other teens are assigned jobs collecting and dumping garbage and keeping living quarters clean, as well as assisting in the mess hall, washing dishes. They are paid a small wage for these jobs on the ship, something new to Sjeffie after years of un-paid labor in the internment camps. Each of them gets a ra-tion of four packs of Navy Cut cigarettes each week, even the fourteen-year-old boys. Sjeffie gives the cigarettes to his parents, who later give them out as gifts to smokers when they arrive back in Holland, having little else to offer when they visit relatives and old friends.

The SS *Willem Ruys* takes a six-week-long route through rough and sometimes explosive-mined waters, via the Suez Canal, past Greece and southern Europe, and on to Holland. Just before entering the Suez Canal, the ship docks in Ataqa,

Egypt. There, the passengers disembark and are taken by train in groups to a giant warehouse in an expanse of desert, the heat causing the air to warp in waves. In front of the building, in a surreal scene, a group of Italian prisoners—Mussolini's soldiers captured during the war—play big-band music as Sjeffie and the refugees file into the warehouse. Inside are long aisles with individual stations of supplies piled high on tables. Each person is to receive one item from each station, including a winter coat, a scarf, long underwear, shoes, and a blanket, for the new climate in Europe. All the items have been donated by American and Canadian welfare organizations to help the refugees get back on their feet. It is the luck of the draw exactly which items each of them is handed, and children cast jealous glances at one another as they are given bright orange plaid coats while their siblings are given nice gray ones. Still, nobody dares to complain out loud about what they are handed as they walk down the line. Then they file back out of the warehouse, past the Italian band playing "Take the 'A' Train," and make the journey back across the desert to the ship. A few days later, they are very grateful for their new clothing as the weather on the ship's decks rapidly shifts from equatorial heat to winter cold past the Gulf of Suez.

After marveling at the changing landscape as they move through the Suez Canal, Sjeffie and the other passengers emerge on the other side, cruising through the Mediterranean to the south of Greece and the tip of Italy. Finally, they pass the Rock of Gibraltar in the narrow strait between the tip of Spain and the north coast of the African continent. Sjeffie learns that the rock jutting straight up out of the sea is one of the two Pillars of Hercules in Greek mythology, the furthest reach of Hercules's twelve labors and, according to Plato, the gate to the "Realm of the Unknown."

The *Willem Ruys* forges right past the rock, into the wide Atlantic. When it rounds the coast of Spain, the landscape changes again, and Europe feels very close. And one afternoon, they slide into Amsterdam's harbor, where hundreds of people stand along the port wall waving and throwing confetti and welcoming their fellow citizens back to the motherland. My grandfather's brother Jan and Jan's wife, Jeanne, are among them, welcoming the Dutch East Indies side of the family to Europe. Sjeffie shakes their hands and looks around him, unsure of what to think. They all take the train to the seaside town of Scheveningen, near The Hague, where Jan and Jeanne make room in their two-bedroom apartment for the family of six to sleep. In the days following, they arrange for Sjeffie and his siblings to attend an *overbrugging* (transitional) school to prepare for entering the Dutch school system.

As they settle in and Sjeffie takes in the unfamiliar tall buildings in a tightly packed country, the gray skies and dirty city pigeons, the bite of a cold air he's never lived with before, the initial hopefulness he felt as they arrived begins to fade. He doesn't want to say it out loud, because he knows he is lucky to be alive. But another unwanted knowledge is settling into his body along with the chill of the North Sea: He is Dutch, but the Netherlands is not home.

—

Zutphen, the Netherlands, 1947

Eventually, Sjeffie's family settles in Zutphen, back in Gelderland, where Sjeffie attends high school and drops the childish "ie" from his name to become Sjef. Intelligent, proud, and driven to learn, he had caught up extraordinarily quickly in the transitional school and has now become competitive with his Dutch peers. He's fascinated by physics, math, and especially aeronautics, an interest developed during the years spent looking at the sky during the war, noting the different types of military aircraft, from the Japanese Zeroes to the Allied planes that brought news of the prisoners' rescue. On the weekends, he joins other teens in an aeronautic club building and flying kites and radio-controlled model airplanes. He joins another club an hour away by bike, where they fly real gliders. He convinces the school headmaster's son to join him, a boy who later becomes a pilot for KLM.

Sjef finds comfort during these years with his eyes looking down in books or up in the sky. He doesn't really have close friends. A psychologist friend of his father's labels him a "secondary reactor," someone who is slow to develop relationships. He is slightly introverted. He does make friends superficially in school, but he doesn't try to hold on to them. Mostly he feels isolated and homesick for Indonesia during his teen years.

Drang is a Dutch word that is not entirely translatable into English. Loosely, it means an unrelenting urge or drive, but the word also carries an implication of deep yearning born of absence. I have this image of a homing pigeon that is released above the ocean. If you tore down its coop, would it fly in confused circles over that spot in perpetuity, never landing, driven by the internal drang of home, home, always home? As a teen, my father writes multiple urgent and detailed letters to the minister of foreign affairs in the Netherlands, proposing the establishment of a refugee community for them in the tropical climate of Papua New Guinea. He argues that certainly there is an uninhabited patch of land there that they can live on, comparing the expelled Dutch-

Indonesian colonists to the Jews, for whom the homeland of Israel is officially established during those same years. He writes that he and the Dutch-Indonesian colonists need the tropics, that they need a homeland too. They are earnest words from a homesick teenager. He checks the mailbox in their new house in Holland every day for a response, but it never comes.

The Netherlands is cold and gray and wholly foreign to a boy who is used to running around on bare feet, scaling coconut trees, and eating mangos on the beach. Having been ignored by the minister of foreign affairs and accepting that he will never be able to go back to Indonesia, Sjef turns to the next option: the United States. He sees the United States as having saved his life in the war. He reads about America, listens to American music, watches American movies. John Wayne, the American West, the Andrews Sisters, Perry Como, Bing Crosby on the radio. John Steinbeck and warm California, with its Pacific Ocean and orange groves. And of course, the repeated clichés about America: the American Dream, freedom. In America, a person can be anything, achieve any goal. He cannot wait. At sixteen years old, Sjef tells his parents one weekend that he is going to the glider club with friends. Instead, he cycles all day to the German border because he knows there is an American military base on the other side of it. He plans to stow away on the first plane out of that place. He doesn't know how; he just knows he needs to keep going. At the border, uniformed agents stop him. "Passport?" they say. Sjef blinks. He feels his face go hot. "Uh, no . . . no passport," he says. The agents look at one another, amused. They laugh at him. They offer him a cigarette and tell him he can come no farther. He declines the cigarette and turns the bike around, begins to cycle back to where he came from. Back to the Netherlands, trudging up the school steps in the unfamiliar snow with children he has nothing in common with, wearing hard leather shoes on his feet, watching black crows chatter in the trees instead of cockatoos, biding his time.

This story about stowing away on a military plane baffles me when he first tells me. "What were you going to do if you succeeded?" I ask him. "You must have believed you were going to succeed or you wouldn't have gone. You were really prepared to tell your parents that you were going to fly gliders and then never see them or the rest of your family ever again?"

"Yeah, I don't know. I guess so," my father says. I see in his desperate attempt to leave the extent to which the war took home from him, not just Indonesia or his house, not just his Dutch-Indonesian identity, but that deepest sense of home, the home of family and kin and citizenship, the home where you belong to a unit. After years of fending for himself in a men's labor camp, he didn't know how to be a child in a family again.

But my father is a persistent creature. He tells his father that he wants to go to America when he finishes high school. He is obsessed with the idea. His parents can't stop him from leaving once he turns eighteen. And they want him to pursue his goals. So they try to help him. My grandfather calls his brother-in-law Henk in Bolivia to ask for advice, because Henk knows a lot of Americans. Diploma in hand, my father prepares to leave the Netherlands, this pit stop between Indonesia and the United States of America. He doesn't feel any sadness leaving his classmates or his house in Eefde. He feels nothing but eagerness. He's going to do great things, and it isn't going to be in Holland. Every month, ships set off for New York, bringing people to new lives.

In the very near future, my father will be on one of those ships too, on his way to a long life in California, where he will marry and have children. He will build a home. He will carry the war with him, but he will also carry an unfaltering survival mentality, the lessons of self-sufficiency. He will carry the fight across the ocean and into a new world.

PART II

MOTHER

People say you're born innocent, but it's not true. You inherit all kinds of things that you can do nothing about. You inherit your identity, your history, like a birthmark that you can't wash off.

—HUGO HAMILTON,
The Sailor in the Wardrobe

6

FASCISM ON THE RISE

Hoog Soeren, the Netherlands, 2015

I am on my way to return a rental car when I abruptly pull off the highway at the exit that leads to the tiny village I lived in for a year as a child. The last time I traveled these roads, I was following the hearse that transported my beloved aunt Hannie's body back over the heath, through the woods, and finally to a plot in a tiny graveyard. I'm in Gelderland, a province right in the middle of the country. This is not a planned detour, as I am already late returning the car. As though called by sirens hiding in the waves of heather, I follow signs until I am on the road that carried me so many times to chimney smoke and spruce and the mushroomy scent of the forest floor I knew for so many years as a child. It's remarkable how I still know every corner of this place, from the mossy spot at the edge of the heath where the wild boars like to root to the train tracks near the big chestnut tree on the other side of the woods, where my cousins placed coins to be flattened by the trains that came through. I know all the overgrown hollows of World War II dugouts where my mother took shelter from bombs as a little girl. I appropriated the bomb shelters as faerie houses when I was a little girl, too young to understand that my mother took cover in them when she was my age, sirens wailing and bombers flying overhead.

Now, steeped in memories, both mine and my mother's bleeding together, I pull over on the empty road and walk out into the heath, the purple blooms ethereal under hovering mist. It is dead quiet, the kind of quiet you experience only in the country, though for me there are the whispers of many ghosts. I no longer have family living here. But this landscape is still mine; it belongs to me, registers as deeply familiar to my senses. This is where we children piled into my aunt's orange VW bus and drove out into the dark with flashlights to look for wild boars and rutting deer that called out to their mates and locked antlers in battle. As a preteen girl visiting my aunt in the summer, I saw the teenage sons of the Dutch royal family who lived in the palace nearby riding their horses in these woods, and I fantasized that a prince would stop his horse and ask me to be his girlfriend. I get back in the rental car and drive out to my aunt's former farm in the next village, Kootwijk. I look up at the window of my old bedroom, tucked underneath the eaves, and wonder who sleeps there now. In the meadow where I used to catch frogs, two enormous draft horses now graze. I drive to the two-room schoolhouse where I spent first grade, and where my mother also spent first grade. It has been converted into a duplex. Volvos are parked in the driveways. Potted plants stand defiantly in the windows. The people who live there are intruders, and I hate them.

My mother has a deep nostalgia for this province where she spent her childhood. I've inherited it from her, having spent every summer there while I was growing up and having lived there for a year when I was little. My mother and I were always missing it. Are always missing it. It's home for my other identity, the Dutch girl who lives on the heath in a green farmhouse in a tiny Calvinist village. Technically it is my aunt's home, but the year we live there and all of the summers we spend tucked into its many bedrooms become part of me. The yellow and red clogs lined up in the mudroom, the gooseberries growing along the fence, and the hornets' nests in the tall grass by the sheep shed. The dirt paths through the forest where we race our bikes, the secret family chanterelle hunting spot behind the old electric building. Here, there is the specific smell of horse manure and Border collie fur mingling with the antique wood of the piano and the damp of the cellar where the onions and potatoes are stored, a smell just as much mine as the smells of home in Los Angeles. I drive around for an hour, then get back on the highway to return my rental car like the tourist I am.

—

Apeldoorn, the Netherlands, 1940

In the dark of predawn, there is a muffled ringing. There is rustling as sleep is rubbed from eyes, and a fumbling under the pillow, where the alarm clock is. Fingers search for the button to silence it without bringing it into the open, where it might wake the man who lies slack-jawed and snoring on the other side of the bed, who insists he never be woken before 8:00 a.m. and complains that the clock's ticking disrupts his sleep. Silently, a woman in her midthirties pulls the covers from her body and creeps through the bedroom, grabbing a woolly sweater on her way out. She is Maria Catharina de Kock, my grandmother. As the small house sleeps, my grandmother lights a fire in the potbellied stove and starts breakfast, scrambling four eggs to feed five people. She slices some hearty whole-grain bread, saving the ends of the loaf for herself. Then she climbs the stairs to wake her husband and their children.

Hannie, the eldest, is eight. Then there are the boys: Bert, seven, and Pim, three. My mother, Elsje (pronounced Elshe) is just one year old. Hannie, already dutiful at this young age and loyal to her mother, changes Elsje's diaper and brings the baby downstairs, putting her in the playpen. The other kids sit at the table, eating. My grandmother knocks softly at the bedroom door to wake her husband, my grandfather. Adrianus Cornelis de Kock. He stretches, yawns. "Did you make tea yet?" he asks my grandmother with a sleep-weighted voice. He groans as he gets out of bed, scratching at the white undershirt covering his belly. He steps into his trousers, runs a wet comb through his hair. In the kitchen, he shovels eggs and bread into his mouth wordlessly, washing them down with the hot tea my grandmother sets in front of him. A half hour later, he is on his bicycle, headed toward the technical college, where he teaches thermodynamics and physics to young men preparing for careers in the auto industry. Hannie and Bert also get on their bicycles and head to school together. Then my grandmother finally sits down to nurse my mother while Pim pushes a wooden block around on the floor like a car. They are living hand-to-mouth at this point, like many in the Netherlands are after the Great Depression, which manifested there later than in the rest of the world, via a slow nagging burn rather than a sudden crash followed by recovery. Adrianus is lucky to have a job at all, and there is a rented roof over their heads and food on the table. Still, he is a man who wants better, who feels he deserves more than this.

—

My grandfather is a proud man. He is also an intelligent man. He has studied cryptology for years and is able to crack advanced codes. He has a degree in astronomy, but he feels his intellect isn't valued, at least not by this post-war, post-Depression society that sees the wealthy getting wealthier with commerce, and the rest of the working stiffs floundering. He makes a low wage teaching for the technical college in Apeldoorn, something he feels should be compensated in equal measure to other occupations requiring a degree. Has it always been this way for educators? I imagine my grandfather standing before his class of aspiring auto mechanics, trying to teach them physics. He speaks at a level beyond them and becomes frustrated when they don't understand. His ego is wounded as he considers where all his years of study and a Ph.D. have landed him: working for pennies teaching math to aspiring auto mechanics.

That ego, combined with his circumstances, makes my grandfather vulnerable to the messaging of national socialism percolating at that time.

The national socialist party in the Netherlands is the Nationaal Socialistische Beweging, or NSB. Established in 1931 by Anton Mussert to address the very issues that gnaw at my grandfather's sense of injustice, the party appeals to an idealist contingent of the population, including some Dutch Jews. What they all have in common is the feeling that the government has abandoned them in favor of the wealthy classes who run Dutch society. In fact, civil servants are prohibited from joining the party. This is a party ostensibly for the people, antiestablishment, though it definitely does not espouse democracy. The NSB favors a strong authoritarian ruler to distribute the country's wealth equitably, and the abolishment of voting rights—in the belief that if people are allowed to vote for politicians, competition and greed will inevitably get in the way of self-disciplined equality. In 1933, the NSB holds its first meetings, and my grandfather is a member from that year forward. In 1935, after the Great Depression has seen many people lose almost everything while others profit enormously, the NSB wins its first seats in Parliament, and begins to gain traction with its "A New Netherlands in a New Europe" nationalist message. The members focus on dismantling the wealthy ruling class, and in the first years, they espouse nonviolence and strategic positioning as tactics to gain power within the existing government.

For a man like my grandfather who feels himself slighted and that his talents are overlooked in a hierarchal class system that values only commerce and not intellect, a proud man who thinks the existing system is run by idiots, the NSB's message is irresistible. The movement preaches the country's interests over group interests, and group interests over individual interests. The national socialists advocate for a strong leader who will make decisions that ostensibly benefit the whole country rather than the few, and for an economy focused on equal distribution of labor and wealth. In order to achieve this, they claim it is necessary to revoke the voting rights of the country's citizens. I suppose that to my grandfather, it must have seemed more important to be granted the promise of a fair and equal system that would punish the corrupt and knock the wealthy off their gilded pedestals than to have his voting rights guaranteed. But those who support fascism usually fail to recognize that they are supporting fascism until it is too late and they realize that they've been waiting for their promised reward from snake oil salesmen. At what point does naiveté become negligence?

While there has been a great deal of literature written

about the false image of tolerance in the Netherlands before the Second World War, and though anti-Semitism was more common in the general public than the postwar Dutch were willing to admit, generally speaking, there is an institutional policy of tolerance for Jews within the NSB prior to 1935, with an estimated 150 of the 30,000 members being Jewish. In 1933, in a retort to anti-Semitic party members, Anton Mussert specifically addresses the NSB's Jewish members, stating, "You have your place in our ranks with full conviction. You remain worthy of this standing, and you may have the satisfaction of having done your duty to all our people despite suspicion and scorn." He further states that the "Israelites are just as welcome as other people" in the party, and insists that "National Socialism in the Netherlands does not have to be or become anti-Semitic, because here in the Netherlands there are Jews who are wholeheartedly committed to the well-being of the Dutch nation, because they help form one inseparable whole and wish to continue doing so."

But all of Mussert's grand words about unity and Jewish inclusion ultimately prove to be empty. In 1936, with Germany gaining power in Europe, some party leaders float the idea that they should ally themselves with Adolf Hitler, and criticize party leader Mussert for allowing Jews into the party. The internal fighting causes the party to lose strength, as cooperation dissolves. More radical leaders and the five NSB Parliament members begin pushing the pro-Nazi agenda further in the government and openly flout parliamentary procedure with disruptive outbursts and verbal abuse. They eject the Jewish party members during this period. Later, when the Nazis begin to deport Dutch Jews, the more prominent NSB Jews, who belong to the group of sixty-four so-called Mussert Jews, are sheltered by Mussert and sent to live at Villa Bouchina, a rectory in Doetinchem. Mussert is eventually overpowered, and the nine remaining Jews taking refuge at Villa Bouchina are arrested by the Nazis and sent to concentration camps, where three of them die.

I don't know why my grandfather didn't leave the party between 1936 and 1939, as it became clear that the NSB was descending into fascism with increasingly anti-Semitic and pro-Nazi rhetoric. However, there are clues that my grandfather was unhappy with the party and made attempts to distance himself and perhaps even leave the party when the NSB became more aggressive and the general population turned against members. In my research of his dossier at the National Archives, I find a letter addressed to him, dated January 1939, from Mussert himself:

> Comrade, Thank you for your letter on the 9th of this month. Of course, your number remains permanently assigned to you. Those who are being terrorized shall soon be able to continue to bear their share of responsibility to the cause within a new system. Thank you for everything you have done for the movement. It is my assertion that you will never be able to renounce your National Socialist membership. The leader, Anton Mussert

My grandfather's original letter to the party is not included, so I can't know to what extent he attempted to extricate himself from the party and what the reasons were for his communication, but the letter makes clear that he was under thinly veiled pressure by the leaders, being told that he could never renounce his membership. I imagine that my grandfather was intimidated and perhaps more than a little afraid as he realized the position he was suddenly in with the NSB's turn toward the Nazi party and war threatening the Netherlands: leave the protection of the party and become their target even as the anti-NSB community shunned him, thereby becoming persona non grata to both sides, or stay with the party that could shield him as it gained power in a political climate that was escalating toward war? He had four children. He argued with his brother-in-law Jan, a police officer, who disagreed with the NSB. I have heard from multiple older people in the family that during these arguments, he said, "If you've said A, you have no choice but to say B. It's too late for me to back out now."

According to all sources, my grandmother has no time for politics. My grandfather drags her to one meeting at the urging of party leaders who want families to be dedicated to their cause, and she signs the form they push under her nose. In the archives, I find political posters for this campaign to involve women and wives of members: "The woman who thinks also votes NSB." But my grandmother is not interested in politics or the nationalistic nonsense, and she never returns to a party meeting, nor does she vote in any elections. She has floors to mop and meals to cook, scarves and gloves to knit, hems to sew, tablecloths to scrub clean, fights between children to referee.

—

In October 1939, my mother is born into this household. Whereas the images of my father's family in Indonesia have a formal Protestant stiffness to them, coupled with the formality of upper-crust white colonial privilege, the black-and-white photos of my mother's family depict the casual familiarity of the lower middle class. They lounge lakeside on a picnic, their bikes lying in the grass next to them. My two-year-old mother stands at the water's edge in a hand-knitted bathing suit, her belly round, her dark brown eyes serious even at that age. There is an easiness in how they interact with their environment in these photos. When I am growing up, there is a photo of my grandmother that hangs in the hallway in our home in Los Angeles. She is in the woods, searching for wild blueberries. Foraging for blueberries and other wild edibles is a family activity that is carried on into my generation, a tradition passed down from my mother's family, a clan deeply involved with nature and place. The older kids join the *padvinderij*, "trail-seekers," the Dutch version of the Boy and Girl Scouts. As teenagers, they all join the NJN, the Netherlands Youth League for Nature Studies. The family often takes walks together, and my grandfather lectures the children about plants and rocks and animals along the way, his hands on his back as he walks, pausing to pick up this or that object and quiz the kids about it. I can see him clearly in my mind, though I never met him, because my uncles are also this way. "*Boletus edulis*," he says, holding up a specimen. "Now, how do we know this is a King Bolete and not *Tylopilus felleus*? Whoever can answer first gets butter on their bread tonight."

Unlike my father's family, my mother's family is not religious. My mother's father is an astronomer, eyes pointed skyward into the ether. Not looking for God but looking at the miraculous, logical machine of nature as the planet spins around the sun. Nature is sacred in my mother's family, and continues to be so, with almost all of the children of my

Eerkens's family on front steps in Benkulu, Sumatra. *(left to right):* Aunt Jo holding Doortje, Grandfather Jozef Eerkens Sr., "Aunt Soer" with Fieneke, Grandmother Elisabeth holding Sjeffie (Jozef Jr.) 1935.

Doortje and Sjeffie playing with a baby tiger, Bengkulu, Sumatra, circa 1933.

Grandmother Elisabeth's students with family *(in front, left to right):* Fieneke, Sjeffie, Doortje) at graduation, prior to family's departure from Bengkulu, 1936. *(Courtesy of Collection Tropenmuseum, National Museum of World Cultures. Creative Commons license 3.0)*

The family around the car, circa 1937.

Sjeffie and baby brother Keesje, Semarang, 1938.

Swimming in Old Tjandi, circa 1938.

Aunt Jo visits the Eerkens family in Semarang, 1938.

Eerkens kids with babysitter "Elly," 1938.

Fieneke, Doortje, Grandmother Elizabeth *(behind)*, Sjeffie, and neighbor Friedl, circa 1938.

Grandfather Jozef
Eerkens Sr. and his
children, Semarang,
circa 1938.

Tropical Eerkens
children eating
mangos. *(left to right)*:
Keesje, Doortje,
Fieneke, Sjeffie,
Madiun, circa 1939.

Grandfather
Jozef Eerkens Sr.
rowing a boat on
Lake Sarangan
with children,
circa 1940.

Cousin Kees *(left)* arrives in April 1941 from Bolivia to go to school. Less than a year later, he will be interned in Camp Lampersari with the rest of the family, and then Camp Bangkong men's camp with Sjeffie *(right)*.

(left to right): Sjeffie, Cousin Kees, Fieneke, Doortje, Madiun, circa 1941.

Eerkens family home on the Ingenluijflaan 49 in Madiun, 1941. When the Japanese invade a year later, their officers will occupy this home.

Grandfather Jozef Eerkens's tin cup for his daily ration of food in the camp. Medium apple for scale.

Rare photograph from inside the internment camps. Women on kitchen duty cooking rice in a giant cauldron over open flames in Camp Lampersari. *(Courtesy of Valentin Schreiber, Creative Commons license 3.0)*

School buildings in refugee camp Kandy after the war as families fled Indonesia with the help of the Red Cross during the Bersiap/civil war, Sri Lanka. The Eerkens family stayed there approximately five months before being repatriated to the Netherlands in April 1946.

Eerkens family back in the Netherlands, Eefde, circa 1948.

Sjeffie in the aeronautics club, Eefde, the
Netherlands, circa 1948.

Sjeffie and new friend on the *Edam*, heading to New York, September 1950.

Sjeffie visits the grave of "Aunt Lien" in Kalibanteng memorial cemetery in Semarang, Java, in 2015. Aunt Lien, a close friend of the family, died in Lampersari Camp at age thirty-six.

Sjeffie visits his former men's prison camp, Bangkong, for the first time in seventy years. The facility is now a school, and beautifully landscaped and maintained. Semarang, Java, 2015.

mother and her siblings going into the natural sciences, and all of us camping, foraging, gardening, and bird-watching. I read the NSB literature and notice a display of pride in old agrarian Holland, like when the party abandoned the Roman calendar names of the months in favor of names related to farming and nature. Starting with January, the new names are: *hide-tanning month, wood-gathering month, spring month, grass month, bloom month, summer month, hay month, harvest month, fall month, sowing month, slaughter month,* and *winter month.* I sometimes wonder if my grandfather was attracted to the NSB because of this strange echo of paganism in the movement that honors agricultural traditions and man's relationship with the land. For my grandfather, nature can be trusted; it is an ordered, reliable, and predictable system. The party he pledged his allegiance to, however, was far less trustworthy.

7

THE OCCUPATION

The Netherlands, May 1940

My mother sits in her playpen chewing on a wooden teething ring while tanks roll past her home in Apeldoorn, shaking the floorboards, causing the chimes on her mobile to jingle. My mother is six months old on May 10, 1940, the day that Germany invades Holland. Two days later, the German forces enter her small town, leaving officers behind to oversee the handover of power.

Civilians, shaken and ashen-faced, pass through the town as they move in from the south, fleeing the blitzkrieg of Rotterdam, which has been flattened by the German Luftwaffe's relentless aerial assaults. The Germans shatter every old church, every last historic brick in the inner city. Close to nine hundred dead bodies lie in the smoldering remains, and eighty-five thousand stunned inhabitants are suddenly homeless. The news is extremely grim, and the Netherlands, which had hoped to remain neutral in Germany's war, now finds itself under a furious attack it simply cannot fight off.

It takes only four days for the country to fall. All through-out Apeldoorn, people weep as the Nazis move in.

But in my mind, this never included my mother's father. Before my research, when I imagined the invasion of the German troops, my grandfather was not weeping as he watched soldiers enter his town. This is what I once imagined: my grandfather standing on the sidewalk with his arms crossed in front of him when the tanks roll by, smug and pleased. Maybe he waves at the German soldiers or gives them the infamous stiff-armed salute, a grin on his face. I imagine the scene in the most evil way I can, because I need a villain. I need him to be a caricature to reconcile this secret fact I know about him with the narrative I have received in school, in popular culture, about what Nazi sympathizers look like. I need him to not be too much like me, his granddaughter. So I compartmentalize. It isn't until I read his letters that I realize he actually loathed the Nazis, that he felt his country was being invaded, and that my black-and-white image of the war is extremely simplistic. So where do I put him now when I try to reconstruct this event in history? On which side does he belong? What if he's somewhere in between?

Four days after the invasion, there is no more fighting. The Germans set up headquarters in every Dutch city hall, stringing up banners and hoisting the Nazi flag up the flagpole outside the royal palace in Apeldoorn. Young men in the Dutch resistance movement throw Molotov cocktails until they are subdued and arrested, but aside from a small civilian backlash, there is no military fighting for the first years of the war, something that surprises me when I learn this later in life. Throughout my teens and into my twenties, I imagined the war as years of continuous military fighting, Dutch and Allied soldiers against the Germans. Bullets flying, snipers on rooftops, ambushes of convoys, for years on end. The truth, I learn, is much less dramatic. Unlike my father's experience in the Dutch East Indies, after the capitulation in the Netherlands, life goes on as usual for the majority of the Dutch public, with the exception of German soldiers and officers hanging about their towns and cities, running everything that was previously run by the Dutch and drinking beer in their pubs at night. The women still go to the shops, the men still go to their jobs, the trains run on schedule, and the kids are in school. Some Dutch Jews, afraid of rumors they've heard, do leave during this period, but the majority stay.

What there is instead of fighting in the streets is tension. There is hatred of the Nazis, and seething resentment of NSB members, who strike a deal with the Nazis in order to remain the sole party in operation under the German rule. It quickly becomes clear that the Nazis are calling all the shots. In his meetings with Hitler, Mussert attempts to be named the leader of a German-allied yet independent nation, but this request is denied. Instead, Mussert is given an honorary title, Leader of the Dutch People, a symbolic pat on the head for his cooperation with occupiers, and sent to his headquarters to await orders from the Nazi leaders. The Nazis appoint new mayors, all from within the NSB party, and opportunists emerge from within the Dutch population. The NSB party swells in size, acquiring over one hundred thousand new members during this period. Many of these new members support the Nazis, but just as many believe that joining the party will protect them. Some join in order to profit.

In June 1940, the Dutch royal family flees to London, fearing for their lives. Mussert uses this to strengthen the NSB's position, taking advantage of people's feelings that they've been abandoned by their queen, whose privilege has allowed her to flee while they remain in the motherland, though most certainly the royal family would have been murdered by the Nazis if they had remained. In fact, rather than abandoning her people, Queen Wilhelmina broadcasts a weekly radio address to the country from her refuge in London, insisting that she is still very much with them. In response to this, the Nazis accuse her of provoking people to stage nationwide strikes and rebel, and so they make the owning of a radio illegal. In the Dutch archives, an anonymous poem, "Goodbye to My Radio," appears in an article on the seizure of radios:

> *My radio, my dearest friend*
> *We soon will have to part*
> *As that German thief has stolen you*
> *To chastise me, your owner*
> *For I pin my only hopes*
> *On the messages from Britannia . . .*

While the rest of the country has to turn in their radios, NSBers are allowed to keep theirs, and in fact are offered the very radios that have been confiscated from their neighbors. They are passed out to NSB members, but my grandfather refuses his, saying he doesn't need a radio. He does help his brother-in-law Jan, the husband of my grandmother's sister Ket, with fixing and hiding an illegal radio. Jan is both a police officer and an active member in the resistance, so my grandfather knows that helping him with the radio is highly illegal. But according to his and Jan's written statements, my grandfather doesn't believe that some people should have things that others don't, and he's critical of the Germans and their radio double standard, so he flouts the rules to help Jan and the resistance.

This is the kind of mixed information that muddles my perception of my grandfather's activity in the NSB. I bump up against these conflicting behaviors continuously, causing my feelings about my grandfather to sway wildly from one end of the spectrum to the other. When he and my grandmother go to visit her sister, he and Jan have heated arguments about politics while they work on the radio and drink jenever in the shed. The more they drink, the more the disagreement escalates. Jan scolds my grandfather and calls the Nazis animals, asks him how he can support a party that supports the Nazis. My grandfather yells back that he doesn't support the Nazis, he supports the NSB. Jan says it's the same thing.

Meanwhile, even as he argues in defense of his membership in the NSB, my grandfather helps Jan with his illegal activities for the resistance, and he knows that Jan uses a typing course held in his living room to pass secret messages to other members of the movement.

In the first few months of the occupation, the Nazis don't take any overt action against the Jewish population of the Netherlands, which numbers at that point around 140,000 people, mostly concentrated in Amsterdam. Perhaps this lulls people into a false sense of security. According to several historical accounts, the Dutch public is naive in the beginning, believing the Nazis won't actually do anything to their Jewish citizens, who are well integrated into Dutch society. In Amsterdam, one in ten citizens is Jewish, including some of the most prominent families in the city. In fact, to this day the Dutch nickname for Amsterdam is Mokum, the Yiddish word for *safe haven*. Prior to World War II, the quarter near the Nieuwmarkt is a bustling area of Jewish businesses where many non-Jews also shop. However, in November 1940, Jews are suddenly removed by the Nazis from public positions, in particular those in the education sector, such as university faculty. All the other faculty members at universities receive a letter, which they are instructed to sign:

> *The undersigned declares that to the best of his/her knowledge, neither he nor she, nor his/her spouse, nor his/her parents or grandparents, have ever belonged to the Jewish belief or community... The undersigned understands that providing false information will result in immediate termination.*

This leads to student protests, but the demonstrations are ineffective. Faculty members who protest the firing of their colleagues and refuse to sign the declaration are immediately arrested by the Nazis and sent to prison, where they remain until the end of the war. The Dutch population, while agitated, either still don't fully understand the danger their Jewish neighbors are in or are complacent and complicit, or a combination of both, depending on whose historical narrative is believed. It's impossible to know one singular truth in this, as with any perspective of history. What is known is that not enough direct action was taken in response to the early arrests of professors and firings of Jewish public employees. The next uprising doesn't happen until February 1941, when a small group of Dutch Jews is arrested and deported. Anger against the Nazis rises among Jews and non-Jews, and a fight breaks out between NSB members and members of the resistance on the Waterlooplein in the Jewish neighborhood. An NSB member is killed, and this is all the provocation the Nazis need. The day after the fight, they put barbed wire around the Nieuwmarkt neighborhood, raise the bridges, place guards at the entrances, and create an island-ghetto, prohibiting movement into or out of the neighborhood. It is forbidden for non-Jews to enter unless on official business.

Today, the Nieuwmarkt neighborhood is one of the liveliest in Amsterdam, and I spend much of my time there when I'm in the city. Looking at a photo of the same square surrounded by a barbed-wire fence, Jews on one side, non-Jews chatting with them on the other, I am shocked by how casual they appear. I think of how easily the unacceptable can begin to look acceptable when people are inside an experience. There are Jews who have already gone into hiding by this point, recognizing the danger, but I wonder about the rest of the community. This photo of the ghetto was taken a full year and a half before the Frank family went into hiding. I wonder if people believed that this was as bad as it could get.

The Dutch practice of meticulous record-keeping works against the Netherlands' own citizens, as the addresses and names of all Jews have been neatly noted in the city halls and synagogues, giving the Nazis all they need to efficiently round up the Jewish population. These people are called to the Nieuwmarkt square to register at tables with the Nazis or face punishment, and each of them receives a Star of David armband they must wear in public. Frightened by the beatings and detainment they have seen happen to others who resist, they comply, standing politely in line and volunteering their names, birthdays, and home addresses, many sealing their fates. They have no idea what awaits them in the camps or the capacity for depravity in human beings. This Dutch efficiency and tendency toward bureaucracy is one of the main factors in the Netherlands' having the highest percentage of its Jewish population killed among all Nazi-occupied countries in Western Europe.

After the creation of the Jewish ghetto in Amsterdam, more fights and protests erupt throughout the city, causing Nazi officers to be injured. In revenge, the Nazis conduct their first large-scale pogrom on the afternoon of February 22, 1941, a Saturday. Driving their trucks into the Nieuwmarkt neighborhood, 600 Nazi soldiers flood the streets, rounding up 425 young Jewish men between the ages of twenty and thirty-five. The young men are held in a school and later sent to concentration camps, where all but two will die. In response to the pogrom and the detention of the young men, who are at that point still in the country, many workers in the city of Amsterdam go on collective strike, led by the non-Jewish dockworkers in the shipyards and the communist party of the Netherlands, which distributes a flyer:

STRIKE! STRIKE! STRIKE! Organize a strike in all businesses! Fight the terror! Demand the immediate release of the arrested Jews! Show solidarity with the heavily stricken Jewish members of our working population! Halt the entire Amsterdam commerce for one full day!

The flyers work. All commerce and public transportation come to a grinding halt that day. Other strikes in cities throughout Holland follow.

Sadly, they do little to stop the assault on the Jews, and the leaders of the first protest strike are executed.

After the February strikes, Jews are mercilessly rooted out of the city. The sound of boots echoes against the tall brick houses in the narrow streets of the city. Fists pound on doors, and if no one answers, doors give way with a violent splintering as Dutch Jews are taken from their homes and put onto trams to the Amsterdam Central Train station. From there, they are taken to Camp Westerbork for processing, and then are sent on to Auschwitz, Dachau, or Bergen-Belsen.

The fact that most of the Dutch Jews are processed through Westerbork, 180 kilometers northeast of Amsterdam, is a bitter irony. In perhaps the cruelest twist of the occupation, in 1942 the Germans seize the Westerbork refugee camp, which had been established in 1939 by the Dutch government and wealthy Dutch Jews to take in Jews and Romani people fleeing the Nazi-occupied areas of other countries. It is filled with Jewish refugees who are like sitting ducks when the Nazis invade the Netherlands. The Nazis put them on trains to the concentration camps almost immediately and turn Westerbork refugee center into a transit camp where over one hundred thousand Dutch Jews, including Anne Frank, as well as one thousand Romani and members of the resistance, are held before being sent to their deaths in extermination camps.

To this day, the trauma still runs deep in Amsterdam. My cousin told me about an old man he knows who grew up in a Jewish neighborhood of Amsterdam near the Amstel station. He was the only gentile living in the neighborhood, and all of his friends were Jewish. One day they came to his house with their parents to say goodbye, bearing gifts. "We'll be back," they said. "Don't worry." But not a single one ever returned. He lost all of his childhood friends and his entire community in one week. This man left the Netherlands and moved to France, unable to bear ever returning to his city.

While Amsterdam was emptied of its Jews, my grandfather was ninety kilometers away in Apeldoorn, which had seen one Jewish teacher fired from the local high school. In the letters he wrote after the war, my mother's uncle Jan maintained that my grandfather was not anti-Semitic. Other witnesses at his trial also insisted he was not anti-Semitic. He himself said he was not anti-Semitic. All of his children insist he wasn't anti-Semitic. As members of the resistance, Jan and his wife had *onderduikers* in their house, people in hiding from the Nazis. My grandfather said nothing when he visited them on weekends. The neighbors had a Jew hiding in their home whom my grandfather knew about. My grandfather said nothing to anyone throughout the war about these onderduikers. My relatives all tell me that he had several Jewish friends and colleagues before, during, and after the war, friends whom he defended.

In his dossier in the archives, I find a defense witness statement from his brother-in-law Jan:

13 June 1945

[De Kock] knew all kinds of information that in the last years of the war could not be brought into the

light of day. For some time I had the family Fontijne
in hiding in my home. De Kock knew about the en-
tire situation and kept it secret. During the time that
radios were confiscated, he even helped me to hide
my own radio. In a shed behind my house I was hid-
ing four horses that should have been confiscated
and two contraband bicycles hidden for the farmer
Schenk. De Kock came to my house, saw every-
thing, was greatly amused by it all, and always kept
it secret.

Jan Enzerink, Police Agent, Dordrecht

So how do I reconcile this portrait of my grandfather with
the article I discover on microfiche in the National Library
of the Netherlands in The Hague titled "Crisis of the Sciences"? Written by A. C. de Kock in 1942 for the NSB journal *New Netherlands*, it reads, in part,

The Jews, one could say, have shown that they are
capable of practicing science and even can be fairly
successful. One could rattle off a whole list of names:
Einstein, Lipschitz, Spinoza, Minkowski, etc. . . . But
hard science, as degenerated as it is today, is no lon-
ger characteristic of our race . . . When the Jew from
time to time succeeds in the current science, which has
become disorderly partly because of him (as well as
Humanism), that does not necessarily prove that he
has anything to offer us in this area . . . On the con-
trary, it would certainly appear that the Jew has noth-
ing to offer that would be of any interest to us, no
more than the Papua, the Chinese, the Eskimoes, or
the African Negroes . . .

These are the words of my grandfather, someone supposedly "not anti-Semitic," someone who supposedly had Jewish colleagues and friends whom he spoke highly of, writing clearly anti-Semitic, racist nonsense for a racist NSB publication. Was he pressured to write it? My cousins, much older than I, tell me that my grandfather was an intelligent man with Jewish academic colleagues whom he respected, and there is no way he actually believed what he was writing in the article. So why did he write it? They have theories. *He was paid to write it and sold out to feed his family. He was threatened. He was afraid of being seen as disloyal. Ego; it made him feel important to be asked to write an article.* Perhaps he was secretly more racist than his friends and family knew and felt superior to his Jewish friends. Sadly, nobody alive today knew he wrote this article until after his death—he never spoke of it. He refused to discuss any aspect of his involvement with the NSB later in life. I don't know what the truth is about this article, or about his continued involvement with the NSB. He has taken his explanation and any possible defense he might have had to his grave.

Further, there is a giant question mark for me regarding the arson of the Jewish synagogue in Apeldoorn. The Jewish population of Apeldoorn isn't as large as that in Amsterdam, but they have a synagogue, a stately brick building with stained glass windows. One night in August 1941, it is set on fire. Three NSB members are caught in the act at 3:00 a.m., shaking gasoline from cans around the perimeter and onto the front door, striking matches. Their names aren't printed in any of the newspapers, but as an NSB member, my grandfather must have known something via the local rumor mill, even if he wasn't directly involved. The synagogue is only a ten-minute bike ride from his home, after all. If my grandfather had been alive in my lifetime, I would have liked to ask him about this, about the article and what he knew and when he knew it, what he really believed, whether he was pressured, and why he continued on in the party. But the documents—ink on paper—and the words of people who knew him who are still alive are all the evidence I have, and they are at odds with each other.

In a video I watch, a man close to my mother's age stands at the grave of his father, who was in the NSB. "The first time I came here, I was so angry," he says, "because of what he did. I think, Jesus, what is going on inside you that you would make a choice like that? I just can't understand . . . The problem is that as a child, you can't ask them what actually happened. [They] didn't want to talk about it." Grappling with the actions and the beliefs of your ancestors is a one-sided conversation. I will never have all the answers I want about my grandfather, and without a diary or letters in which he wrote freely, I will never have the chance to hear his side of the story. Recently, my cousin and I traveled to visit my grandfather's grave site, which we had never seen. The family had received word that the body might have been disinterred. The site had never been paid for or maintained. I don't know why we wanted to go. In the car on the way to the cemetery, we talk about our frustration that we will never get to ask him "Why?" The cemetery where he is buried is grim and gray, abutting a mobile home park. Almost too perfectly, a pair of black ravens sit on a gravestone in the drizzle, calling out. Our grandmother was not buried next to him. All expense was saved burying him, and he was buried in a public grave in the county where he died. At his grave site, we discover that he's not alone. He's sharing his grave with a stranger named Izaak. Izaak is buried on top of him in the same grave, something that we learn was done in public graves during the 1960s. My grandfather's gravestone is plain and worn away, covered in lichen. We stand in front of it, looking down, getting no answers to our "Why?"

In 1941, my mother is two years old, toddling about the house, walking through the woods nearby, sitting on the banks of the Hill and Dale nature park with her brother Pim, now five. When school lets out, her face lights up as she sees her brother Bert, now eight, and sister Hannie, now nine, come in through the back door into the mudroom and set their book bags on the ground. Across town, thirteen Jews are removed from their homes in Apeldoorn and sent to concentration camps. My grandfather, like all Apeldoorn community members, will be told of their deportation, though he doesn't know what their ultimate fate will be in the "detention" camps.

At the end of 1942, my mother is three, and scooting around on her tricycle. Pim is practicing writing his letters: *P-i-m*. Meanwhile, all Jewish bank accounts are frozen, and in Apeldoorn, another two hundred Jews are removed from their homes during Nazi *razzias,* their doors kicked in, and men, women, and children dragged out into waiting trucks.

In early 1943, my mother is four. My grandfather is still working at the auto mechanics' school, cycling there and back every day. His Jewish students and colleagues are missing, and for most of the remaining faculty and student body, maybe it's easy to forget they were ever there. He comes home, grabbing the newspaper off the stoop, and pours himself a cup of tea. Across town, thirteen hundred people in a Jewish mental hospital in Apeldoorn who had been allowed to stay up to that point are led out of the facility, loaded onto trucks, and deported to concentration camps, thereby emptying the city of all its Jewish citizens, with the exception of the onderduikers in hiding.

By all accounts, both by witnesses in his postwar trial and by people who knew him, my grandfather condemned these acts to those who challenged him on his NSB membership. He agreed in their political debates at the time that the Nazis had gone too far, and that the NSB should never have allied themselves with the Nazi party to begin with.

But did he rethink his NSB membership? Is knowing about one onderduiker in hiding and saying nothing an excuse for knowing about thousands of others being pulled from their homes and put on trains and taking no action to stop it? We could ask the non-NSB citizens the same thing. Here is where I always get caught up: If my grandfather was afraid of the repercussions of turning his back on the party, does it make any of it OK? What about the others, the hundreds of thousands of residents who cursed the Nazis, who weren't in the NSB, but who bought their Jewish neighbors' silverware at the market stalls and moved into their homes for a bargain?

My mother was a toddler during the worst of war, during the razzias and the increasing anger. She recalls very little of that period, and her parents did their best to shelter their children. But her older siblings who were in school remembered a lot. They had very few friends during the war. Hannie was so ashamed, she often sat with her head down in the corner. As an adult, she told me she was thankful that the teachers didn't throw her out of their classes and that the other children tolerated her presence. Still, while she and her siblings were tolerated, most of their classmates were forbidden to play with them, as they were "dirty NSBers." At school, they ate lunch alone. They weren't invited to birthday parties, except for those of the other children of NSB members. The neighbors cursed under their breath when they passed. All across the country, taunting songs were sung to and about NSB members in the streets. As she was under the age of five, my mother doesn't remember the songs being sung to them, but her family would not have been an exception.

I learn about these anti-NSB songs not from my mother's family but from an eighty-three-year-old woman whom I am introduced to in 2014 while on a writing retreat in Gelderland, in a village that saw a lot of fighting at the end of the war. The woman recalls being a child during the war in the village, where she spent her whole life, and having an NSB member as a neighbor. We sit in her garden and drink tea as I ask her about her memories of the war. When I mention writing about the NSB and my grandfather, she misinterprets this to mean that he fought the NSB, and she says, "Oh, we kids used to tease the NSBer on our street. We ridiculed him and his son!" and begins singing enthusiastically, apologizing for her shaky voice.

> *Ohhhhhh Jan de Bree, you're a traitor to the country*
> *Ohhhhhh NSB, we're going to break your neck*
> *You in your lil' black uniform, you're actually in*
>   *mourning,*
> *When Queen Wilhelmina comes back, we'll beat*
>   *you black and bluuuue.*

When there is no more meat to eat, we will butcher
    yooooou.

She laughs. "That's what we kids always sang about that nasty NSBer, Jan de Bree, and his son, who lived on this street. NSBers, you could see it in their eyes. Just mean." There is an awkward pause as I try to formulate an elegant way to correct the misunderstanding that has transpired between us, but there is no tactful way to say it.

"Um, actually, I meant I am researching the NSB because my mother's father was a member."

She blanches and stammers, "Ohhh. Oh, I thought— It was just kid songs. We didn't know any better. I didn't know."

"It's OK," I say. "Actually, this is good. I'm glad you shared this with me. Nobody ever wants to tell me how people really felt about the NSB members once they know about my grandfather. They're afraid of being impolite. But I want to know how it really was. I can't understand if I don't know how it really was at the time."

Later, I research anti-NSB songs and discover many others. One I find especially interesting:

On the corner of the street is an NSBer,
It's not human, it's not an animal, it's a Pharisee-er.
With a newspaper in his hand, peddling his rag,
Selling out his Fatherland, for a coupla cents.

I am struck by the lines about NSBers not being human. I wonder how the children of NSB members internalized that messaging about their parents during the war. I wonder how that message influenced their relationships with the people they relied on for all of their needs, emotional and physical, at a young age. The Dutch, filled with rage and grief as they watched their neighbors being arrested and taken away, had little recourse left beyond verbal protest. So they did not hide their feelings about the collaborators during the war, and the children watch, extensions of their parents. "*Fout!*" my three-year-old mother hears yelled at them as she walks through the farmers' market holding her mother's hand. "*Fout!*" my mom's big sister, Hannie, hears yelled at her as she bikes to school. "Dirty, filthy Nazi-lovers! *Fout! Fout! Fout!*" *Fout*. Wrong. *Fout* means not just incidentally wrong, but inherently defective and flawed, a deeper, unchangeable, all-encompassing kind of wrongness. How does a child like my mother metabolize that label on her and her family as she grows up?

—

Apeldoorn, the Netherlands, 1943

In early 1943, Hannie is enrolled by my grandfather in the *Jeugdstorm*, the NSB youth group for kids aged ten to seventeen, based on the Nazis' Hitlerjugend. On weekends, Hannie is expected to put on a uniform that looks much like a Girl Scout's uniform. She bikes across town to attend the meetings, where they do calisthenics and track-and-field exercises to keep their bodies fit. Healthy body, healthy mind! The blond, blue-eyed girls memorize songs and march back and forth on the frost-covered field at the local high school while singing in unison, their breath puffing from their faces in little clouds:

> *Our drumbeats sound throughout the land, marching with the Youth Storm!*

The flags are waving in our hand, the flags of our
   Fatherland!
Stormer's youth! Stormer's youth! Stormer's youth
   is marching!

Hannie, now eleven years old, shuffles along in formation in the cold, gray afternoons. She's thoroughly embarrassed and doesn't feel moved by the flag or the fatherland or these women standing in front of her shouting with their mega-phones in their woolen skirts, ties, and silly hats. She's a sweet, sensitive girl who likes everyone. She doesn't understand why she's supposed to mistrust Jews or feel proud to be a Germanic girl. To the contrary, her face flushes with shame when her non-NSB classmates bike by the field, and she tries not to catch their eyes. She would much rather be reading a book, walking in the woods, or even doing her homework. When it rains, the Youth Storm leaders force the children to sit inside and watch Hitler's speeches projected onto a white screen, or they force the kids to write stories about being proud Dutch children for the Jeugdstorm news-paper, *The Storm Seagull*. Hannie daydreams and fails to ap-ply herself to the cause with gusto. She is talked to sternly by the Jeugdstorm girls' leader about her importance in the movement. "Young lady, your country is counting on you. Is that bird you're staring at perhaps more important than your country?"

Hannie bikes home and bursts into tears as she walks in the front door. "I don't want to be in the Jeugdstorm any-more," she says to her father. "Please, please, Paps, can I quit?" My grandfather nods.

"OK. If you really don't want to do it, I will see what I can do." He goes to his desk and pulls out a sheet of letter paper. A week later, a response comes back to him from the regional girls' director of the Jeugdstorm.

April 4, 1943

Comrade,

In regard to your letter of April 2, the following: You write that when your daughter is required to go to the Youth Storm, she has no free time left over due to all her studies, and this seems to you to be unhealthy for a child of eleven years old. Would it then not be a better solution to not have a child of eleven years old study so much? The Youth Storm is not stressful but in fact anti-stress, and is a moral obligation, Mr. De Kock! I would have expected more understanding from you as a national-socialist about the forthcoming new times and some sense of duty to your other comrades, whose own children are committed for the full 100% to realize their ideals, and are willing to sacrifice insignificant personal past-times. This is not a game anymore, but deadly serious. It is sink or swim now, and children cannot learn this early enough, comrade! I therefore see no good reason to excuse Hannie. However, you can consider her expelled from the Youth Storm as of the 1st of grass month. I would have liked to have seen her contribute something to this point. She is seven weeks behind, something which you should not have allowed to happen. If Hannie had been told at home what her duty was as a Youth Stormer, this would not have happened.

Her uniform pieces are owned by the Youth Storm and remain our property with her departure. Please

have her drop them off as soon as possible. They are:
a blouse, cap, tie, tie clip, and badge.
 Stay the course!

    The Regional Girls' Youth Storm Director,
        C. Wedekind

Some NSBers profit financially from their membership in the party, being appointed to important positions and getting salary increases, but my grandfather, sticking to his socialist ideals, rejects such opportunities. He is offered a better position at a better school but keeps his teaching job at the auto mechanics' school, despite his low pay and lack of prestige having been a major point of frustration for him. He is offered a radio, illegal for all Dutch people not in the NSB, which he refuses. He is offered more food coupons during the rationing that takes effect throughout the Netherlands during the war, but he declines, and my grandmother stands in the same lines as everybody else.

Throughout the Netherlands, Jewish homes are looted during the war after their residents are sent to the camps. Priceless artwork, furniture, clocks, silverware—everything is stolen, leaving the buildings abandoned and bare. Later, the homes will be bought for pennies on the guilder by non-NSB Dutch investors. My grandparents never received any property from Jewish homes, even though both NSB and non-NSB Dutch participated in this practice. While this fact doesn't absolve my grandfather of his sins, it begs the question of how clear the divisions are between the righteous and the collaborators they condemn.

When my uncle and I walk through the former Jewish neighborhood in Arnhem, it occurs to me that these homes sat empty after their inhabitants were deported and murdered. It's a lovely neighborhood, with typical brick town homes near the historic city center.

"What happened to these houses when the Jews were sent to the camps?" I ask him.

"Dutch people bought them for next to nothing. Dutch people bought anything that wasn't already looted," he says.

This is something I never considered before. NSB members were not legally permitted to buy these properties after the war, so I realize now that any property not looted by the Nazis at the time of the razzias was bought or looted by those on the other side, the "right" side, something that seems perverse.

"You mean the people who were protesting the German occupation then turned around and got a bargain house or furnishings?"

"Basically," says my uncle.

At the same time, I understand that with the exception of the Nazi officers and NSB members willing to profit from advantages, everybody suffered during the war, particularly at the end, as the Allied troops fought to take back territory from the Germans and bullets and bombs hit civilian homes as the air raid sirens screamed. With the Germans controlling the railways and waterways, there was a food shortage. The Dutch population suffered, regardless of which side they supported.

My mother's family is no exception in 1944. They eat stinging nettle soup when there are no vegetables, knit underwear out of yarn from old sweaters. "Things will be better soon, kids," my grandmother tells her children. "The war will be over soon." How mistaken she is, as she halves, and halves, and halves again the number of potatoes included in each meal to make her rations stretch a few more days.

8

END OF THE WAR,
BEGINNING OF THE WAR

The Netherlands, 1944

In June 1944, the Allied forces land on the beaches of Nor-
mandy in France. My mother is now four and a half years
old. D-day is the beginning of a furious effort to liberate
Nazi-occupied countries, as troops begin fighting their way
toward the Netherlands. In September, they reach Belgium,
and the Dutch hear rumors that the liberation operation is
under way. This leads to Dolle Dinsdag, on September 5,
1944. Mad Tuesday. Believing they are about to be liberated, people celebrate in the streets and await the Allied
troops. *De redding is nabij!* "The rescue is near!" radio announcers call into people's living rooms. In most living
rooms, the response is jubilation.

For collaborators, however, it's complete panic and a reck-
oning. They are certain they are about to be killed or arrested. About half of the NSB members, particularly those
in leadership positions, pack their suitcases. Nazi leaders

inform them that they should flee to Westerbork, where they
will be transported on to safe houses in Germany. Some
thirty-five thousand NSB members take them up on this offer
and flee to temporary camps and Camp Westerbork, which
is still occupied by Jews who are also due to be transported,
but to entirely different fates. In an unattributed diary cited
on the "Drenthe in the War" website, a Jewish Westerbork
prisoner purportedly writes,

> *The first NSB'ers have arrived, most in cars stuffed*
> *with suitcases, baby buggies, chests and blankets. The*
> *stream of NSB refugees flows through the camp. On*
> *foot, in cars, on bicycles and wagons, and at the end*
> *on freight and passenger trains, they arrive. We are all*
> *staring at each other, we can't believe our eyes. "Now*
> *it's your turn," that's what all our faces say.*

My grandfather chooses not to flee. He doesn't believe he
has done anything to put him in danger. He doesn't feel complicit and naively assumes that the authorities will look at
his circumstances and agree with him. So my mother and her
family stay where they are, in their house in Apeldoorn.

But the Netherlands' liberation will not come that easily,
and Mad Tuesday turns out to be a false alarm. The Allies
enter the country to ticker tape parades, but they are en route
to fierce battles and roadblocks, particularly along the country's rivers, where bridges are the key to controlling the territory. The Allies aren't assured of success; the Germans put
up a furious fight. They block bridges to cut supply lines, a
tactical move to starve the country and force the Allies to
back down. In return, the Allies focus on gaining control of
some bridges and bombing others in order to prevent the

Germans from moving troops to fight them, an operation made famous by the film *A Bridge Too Far.*

In Operation Market Garden, thousands of Allied troops are dropped from planes with the goal of taking key Dutch bridges, including the main bridge over the Rhine river at Arnhem. But weather and other circumstances create a chain of disastrous events. The troops are dropped far from their targeted landing sites, and as they make their way through the Dutch countryside, high-stepping through soggy fields past dairy cows, they unexpectedly encounter German troops. Fierce fighting between the troops goes on for several days, with Allied and German soldiers alike losing their lives, their corpses loaded onto stretchers in the days that follow, to be sent home to their families in bags.

After nine days, the Allies fail to take control of the intended bridges, which was key to expediting the Allied forces' advance into Germany. The Dutch are not liberated. The failure of the Market Garden campaign means that the war will last another year, one of the most difficult of all the war years for the Dutch citizens as German troops double their efforts to retain territory, engaging in ferocious fighting with the Allies. In Gelderland, the province where my mother lives, the fighting is particularly bad. The woods near Apeldoorn are filled with munitions bunkers and German soldiers guarding them. Bullets whistle past the trees her brothers love to climb. Booby traps are dug into the cool, damp soil and covered back up with moss.

Air raids are common during this time, and families are ordered by the Nazis to black out their windows at night so they can't be seen by Allied bombers from the air to use as guides. My mother, now five, listens to the growing and ebbing moans of air sirens that sound like a cat in heat, rubbing her eyes in her little bed. Her eleven-year-old brother Bert whispers in the dark, "Elsje, don't be scared. Come on, you have to get up. We have to go to the cellar." The door to their bedroom opens, and my grandmother scoops Elsje up to carry her down, with Hannie behind her carrying blankets and pillows pulled from their beds. Many nights are spent in the cold cellar on mattresses between the potatoes and the jars of blackberry jam. Elsje listens to the airplanes drone overhead, explosions in the distance, afraid of the noises but not sure what they mean. Her siblings know. They help my grandmother by playing with Elsje. They tell her stories about the twin babies Mapje and Papje who are found in the forest after wandering away from their mother and raised by rabbits in a warren under the ground until Elsje falls asleep, the cellar around her filled with her rabbit siblings in their rabbit hole.

On October 14, 1944, my mother's family gets a devastating reminder that the war is not over. On that afternoon, my mother and my grandmother visit my grandmother's father and stepmother in Zutphen, a town about an hour and a half from Apeldoorn by bike. My mother's grandparents run a printing press and a stenography training school out of their home. My mother loves visiting her *oma* and *opa*. It will be Oma's birthday the next day, Sunday, but they celebrate today. My mother sits on Oma's lap and they read books together. She gets apple cake with whipped cream. Opa is helping the stenography students who are practicing in the study, but he pops in to kiss her.

At 3:15, my grandmother looks at her watch and says they need to get going to make it back to Apeldoorn before dark. They drink the last of their tea. My grandmother stacks the cake plates and offers to wash them, but her stepmother says, "Leave them. I'll do that. You guys need to get going."

My mother hugs her opa and oma and thanks them for the cake.

"Oh, my pleasure, sweet thing. Be a good girl," Oma says, helping Elsje on with her coat and buttoning it up to her chin. She kisses my mother on the forehead.

My mother and grandmother put on their scarves and hats, mittens for my mother. Elsje's grandfather winks at her. "See you soon, *meiske*."

My grandmother kisses her father goodbye and then lifts Elsje onto the child's seat on the back of her bicycle. There's a damp fall chill in the air, and she isn't looking forward to the long bike ride back after the cake and the warm house.

At the same moment, twelve British RAF planes that have taken off south of London cross the channel into Dutch airspace. They fly low over Apeldoorn in the direction of Zutphen at the same time that my grandmother and mother pedal over the IJssel Bridge headed toward Apeldoorn. About twenty minutes into their ride, they intersect with the squadron, flying in the opposite direction. In the distance, my grandmother hears the air raid sirens in Zutphen caterwauling. She stops, wakes my mother, and lifts her quickly off the bike, which drops into the grass as they jump into one of the bomb shelter ditches dug into the side of the road.

Moments later, they hear the bombs. It's a thunderous noise of 137 bombs making impact for over ten minutes, shaking the ground. It is 3:53 p.m. My mother clings to my grandmother in the ditch. Elsje pops her head out of the shelter to look back at the massive cloud of black smoke rising above Zutphen before being yanked back down by my grandmother. My grandmother has seen the bull's-eye roundels on the wings of the planes and recognizes them as

Allied planes. She assumes their target is German troops. What she does not know is that the target is the Dutch bridge, which has a railway across it and is used by the Germans to transport ammunition.

By the time my mother and grandmother cycle into Apel-doorn an hour later, tired and chilled, the news has already reached there: The bombers have accidentally overshot their target and taken out not just the bridge but the neighborhood next to it as well. In their street, the neighbor children taunt my five-year-old mother with the one part of the story she will recall vividly for the rest of her life. Skipping alongside her and my grandmother as they pedal up to the house, the neigh-borhood children call, *Your granny and grandpa are dead, deh-ed, deh-ed, deh-ed. Ha-ha, you dirty NSBer!* My mother's grandparents, whom she had been drinking tea with hours before, have been killed instantly in the bombing.

—

Zutphen, the Netherlands, 2015

Today, my great-grandparents' house is number twenty-two on an audio tour of historic Zutphen. On the internet, there is a downloadable recording for tourists, along with photos of the exterior of their home both before and after the bomb. A virtual museum docent recites the details of site twenty-two on our city walking tour in his measured, museum-quality voice:

> *Stand with your back to the IJssel River. The Brug-straat and the IJsselkade lie in the center of the stricken area. On the corner of the Brugstraat and the IJs-selkade lived the family Barto. At the time, stenogra-*

phy courses were offered in their house. Because of that, there were usually more people in the building than just the family members themselves . . . The house of the Barto family collapsed after the neighbor's house was hit by a bomb. Mr. Barto and his wife, who would have had her birthday the next day, did not survive the strike. And there were more victims on this spot, including one dead and one wounded student.

According to my mother, the wounded student survived because my grandfather threw himself over her body during the bombing.

I visit the memorial for my great-grandparents in a wooded area of the Zutphen cemetery for war casualties. My great-grandmother's name is misspelled on the marble commemorative stone. I walk to the riverfront where their home once stood, amid a row of homes, looking out on the bridge and the broad, slow-moving IJssel River. My great-grandparents would have looked out over the water at the children fishing for eels on the banks, the long barges passing through, lovers strolling along the waterside path with dogs in tow. Toward the end of the war, they would have seen tanks crossing the bridge, the lamps rattling as their stenography students looked up, alarmed, from their machines. I have to imagine all of this, because the only photo I have ever seen of their house from the time they lived there is of the rubble of brick and glass and a jagged hole the bomb tore through it. As an adult, my uncle Pim attends an exhibit about the war in a military museum, and realizes with a shock that he is looking at another angle of his grandparents' home, a particularly unique angle. The photo has been taken from the belly of the airplane that dropped the bombs, and it shows a bird's-eye view of the house, a bomb captured on film in the air directly above it, suspended in time in the seconds after its release. Somewhere just out of frame in the landscape below are my grandmother and my mother, cycling back to Apeldoorn.

Today, there is a bland, concrete square block of an apartment building on the site of my great-grandparents' former home, the kind the Dutch were proud of calling "contemporary" in the 1960s and '70s, the kind that I abhor. Somewhere on the sidewalk there is supposed to be a small brass square embedded in the pavement to commemorate the lives lost in the bombing, but after circling the building twice, I cannot find it anywhere.

—

Apeldoorn, the Netherlands, 1944

Not only does the war continue for the Dutch after Mad Tuesday, but in September of that year, the country enters into one of the most difficult periods yet, the Hunger Winter, also known as the Dutch famine of 1944–45.

After D-day, the Allied troops manage to liberate the southern part of the country, below the rivers that slice the country in half. But the northern provinces continue to be stranded after the failure of Operation Market Garden. In September 1944, there is heavy fighting along the rivers, and the residents of Arnhem are told to vacate their homes or risk being bombed. So it is that Hannie comes out of the woods one afternoon after foraging for chanterelles and sees them coming down the road into Apeldoorn like a zombie invasion: fifty thousand emaciated people dragging wheelbarrows and wagons, exhausted and gray-faced. Behind

them, their city is crushed and set ablaze as the Allied soldiers battle the Germans for control. These are the lucky
ones. On the road behind them also lie the bodies of their
former neighbors, people in the wrong place at the wrong
time as they fled under fire. The Arnhem refugees pour into
Apeldoorn and the surrounding towns, putting even more
stress on a dwindling food supply as the region heads into
winter.

As a result of the failure of Operation Market Garden,
the Germans now control the bridge, and with it, the only
route to transport goods and food by train to the northern
parts of the country. The Dutch railway workers attempt to
aid the Allied effort by striking and preventing the Germans
from transporting their troops, ammunition, and supplies
over the rails. In turn, the Germans retaliate by placing an
embargo on the shipments of food to the north, a common
tool of war. In cities like Apeldoorn, the people are starved
out in a deadly game of chicken. People already have to use
ration books during the war due to the limited food supplies,
but now their ration books don't buy anything at all, because
the stores are empty. No bread, no potatoes, no eggs, no
meat, no cheese, no fruits or vegetables. People trade anything they can: a piano for a wheel of cheese or a couple
dozen eggs, a wedding band for a sack of potatoes. If there
is food in the shops, the rations now allow only approximately one thousand calories a day per adult anyway, which
isn't enough to sustain them. In the streets, everybody is
gaunt, their cheekbones jutting out as they smile. When they
still smile.

When the Germans partially lift the embargo, allowing
the canals to open for transport of food by boat, it is too late.
The country is in the midst of one of the coldest winters in
its history. The rivers are frozen solid, and no boats can travel

up them anymore. The snow piles high on the roads. No food enters the region.

During this period, 4.5 million Dutch people survive only because of soup kitchens established by charities and the Red Cross, while 20,000 succumb to starvation during this last stretch of the Nazi occupation.

In Apeldoorn, the snow creeps higher on the garden fence, and my mother, five years old, sinks in it to her armpits. The De Kock family heads into the woods to dig for anything edible and to hunt small animals, but they aren't the only ones, and many of the woods in that area are cordoned off due to the German munitions storage under their cover. The blackberries, blueberries, and mushrooms frozen in storage from the previous summer are quickly depleted. Rabbits, deer, and wild boars are spotted less often as the woods are stripped by hungry people. By midwinter, the family has nothing. My grandmother serves the children runny soup with boiled tulip bulbs from the cellar, but still their stomachs rumble at night.

One night my grandmother and grandfather sit down at the table with their eldest child. Many people have been going on "hunger tours," traveling to the far north on foot or by bicycle to the farms in Friesland and Groningen, bringing anything they have left to barter. My grandfather has to stay at his job at the auto mechanics' school to avoid losing it. But two people will have to go for food, or the family may starve. My grandparents look at their twelve-year-old daughter. "Hannie, do you think you can handle the trip with your mother?" her father asks. She nods solemnly.

It's decided. Hannie and my grandmother will go on a hunger tour. They will go north to get potatoes and vegetables and meat on their bicycles with wooden wheels, as all the rubber has been turned in for the war effort or taken by the Germans. The wooden tires will add time to the journey. The deep snow and cold will add even more time. Altogether, it will take ten to twelve hours each way, so they leave very early in the morning, in the dark. Friesland, the northernmost Dutch province, is 150 kilometers from Apeldoorn.

I talked about this trek with my aunt Hannie the year before her death in 2009. "We had to cross a river," she said. "But the Allies had bombed the bridges to slow down the Germans, and in places, the narrow railway bridge was the only way across, guarded by the German military to allow trains of their soldiers and ammunition to cross. So when we got to the IJssel River, we had to stow away on a train carrying German soldiers."

After three hours of biking, they reach the river and wait just before the bridge for the train, shivering in the subzero temperatures just beneath the berm. The train slows to a crawl when it gets close to the bridge, and they scramble up the embankment. Amazingly, German soldiers appear in the vestibule of the train: smiling young men in olive-green uniforms holding out their hands to them, offering to help them aboard. They pass their bicycles up to the men, then are lifted into the train themselves. The German soldiers hide the bicycles and bring Hannie and my grandmother to their seats, telling them to get down low in case the officers pass the train on the other side and spot them. These soldiers know nothing about the stowaways' NSB affiliation, so as far as they are concerned, they are helping regular Dutch citizens. They are just boys enlisted against their will by Adolf Hitler and forced to fight. They see a girl and her mother trying to get food, like so many others on this trek to the north. Inside the train, there are no enemies. The men dig through their duffel bags and give my grandmother and aunt their own army rations—crackers, sausage, chocolate—which they rip open and eat quickly. They drink from the men's canteens. When they reach the other side of the river, they have to jump out before the train picks up speed again, and the soldiers pass them their bikes, waving to them as the train slowly moves on, carrying many of these young men to their deaths in the final months of the war.

From Zwolle, where they've now successfully crossed the river, my grandmother and Hannie continue cycling north in the snow. After twelve hours, they arrive in the farmlands of Friesland at dusk, the windmills rising from the flat horizon like agricultural lighthouses to the weary travelers. Cycling from farm to farm, they knock on doors to barter with the farmers, exchanging their money and jewelry for a comparatively small amount of food. Then they cycle to the coastal Frisian city of Zoutkamp, where they have family that also gives them some food. They load their bicycle bags with potatoes and beets, a few cuts of meat, loaves of bread, and more, and then immediately begin to ride back to Apeldoorn, where hungry mouths and young children are waiting.

They have already cycled for twelve hours, and they are exhausted. After about four hours, my grandmother calls through the dark to Hannie, who is cycling with her head down ahead of her. "Hannie! I have to stop. I have to rest!" So they rest on the side of the road, collapsing directly into the snow. They nearly die there. "We were so tired that we started to fall asleep," my aunt told me. "Our bodies were just completely spent. But we knew that if we fell asleep, we would freeze, so we kept saying, 'OK, in thirty seconds we have to stand up and keep going.' But we couldn't do it, and the more time that passed, the harder it became to stay awake and stand up."

In the distance, a light burns through the window of a farmhouse, the orange glow fanning out over the snow like spilled sun. They can almost feel its warmth. Inside will be a fire crackling, a cup of hot tea offered to them. The house is only about a hundred yards away, across a field. "Mom, we have to walk to that farmhouse down there and ask if we can come in or we will freeze to death," says Hannie, standing up. My grandmother nods and slowly stands, wobbling on her legs like a newborn calf. She and Hannie look across the snow, a sea of blue between them and the orange light. They stand like that for several minutes, staring. "I can't," my grandmother finally says. They are too weak to walk.

"I don't know how we did it," Aunt Hannie told me, "but somehow we got back on our bicycles, and we said, 'We can't stop again, no matter what, or we'll die.' So we just kept cycling." When they return, they have been on the road for twenty-four hours, cycling for almost all that time. Hannie is carried by her father to her bed and sleeps for thirty-six hours straight, a record that holds in the family to this day. But they have food again, and they carefully ration it. Elsje is a very little girl when she watches her mother and big sister come in from the snow, half dead from exhaustion with bags full of food. Food becomes a charged thing for her in adulthood. The rationing of it, the fetishizing of it. Later, my mother will become a dietitian. My aunt Hannie, for her part, will become convinced of an economic collapse in the run-up to the millennium as the media floats doomsday scenarios about computers going haywire. The first thing she does to prepare for the year 2000 is to panic-buy a brandnew bicycle, even though she already owns one. The "millennium bike," as the family calls it, sits unused in her shed for years as the year 2000 comes and goes without incident, an expensive symbol of war trauma.

This near starvation of the family becomes a point of contention for my grandfather later as he defends himself, because they didn't have to starve. He could have used his membership in the NSB to get extra food, get money, and gain status. In fact, other NSB members trade in their working-class jobs to become mayors of cities all over the Netherlands, as the Germans allow only NSB members to hold local political positions. The fact that my grandfather's family suffers alongside the rest of the Dutch population and that he doesn't use his position in the NSB for favors becomes a point of defense in his trial later. "I never profited from my membership in the NSB during the war," my grandfather writes to the judge. At trial, others testify that he was offered positions that would have put food on his family's table and money in the bank, but as a socialist, my grandfather refused these positions, unwilling to accept favors. Repeatedly in the trial transcripts, I read affidavits that say, "He was an idealist, and not a war profiteer. He was not interested in the Nazi agenda."

So it is with a great deal of bitterness in later years that my grandfather realizes that after his difficulty surviving the war years, when the Germans are finally defeated, for him, the war isn't over.

When the Nazis surrender on May 5, 1945, and the Allied soldiers roll through the country in ticker tape parades, smiling Canadian troops waving from atop their tanks, people's fear lifts. Elsje stands on the corner outside their house with her brother Bert watching the troops, delighted by the joy all around her. The soldiers march by, smiling and waving. People hug and dance in the streets. They wave Dutch flags. Elsje is five years old and likes a good party. She doesn't understand that her family is on the wrong political side of this liberation. She waves at the soldiers, and a Canadian soldier stops his green Jeep to beckon her over. She approaches reverently. She gazes up, and the soldier reaches down to hand her a tiny mohair Steiff bear with a brass button in its ear. He winks at her. Elsje feels she is looking at a god. She clutches the little bear to her chest. It's the most precious thing she's ever gotten and the last happy moment she'll know for a while. Because as the relief sets in for the Dutch people, and years of anxiety leave their bodies, in its place comes a wave of hot anger long suppressed, a wild fury about years of living under occupation. It sweeps through the streets, a smoldering that ignites house after house as neighbor talks to neighbor, finally free of their muzzles. One thought consumes them. Revenge.

9

HATCHET DAY

Apeldoorn, the Netherlands, May 5, 1945

As soon as the war ends, payback begins. The country goes into a period of ferocious vigilante justice they call Bijltjes-dag. Hatchet Day. In the months following the liberation of the Netherlands, the Dutch unleash their anger, grief, and resentment on neighbors whom they see as having been complicit with the Nazis who occupied their cities for years. Nazis kicking in doors in the dark of night with barking German shepherd dogs. Nazis pulling Jews out of attics and basements. Nazis strafing their cities at the beginning of the war to leave flaming debris behind in the place of families, terrorizing their sleepy villages so that no Dutch man, woman, or child knows how to sleep soundly anymore. Now that the Germans are gone, it is the collaborators' turn to have their doors kicked in and to be pulled from their homes. On May 10, before she has even returned to the Netherlands from London, Queen Wilhelmina announces on the radio, "In the liberated Netherlands, there will be no more place for traitors."

Anyone who has had anything at all to do with the Germans during the war is subject to the "hatchet" that will be brought down on them during this period. Nazi sympathizers are arrested as traitors. NSB members are forced to eat feces, tied up, and beaten or shot to death in the street. Female NSB members and the wives of NSB members are sometimes raped. Dutch girls who have become romantically involved with German soldiers billeting in their towns, nicknamed *moffenmeiden*, or "Kraut girls," get the worst of it in cities throughout the country. They are held down, shaved bald with razors or even hedge clippers, and marched through the streets with their hands on their heads and signs hung around their necks that read "Kraut Slut" or "Traitor" while people throw garbage at them. Black tar pitch is smeared on their faces. They are jeered at, and a few people throw rocks. "Kraut lover!" they yell. "Dirty Kraut whore!" The epithet is uttered by children and adults alike. In the many photos documenting these public shaming sessions, the wide smiles of glee on the faces of the people in the crowd are a startling contrast to the vacant faces of the girls being held with guns to their heads. They have the faces of people who have left their bodies.

My mother and her family hide in their house, the children crawling under the beds, whenever they hear knocking on the door. I am struck that both my parents have hidden under beds this way within a year of each other, children terrified of raging vigilantes outside.

On April 17, 1945, the knock at the door they've been fearing comes, and my grandfather is pulled from the house by members of the resistance and marched away with his hands in the air and a gun at his back while my grandmother pleads and the younger children cry. The city is celebrating liberation day, and Canadian troops, floats full of dancing people, and marching bands parade through the streets. They march my grandfather, along with other NSB members, along the parade route of angry onlookers to the center of Apeldoorn, where he and the other suspected collaborators are loaded onto trucks to be sent to a detention camp. Then it is quiet, until unexpectedly, another knock comes on June 21. This one is a complete shock.

I can see my mother standing on the front stoop of her home in Apeldoorn, the house on de Jachthoornlaan: Hunthorn Lane. It is 1945. She is holding a rag doll. Her thin legs emerge from under a cotton sundress and disappear into a pair of hand-knit socks and a pair of leather sandals. She squints into the sun. Cyclists pass on rusty bicycles with their wooden tires and crane their necks. Elsje is crying. Pedestrians gather to watch; someone shouts an insult. A car drives by slowly. Her three siblings try to comfort her. Their *moes*, my grandmother, is being marched out of the house by military policemen with guns.

The facts are still fuzzy for my mother, her memory malleable. She was very little. She speaks slowly, carefully, reluctantly, unlike my father. "I . . . I remember things being thrown out of the second-story window for us in the five minutes my mother was given to prepare. She was throwing things out the window. We didn't know they were going to come at all because my mother wasn't active in the NSB," says my mother now. We sit at the table next to her sewing machine and scraps of fabric, and she drinks tea, the tea I brought back from the Netherlands, from the shop where my grandmother always bought it, extra bergamot. My mother's hair is white silver now, shining brilliantly under the lights. Her wrinkled hands smooth over a piece of fabric, back and forth, as she talks. "We weren't prepared for it. I just have this image of things being thrown out of the window, things falling down to us from above." A thick wool blanket and pillows, sweaters, a bag of toothbrushes. My uncle says this part isn't true, but he may have been on the other side of the house, and this is my mother's memory. She says she can still see it. And whether or not it is true, it is her truth and the image that remains with her today.

What is not in dispute: the children's mother, my grandmother, being loaded into a car, a black car from the POD, the Politieke Opsporingsdienst, the Political Investigation Service. Then the POD agents place wire seals on the doors and windows of my mother's house. They post a notice on the front door stating that the home has been seized. Boots stride past the children without stopping. Car doors slam. The engine is started. My grandmother turns to look at her children through the window of the police car, her face stunned. And moments later, the car is gone, headed toward Wezep, the same camp they brought my grandfather to two weeks earlier, the special jail for NSB members. My five-year-old mother is crying harder now, inconsolable. Hannie, fourteen, takes her hand. Their two brothers, ages thirteen and seven, flank them. The officers do not come back. Nobody comes for them. The children stand for many minutes on the curb as the elder sister thinks. The pedestrians move on. Fingers hook to pull curtains furtively aside in the houses of the neighbors. They watch the children standing in the street, but they do not come outside. When Hannie turns toward them and catches their eyes in the sliver of space between curtain and window, the fingers hastily retract and the curtains fall closed. She turns away.

William Maxwell writes about a boy losing his home in the novel *So Long, See You Tomorrow*: "Whether they are part of home or home is part of them is not a question children are prepared to answer. Having taken away the dog, take away the kitchen—the smell of something good in the oven for dinner. Also the smell of washday, of wool drying on the wooden rack. Of ashes. Of soup simmering on the stove. Take away the patient old horse waiting by the pasture fence. Take away the chores that kept him busy from the time he got home from school until they sat down to supper. . . . Take all this away and what have you done to him? In the face of a deprivation so great, what is the use of asking him to go on being the boy he was. He might as well start life over again as some other boy instead."

There is the image of my five-year-old mother again, left standing in front of her home, which has just been locked and sealed off. Too late, she remembers the Steiff bear the Canadian soldier gave her, now entombed in the locked house. In my mother's mind, her mother has been taken away into a black hole, never to return. She and her siblings begin to move down the road, away from the home that is, in an instant, no longer theirs. They walk to the only house where the door might open for them. "Go to the Van den Dools'," their mother had called hastily as she was led away by the police. So the children walk through a city in the throes of Bijltjesdag, past the shops with signs in their windows that read "No wigs sold here to women with shaved heads," and keep their eyes on the cracks in the sidewalk, hoping nobody recognizes them, heading for the home of the Van den Dools, unsure if anyone will still be there. Perhaps they have been vanished too, put in handcuffs and taken away.

After what feels like a long time walking but is likely around thirty minutes, they arrive at the home, and Hannie knocks on the door. Elsje cowers behind her older sister's skirt, holding on to her leg. They hear footsteps. A curtain is pulled aside and falls shut. Then the footsteps come to the door and the door of the house opens. Mrs. Van den Dool regards the children, whom she knows quite well. Her face indicates that she already understands the situation. Hannie's voice shakes as she speaks. "They've taken Mummy away. She told us to come here." Mrs. Van den Dool brings the children inside and pours hot tea for them. The house is very quiet. The wooden grandfather clock swings its pendulum. *Tick. Tock. Tick. Tock.* Elsje looks around her for the Van den Dool daughters, her teenage babysitters, but they are not there. "We sent the girls to Germany, where they'll be safe," says Mrs. Van den Dool. "Mr. Van den Dool was arrested yesterday."

Mrs. Van den Dool cannot keep them. She has too many worries about her own family and no money. The next day, Aunt Ket arrives by train and takes them south to her home with Uncle Jan and their kids in Dordrecht. Aunt Ket is a solid woman, a pragmatic workhorse not prone to sentiment. She herds the children onto the train and sits tensely, hands folded in her lap, staring out the window at the empty fields that slide past into the train's wake. When they arrive in Dordrecht, a city adjacent to Rotterdam that is tattered by bombing from the Germans during the war, my mother and her siblings walk from the train station with Aunt Ket and crowd into her tiny house on the dike. It is very small for the four children and their two cousins. They sleep squeezed together like pencils in a box. As Elsje is falling asleep, she hears arguing downstairs. Aunt Ket's husband shouts, and the words float up through the floorboards. *A bunch of NSB children . . . be able to show my face . . . not our problem . . .* Then Aunt Ket's voice rises. *My sister's children . . . can't just leave them . . . this is family . . . what are we supposed to do?* So the exchange goes until Elsje falls asleep and dreams of angry neighbors with hatchets calling for their heads.

When my mother tells me this, her sense of hurt and rejection is palpable. Where my father learned to detach and become wholly self-contained, my mother's entire adult life has been defined by a raw desire to belong somewhere, with others, to be wanted, to be home. "I heard them fighting," she says of her aunt and uncle. "He was a member of the resistance and he had a reputation to protect. He couldn't have NSB children in his home. They told us they didn't have room for us, but it wasn't just because of the lack of space. They also didn't want us because we were fout, wrong."

Documents in my grandfather's trial dossier that I read in the National Archives seem to support my mother's memory. There are letters to the Ministry of Justice from Jan complaining about his brother-in-law's political mistakes and being saddled with a bunch of unwanted NSB children. Pressured by his wife to take care of my mother and her siblings but wanting to be rid of them and angry about the position it puts him in, he requests that his brother-in-law be released immediately in these letters, "in the hopes that you, in recognition of my own family which played no part nor participated in the stupidity of my brother-in-law, yet is now the dupe, will offer your cooperation in my request and hopefully can offer me an expedient and positive response."

When the request is denied, Uncle Jan wins the battle in the little house on the dike. The NSB children, Aunt Ket's nieces and nephews, must go. The next day, Aunt Ket is very quiet as she places a piece of bread on the plate before each child. She doesn't look at them, and they eat in silence. Finally, she says, "I'm afraid this house is too small for all of us. We will have to find another solution." In the afternoon, she is gone for several hours. When she returns, she is holding a paper from the Renate Home for Child Welfare. It is the third time Elsje has been ejected from a home in a few months. Shortly thereafter, Aunt Ket brings Elsje and her siblings to the Renate Home, a large building with two wings to house NSB children whose parents have gone to jail, boys and girls left in the wake of the mistakes of their parents and the swift retribution of their country. All across the Netherlands there are institutions like this, filled with the thousands of offspring of the fout.

"I'll come to visit," Aunt Ket says. "I promise." The woman from the home smiles at the children. She takes Elsje's hand. "You'll be in the little children's wing." Elsje looks to her older sister with big eyes. Aunt Ket crouches down. "Be a good girl, Elsje," she says. "Don't make any trouble." And Elsje doesn't make any trouble. She makes it her duty never to make any trouble again. She is absolutely silent as the lady from the children's home leads her down the hallway, away from her siblings and Aunt Ket, who is waving bye-bye.

NSB members like my grandparents are sent to jails and the same Nazi camps in the Netherlands where the Jews had been interned during the war, the most famous of which was Westerbork. Because there were so many of them, an estimated 120,000 to 180,000 accused collaborators, some of them spend years awaiting trial. A handful of them don't make it that long, as Hatchet Day didn't end outside the camps, and a number of the NSBers being held for trial are killed inside the camps. In 2012, the remains of nine people were dug up in the woods outside of Westerbork, and these bodies belonged not to Jews but to the NSBers held there after the war. More bodies are believed to be buried there, though it is not known how many. In an article in the Dutch newspaper *Trouw* reporting on the 2012 discovery, Helen Grevers, a researcher at the Netherlands

Institute for War Documentation, wrote, "It was always known that there must have been bodies buried somewhere, the Ministry of Justice has never made a secret of that. There probably also is some documentation of it. Only it has long been unknown where exactly the graves are."

Shame breeds silence. Many of the NSB members refused to speak about their experiences after the war, and my grandparents were no different, stating that it was a closed chapter they never wanted to talk about again. I search the internet for any information about what my grandparents might have experienced during this postwar period and their subsequent detention. I find a very old film online of the liberation of Apeldoorn, which includes the rounding up of the NSBers. I pause the film to study the grainy faces of the figures who walk with their hands up, at gunpoint, through a gauntlet of celebrating Dutch citizens. As a sound track to these images of arrests and public shaming, cheerful marching band music plays, which, out of context of the era, seems perverse. I realize that I am searching through the faces of those being marched through the streets for my grandfather, whose image I have never actually seen, in person or on film. Perhaps he is among them. It's a distinct possibility. But I don't know my grandfather well enough. In the film, men, women, and teenage children walk with their hands in the air, the crowd jeering. One woman's face in particular strikes me, and I pause the video, squinting. This woman could be my grandmother. It isn't, as she was arrested later, but she would have been treated much the same. The woman in the video wears a white sign around her neck, and as she walks with her hands up, guns at her back, she looks down at the sign, trying to read what they've written across her chest. In other films, I watch NSBers held in town squares and made to bend over on platforms while members of the public beat them with chairs and rods. Little children look on with their parents at these beatings, their faces lit up with openmouthed laughter. Amazingly, shortly before finishing this book, I find a photo in a county archive of unnamed NSB men being arrested after the war. A man at the center of a crowd walks with his hands in the air, marched through the streets to the courthouse past jeering citizens like so many others I've seen in other photos. The caption reads: *(b/w) photo. People suspected of being Nazi sympathizers are brought in, 17-04-1945 . . . (In the period shortly after the second world war many innocent people were also arrested.)* I have an eerie feeling creeping through my body that this man is my grandfather, though I never met him and the photo isn't clear. I email the photo to my mother. She responds, "Yes, my love. That's him. I have never seen this photo. Shit." She spends several days crying over the emotional confrontation of the image. When I share the photo with family members, they too express shock. My brother writes, "That is a shocking photo of Opa de Kock being arrested! Wow. I had to stare at that for a while." My cousin Hanke reflects my own reaction, writing, "I've never seen that photo of our grandfather being arrested, and it hit me hard. For me it's suddenly visual evidence of our family history, to which shame, guilt, and question marks are attached."

With the abrupt end to the war, it is difficult for people to reestablish a harmonious and orderly society with collaborators of the enemy living next door. People cannot simply go back to life as normal while anger and pain about their neighbors' actions pervades, and with the vacuum of a clear, operational government left in the wake of the German retreat from positions of authority, it's absolute mayhem. The government realizes that they need to bring in collaborators sooner rather than later, before they are murdered in the streets and in their own homes. Because of the haste, they don't have time to vet every case. They round up everybody who is suspected of having had any connection at all to the Nazis or the NSB, no matter how vague the link. This includes instances of mistaken identity. In a letter he sent to my father's family in Indonesia after the war, my father's uncle in the Netherlands wrote, "Delightful to see how the NSBers were rounded up and the Krauts interned." This reflects the predominant sentiment in the population.

These people will be sent to the former Nazi camps in the Netherlands, and because there are so many, they will be forced to build their own camps. Other videos I find show NSBers erecting the barbed-wire fences for their own imprisonment, as the government hasn't even had time to prepare for this massive influx of prisoners. They'll stay interned in these camps, some for half a year or more, until their cases can be heard at a tribunal. The conditions in many of the camps are horrendous. Prisoners in these camps aren't able to wash, sleep on straw in unheated horse stables, and are underfed. Toilets are holes in the ground. In one camp, Harskamp, 150 prisoners die of starvation, and Harskamp is the only camp where the government conducted any official inquiry—four years after the fact, in 1949–50, after a former prisoner published a pamphlet about his experience there. At the time, the abuses in the camps were largely ignored, and the research of journalist Koos Groen, as presented in his book on NSB families, *Wrong and No Good*, suggests that a minimum of 1,000 NSB members died in this period after the war in the detention camps, with their deaths left largely uninvestigated. His research includes a study of 178 accounts of interned NSBers in the National Archives that indicate that the conditions in all of the camps were equally miserable and included "systematic abuse, systematic starvation, and a high incidence of sexual harassment." Why did these abuses go overlooked for years by the public and the Dutch government? According to an article by Netherlands Institute for War Documentation employee Johannes Houwink ten Cate in the Dutch online "History Newspaper," "Prisoners are tortured and beaten bloody. Guards empty the contents of the latrines on their heads. But the Dutch public doesn't want to hear about the abuses in camps for 'foute' Dutch. Collaborators had broken the national solidarity during the war, and for that they needed to be punished . . . [From a] political-social perspective the trials and punishment of 'wrong' Dutch citizens was effective in the extreme. [From a] humanitarian perspective, the arrests and internment of 'wrong' Dutch citizens was a catastrophe."

It is disappointing to me as I try to piece together my family's story that my grandparents were so affected by their internment that they absolutely refused to ever speak of their experience after the war. Specifically, when I consider the things I have read about these camps, I think my grandmother must have been deeply traumatized, especially given her complete lack of involvement in the politics that put her there. To be identified as a *verrader*, a traitor, someone fout, wrong, when her worst offense was being married to a man who may have been these things, must have felt like a betrayal. And because she doesn't exist as an individual in the record of this history due to her silence on the issue, I project onto her the other narratives that I read, filling in the vacuum of information that her shame left in the family history. This is hardly unique, as I read over and over in the words of NSB children that their parents refused to speak of what happened to them as well. The stories we are left with, the only ones that make it into the history books, become the mismatched pieces we jam into the gaps of our family puzzles. They don't complete the picture, but they're better than empty spaces.

In a video, a woman who was the young adult daughter of an NSB member, arrested along with her parents, speaks about being put into a group of prisoners who are the daughters of NSB-appointed town mayors. She was forced to walk with these women in a circle as they were hit with sticks and hoses. "Are you sorry?!" the guards yelled as they hit the young women. "'No,' we said, because there wasn't anything we could have done about it. They hit us everywhere. [They felt] we had deserved it," says the woman. In her book *From Traitors to Good Patriots*, Helen Grevers quotes a camp guard in an NSB internment camp in Velp: "Why we hit [the internees] I don't actually know. The early days of the liberation were an abnormal time and a chaos. Such behavior toward the political delinquents found its roots mainly in the effects of the liberation excitement which we were experiencing, through which we couldn't fully understand the consequences. Practically all the guards were in that state of mind that they hit the political delinquents."

It is complete confusion as the NSB members come flooding into camps and prisons throughout the country, thousands upon thousands, among them my grandfather. They cram into the barracks, stack themselves into the bunk beds if they are lucky. The rest of them sleep on straw on the ground.

For the NSBers sent to Westerbork, in the barracks right next to them lie dozens of Jewish people who were saved in the nick of time before their transport to Auschwitz and Dachau but haven't yet been repatriated. Many of these survivors have nowhere to go. So they stay in the camps, where they get a bed and food and time to make plans. Once again, as after the false alarm of Mad Tuesday, Jewish internees and NSBers mingle inside the camps. But this time, their statuses are switched, the Jews finally free and the NSBers prisoners. One Jewish survivor wrote to family members,

> *Every day now, large transports of NSB members arrive here. They don't have it easy . . . We Jews no longer have to work, except we now are the supervisors. There are boys here from the Free Netherlands [magazine] and military police for security. They are extremely harsh towards all that is NSB.*

There are not enough guards, and a handful of the Jews who had been liberated only days earlier are now offered jobs as guards.

The violence of revenge outside the camps that the NSBers were presumably saved from with their internment is in actuality just as bad inside the camps, if not worse. There do not seem to be any rules against flagrant abuse of the prisoners, and the Dutch authorities look the other way with regard to human rights violations. The most bizarre humiliations are invented for the accused collaborators. They have to "mow the lawn," forced to get down on their hands and knees and bite grass and weeds off with their teeth. In the worst camps, they are made to walk on glass shards. At night, the guards get drunk and pull the prisoners naked out of bed and lead them around by a rope while they are beaten with sticks and bottles. According to one historian, "Abuse was more often the rule than the exception."

Elderly people, many of whom had done nothing more than vote for the NSB party prior to the war, succumb first. Meanwhile, six months or more go by before those accused get a hearing before a judge. Some of them are innocent, including women who, like my grandmother, had never been active in the NSB but happened to be married to a member. The human rights abuses they suffered are waved away as irrelevant by the Dutch authorities because "if they had been released, they would have been murdered."

Aside from the conditions in the camp, I imagine that for my grandparents, and especially my grandmother, not being able to see their children is the greatest difficulty of their internment. My grandmother gets a letter in the camp from her sister telling her that the children have been taken to the children's home. There is nothing she can do about it, and she feels helpless. She spends her days knotting fish nets or weaving place mats or making handbags or sewing jackets, or whatever her daily labor is, but her mind is on her children in that facility in Dordrecht. She is a mother who cannot go to her children in the night when they have bad dreams. She cannot check her children's foreheads for fever when they are ill. She is trapped behind barbed-wire fences, unable to soothe her children's worries.

—

Dordrecht, the Netherlands, 2014

On a drizzly late-spring day, my aunt, my mother, and I drive into the city of Dordrecht in the southern part of the Netherlands. We follow the GPS to locate the former home of my mother's aunt Ket and uncle Jan, using an address I have copied down from my research in the archives, but the GPS leads us to a dead-end parking lot next to a factory abutting the freeway. We get out of the car and walk down the road, which is, as expected, a dike with some charming old cottages at the opposite end, but none of those is the right house. Eventually, we learn from a woman walking her dog that this dike used to continue but the freeway now bisects it, cutting one half off from the other. We get in the car and drive through a tunnel to the other side of the freeway and locate the other side of the dike, which now has a different name. New homes line this neighborhood, but a horse stable at the end appears to be old, and we stop there. My mother recognizes the stable as part of a farm that the dike house looked out on, but all around it, time has progressed, filling in pasture with cement. We never locate the dike house, though one small cottage is a contender. My mother isn't sure. I realize that asking a woman in her seventies to remember a house she was removed from as a five-year-old may be unrealistic. I snap some photos, and we move on to locate the children's home where my mother stayed when her parents were interned. This address pops up on GPS as being in the center of the city, so we drive downtown and park. Dordrecht is an old city, with cobblestone streets and church spires rising up from the center. It's also a modern city, with the same kind of nondescript apartment buildings we've encountered everywhere. In the drizzle, we locate the address and find a huge concrete block. Inside is a retirement home. We use the restroom in the lobby, and I watch the residents, all appearing old enough to have lived through the war themselves, spoon yogurt into their mouths in the dining room. The trip to find my mother's past here is a failure. I am left feeling a sense of emptiness about the ways that history is literally paved over. I will never be able to know my mother's experience, and will only be able to fill in images based on my research, just as a reader will only be able to create their own vision of the truth based on the information I present. The true narrative is buried somewhere beneath Dordrecht's rebar and concrete.

—

Dordrecht, the Netherlands, 1945

Elsje is in the little children's wing of the Renate Home, separated from her brothers and sister. Hannie is in the older children's wing, and her brothers are on yet another floor. The children sleep in bunk beds in tiled rooms. Elsje misses her mother intensely in the dark of the room. Every now and then she hears footsteps in the hall echo off the walls and waits for the door to open. But it rarely does. Hannie comes to visit her once, but she and Pim contract diphtheria almost immediately and are put in quarantine, and thereafter they don't visit for weeks. Elsje gets lice, which make her head itch. All of the kids get scabies. The meals are adequate, but thin. Elsje watches the staff of the home slather butter on their bread in front of the children, who aren't afforded these luxuries, and she is envious. She loves butter. It has been a long time since she tasted it.

Elsje is ill almost constantly in the home, probably due to anxiety. Her stomach is in knots, and she has intestinal issues that put her in the sick ward more often than she is in her assigned room. Her sleep is restless, punctuated by nightmares, and one night as she tosses in her top bunk, she rolls completely off the mattress and drops to the concrete floor below. She lands on her side and her face smacks the floor, causing it to swell and turn shades of black and purple. After that, one of the women who works in the home takes pity on the bruised six-year-old and begins to take her home with her to her house outside the city on the weekends. At Anneke's house, Elsje gets to play outside with the dog and watch the chickens catch beetles in the dirt outside their coop. There, she gets a soft-boiled egg at breakfast with a tiny spoon just for her, and a bedtime story and a kiss on the forehead before sleeping on soft cotton sheets. She wishes she could stay there forever and be part of this family, this perfect family that is not hated by strangers, and maybe at some point she even expresses to them this desire to stay. It's something that will plague her forever as an act of betrayal toward her own family. All week long at the children's home, she waits for Friday to come so she can go home with Anneke. And after some time, maybe Elsje sort of forgets that she ever had another mother and father. Anneke's family is a tiny sliver of normalcy in the fear-laced loneliness of being six years old and separated from your parents and siblings, rejected by your aunt and uncle, resented by your community as the child of people who were fout, like maybe there is something inherently fout with being born to that family.

In June 1946, my grandmother finally has her trial and is found not guilty of active treason, though she is found guilty of being an NSB member and loses her right to vote. She is released from the camp, as are nearly one hundred thousand other people for whom there is insufficient evidence to warrant a conviction for treason. She may not be guilty of more than signing her name on a form once years before the war, but the mark is already on her as an NSBer, and the punishment has already been delivered. All of the family's possessions are gone. My grandfather's assets have been frozen, and his bank account is now controlled by the state, which pays his bills via a state-appointed accountant. His salary, pension, and benefits have been revoked. Still, the bills roll in and go to collection when the accountant doesn't pay them on time. Telephone service bills for a house they cannot enter, outstanding balances, all accrue late fees upon late fees. The children's home in Dordrecht has also been charging astronomical fees that the family is expected to pay upon release—adding up to a bill of 1,913 guilders (the equivalent of approximately 10,000 dollars in current-day value, when adjusted for inflation). The government's payment for the accidental bombing and deaths of my grandmother's parents in Zutphen doesn't cover all the bills. Because my grandfather is unable to organize mandatory repairs from inside prison on a house in Gorssel he owned that has been damaged by bombing, the government fines him.

Into this state of bankruptcy, bureaucracy, and accruing debts and fines that have compounded while my grandparents have been incarcerated, my recently freed grandmother emerges, walking out of the detention center with only the clothes on her back. She has no home and no money. Like a homing pigeon, she has one destination in mind, and she heads there immediately.

Elsje wakes in the children's home one morning, ill with the flu and confined to the sick ward as she so often is. In the doorway of her room are two staff members and a woman. "Elsje, look who's here!" Elsje sits up in her bed blinking her feverish eyes, cheeks flushed, looking at the thin woman in the shabby coat who is beaming at her. The women look at her expectantly. She smiles. "Is it . . . Aunt Nini?" Elsje asks, a tentative smile tugging at the corners of her mouth. Aunt Nini, her mother's sister, lives in South Africa, and Elsje has never met her before. The woman's face falls, and the staff members look at each other uncomfortably. "No, no, Elsje. Look again. It's your mother!" Elsje isn't sure what to think. Her mother was sent away. She was gone. In her child's mind, this meant she was *gone*, no longer existed. Yet here she suddenly is, this person they insist is her mother, standing in her room. Her mother comes to her, reaches out her arms, her eyes full. Elsje reaches back.

Despite this reunion, my grandmother has to leave her children behind in this home because she has not a guilder in her pocket nor a home for them to go to. Answering advertisement after advertisement, she gets a job near the children's home in Dordrecht, as a live-in maid for a wealthy man, and works for months to save enough to get them out, visiting the children daily. It's a slow process, as the fees for the children's home accrue simultaneously. Three, four, then six months pass, but she hasn't saved enough, and nobody will rent a house to her. When she visits the children in the home, the eyes of the staff members turn to stone. She's an NSB traitor. Her disloyalty has caused her children to suffer, and the staff to have to take over her parental duties and tie shoelaces, wipe noses, and pick lice out of these NSB children's hair. What kind of a mother does this to her children? The judgments move across their faces like clouds. They don't try to hide their disdain. But my grandmother's only choice is to keep the smile plastered on her face every time she visits, the smile of attrition that has become second nature. "Thank you so much for keeping them longer," she says. "I'm earning money now. I'll have enough soon to take them with me and off your hands." Anneke, the woman who brings Elsje home on the weekends, turns to my grandmother with daggers on her tongue. "I've discussed it with my family, and we've decided that we'd be willing to keep Elsje. She's a very sweet little girl. Helpful and obedient. She deserves . . . a *good* home."

My grandmother snaps, her smile disappearing. "Keep her? Is that a joke? She's my daughter, and she isn't available to keep. I love my children." Shaking, she wipes her eyes. "I know what you think, but I am not a bad person, and I wish to take my children out of here."

So it is that a few days later, Hannie, Pim, Bert, and Elsje are retrieved from their respective wings, and their mother walks out of the Renate Home for Child Welfare in Dordrecht with her four children and an overwhelming sense of complete uncertainty about what to do now.

10

STARTING OVER

Dordrecht, the Netherlands, July 29, 1946

My grandmother doesn't have enough money saved to rent a home for herself and the children, so she immediately begins finding temporary solutions, sending letters to friends and family to ask for assistance. The boys, now nine and thirteen, are sent to live with a farmer who needs help with chores like milking cows and mucking out stables. Hannie, the eldest, now fourteen, is sent to live with a family in Hoog Soeren—a tiny village about thirty minutes' drive from Apeldoorn—helping them with sewing jobs. Elsje, too small to work for her keep, is taken in by the family of one of the family's old neighbors in Apeldoorn. Meanwhile, my grandmother keeps working as a maid and searches for a home where the family can be together. But every rental application she fills out is denied. As she becomes increasingly desperate, and as the family that has agreed to take Elsje in begins to ask how long her stay is going to last, they find a solution for her.

They know a family that has a summer cottage in the

High Veluwe, the nature reserve of heath and woods on land owned by the royal family, in Hoog Soeren. As a small summer cottage, it isn't even insulated, the wind whistling through the cracks, but the matriarch who owns the place, the elderly Mrs. Parqui, now needs assistance. They work out an arrangement that my grandmother and the children can live there for very low rent year-round if they take care of Mrs. Parqui during the summer months when she is there. My grandmother agrees immediately, and gathers her children into the tiny house between the cornfield and the woods to try to start life over. The painted wooden house is called "The Red Pan," a play on words, as the Dutch word for the red clay roof tiles on the house is "roof pan" (short for pantile), and a carving of the horned pagan god of field and woods, Pan, dances on the top of the house's peak on his goat hind legs. The cottage resembles a particularly elaborate Swiss chalet, with woodland creatures carved into the gables, forest gnomes in the garden, owl-shaped trellises, and bucks with antlers stenciled onto the exterior walls. At night, the frost spreads across their blankets and they wake up with ice crystals in their noses and their hair frozen to the pillows, but for Elsje, this is the best time in her life, back together with her siblings and her mother under one roof. And they are quite literally under one roof, as they sleep side by side upstairs under the folk-art-painted eaves in two rooms separated by an interior wall that doesn't reach the ceiling. At night, Pim and Elsje lob things over the wall partition to Hannie and Bert, and they sing Dutch folk songs in the dark together until my grandmother, knitting socks and underwear downstairs by the fireplace, calls up to them to go to sleep.

—

Hoog Soeren, the Netherlands, 2015

On a sunny early summer day, my mother and I visit the sites of her childhood—and part of mine—in Hoog Soeren. We pass the school where I attended first grade, and where my mother attended grammar school. We are on our way to the The Red Pan, which is now on the National Register of Historic Places.

I have biked past The Red Pan many times in my life, and my cousins still own my grandparents' summer cottage down the road, so this is not the first time I have seen the house, but it will be the first time I have been inside.

Via a website about the village, I tracked down the current owner, and was surprised to find that the house has remained in the same family all these years and that the owner is Heidi Parqui, the granddaughter of Mrs. Parqui, whom my grandmother cared for. She is a bit older than my mother, more my aunt Hannie's age, but my mother recalls playing with the teenage Heidi when she visited her grandmother at the cottage. So it turns out this will be a reunion not only with the house but with the people who were there with my mother seventy years earlier. Over the years, the area has transformed from the rural religious community I knew as a child to a highly desired area of weekend and summer homes for the rich. Some of the old farmers have held out, regarding the interlopers with disdain as they herd their cows past villas in their blue coveralls and wooden shoes. The Red Pan sits indifferently in the midst of this, a field of corn still on one side, and a rebuilt summer villa on the other. Two muscular, well-groomed horses graze in the sun next to the new villa. Heidi is now old and uses a walker, so she comes to the house only to show it to visitors. Nobody has lived there for years. As a result, the house is preserved in much the same state that it was in when my mother lived there as a child.

My mother shows me the corner where she slept. It's cramped and tiny, but I can understand why she loved it. Heidi spends several hours with us drinking tea on the veranda of the house, reminiscing with my mother. I see it as an opportunity to get my mother's story from a different perspective.

"What did people think about your grandmother giving shelter to an NSB family?" I ask. Oddly, my mother jumps in immediately before Heidi can answer, stating, "Oh, nobody in this village cared about that. They liked us. It was not an issue." My mother loved her time in Hoog Soeren and doesn't want anything to mar her image of it, her longing for acceptance and community still a deep need. As gently as I can, I say, "I know that was your perspective, but I actually would like to hear the answer from Heidi." Heidi looks uncomfortable, and watching my mother's face, says, "Oh yes, sure, they were liked by most people in the village. They always behaved themselves." I push on, despite being aware that my mother may not want to hear unvarnished truths. "Knowing how deeply NSBers were hated, Heidi, I find it hard to believe that there was no issue at all with your grandmother putting NSB-allied tenants in her house. It's OK. I want to know the truth about what people really said back then, behind the family's back."

"Really, nobody around here made an issue of that," my mother answers for Heidi again. I stop her, and say I'd like to hear from Heidi. "Well," says Heidi carefully, diplomatically, "it's true, most people held their tongues. But my uncle and aunt said, 'How can you take NSBers into your home?' Actually, the truth is, they wouldn't talk to my grandmother after that. It caused a bit of a rift in the family."

Grandfather Adrianus Cornelis de Kock and Grandmother Maria Catharina Barto, prior to marriage, 1931.

Elsje at the lake in hand-knitted bathing suit, circa 1941.

De Kock children during the war. *(left to right):* Hannie *(behind)*, Elsje, Pim, Bert. Woods near Apeldoorn, circa 1942.

Great-grandparents, Arie and Bertha Barto, cycling on the bridge with Hannie and my grandmother, their daughter, circa 1942. The bombing of this bridge would later take their lives.

The bridge in Zutphen after the bombing, 1944.

House of great-grandparents, Arie and Bertha Barto, after the bombing that killed them both. Zutphen, the Netherlands, 1944. *(Courtesy of Photo Collection Stedelijk Museum Zutphen, Nederland)*

The Nieuwmarkt neighborhood ghetto surrounded by barbed wire during Nazi occupation in Amsterdam, 1942. *(Courtesy of Charles Breijer, collection Stadsarchief Amsterdam)*

Hatchet Day, the Netherlands. Girls suspected of having relations with German soldiers and other suspected collaborators are shaved bald and paraded through the streets at gunpoint. April 1945. *(Courtesy of William van de Poll, Creative Commons License 3.0.)*

Arrest of my grandfather (center, with arms raised) on April 17, 1945, during Hatchet Day, Apeldoorn. *(Courtesy of Henk van Veen Sr.)*

The House of the Red Pan in winter. Hoog Soeren, the Netherlands, 1947.

In the garden of the Red Pan. *(left to right):* Loes, Hannie, grandfather Adrianus, Elsje, the elderly Mrs. Parqui, whom they helped care for during the summer in exchange for low rent. Hoog Soeren, the Netherlands, circa 1947.

The family back together after the war. *(left to right):* Grandmother, grandfather, Pim, Elsje, Hannie, and Bert *(in back),* circa 1947.

Pim, Hannie, and Elsje on bikes after being reunited as a family. Hoog Soeren, the Netherlands, 1947.

Baby Rob is born and the family adopts a dog after being reunited under one roof in the House of the Red Pan. Hoog Soeren, the Netherlands, 1948.

Elsje and her baby brother Rob. The House of the Red Pan. Hoog Soeren, the Netherlands, 1948.

Grandfather beekeeping on a family vacation spot, Kootwijk, the Netherlands, circa 1961.

Elsje as a young woman in Amsterdam, circa 1960.

Elsje and Sjeffie's wedding, August 19, 1968, Gorssel, the Netherlands.

The de Kock family, grown, after my grandfather's death. *(left to right)*: Bert, Hannie, Rob, grandmother Maria, Pim, Elsje, circa 1970.

Eerkens family in Pacific Palisades, 1976. *(left to right):* Elsje, Boukje, Sjeffie, Jelmer, Mieke.

Elsje visits the House of the Red Pan, Hoog Soeren, the Netherlands, 2016.

Elsje visits the House of the Red Pan, Hoog Soeren, the Netherlands, 2016. The house is now owned by the granddaughter of the elderly Mrs. Parqui (Heidi) with whom Elsje played as a child. Here, they reminisce about the past. *(left to right):* Eva (Elsje's childhood friend from the village), Boukje (Pim's wife), Heidi Parqui, Elsje.

"I think that's remarkable," I say. "Your grandmother was willing to risk her own relationships to help a woman and her children in need." My mother listens to us in silence, then quickly changes the topic of conversation to her memories of the garden. She doesn't want to think about the ways her father's actions radiated outward to affect others.

War scars more than just one layer of a community. It scars both figuratively and literally. It scars people, it scars systems, and it scars landscapes. The war permanently changed this area. Even in my childhood when we visited Hoog Soeren and the nearby village of Kootwijk, where my aunt lived, it always lurked like an apparition between the trees. There has never been a time when I didn't know this beloved, serene place as marked by the memory of violence. From the trenches dug at intervals along the roads, now scabbed over with moss and heather, to the concrete bunkers built into hillsides, World War II was a part of this landscape for me. I learned at a very young age that there were areas my siblings and I were never to play in when we rode our bicycles deep into the woods. Over seventy years later, this is still the case. There are still sections of the forest where we cannot wander freely today. Walking with my mother through the specific quiet that only the deep woods can offer, over paths worn hard by thousands of feet, I peer between branches to the shafts of sunlight filtering through to the forest floor, wondering what lies beneath. During the war, the Nazis used the dense cover of this forest to bury their explosives caches throughout the region. As a child, my mother found a German ammunition belt in these woods, and brought the unused bullets home to make jewelry out of, until her mother discovered them and told her they were dangerous. The big yellow signs with red exclamation marks still stand in certain parts of the forest, jarring people out of their communion with nature. They read: "Danger! This is a cleanup area of a former WWII German munitions depot by the Royal Bomb Squad. Stay outside of this zone and stay on the paths." Today, picnicking parents out for a day in the country might feel the blood drain from their faces when their giggling children toddle from the thickets holding live grenades in their chubby hands. *Look, Papa, I found an egg!* It's the type of scene that still occurs each year or two with alarming regularity throughout the Netherlands.

I wonder what existing in this kind of imminent danger does to a psyche. My mother tells me about the flasher the children encountered in the woods after school when she was a child, shaking the whole community, but the munitions zones and the bomb dugouts, and even the underground bunkers where Jews hid in these woods during the war, were such a constant presence that they were experienced as part of the landscape. I wonder, how does cohabiting with the perpetually active remnants of war, as my mother did, affect one's psychology? How does anxiety manifest in the body and carry on in the children of those who lived in a consistent state of fear? In the woods after our visit with Heidi at The Red Pan, my mother and I walk on past the warning signs we no longer read, treading carefully as a matter of habit.

—

Hoog Soeren, the Netherlands, September 1946

My grandfather is released in the fall of 1946, after serving his sentence of sixteen months of internment, as they call it.

He has no job, no property, and no prospects. What he does have is a wife and children who are living in Hoog Soeren in The Red Pan, all arranged by my grandmother.

Her father's return to the household doesn't make much of an impression on the young Elsje. She already has the restoration of family and the home she wants by then in her mother and siblings. When I ask her about it now, she says she does not recall the day her father arrived at the cottage after being released from prison. Like a car merging onto a freeway, he's suddenly just there among them again, eating at their table, drinking the tea his wife sets before him. While the return of her father specifically doesn't make much of an impression, six-year-old Elsje finally feels content once again having her family back together and a secure sense of home, and this period in Hoog Soeren is marked by a profound sense of happiness. She builds snowmen with her siblings in the winter and goes to school on the back of her mother's bicycle. It's her first year of school, first grade. The next year she will ride her own bicycle beside her siblings, learning this necessary skill early like all Dutch children. In a random search of information about the two-room Hoog Soeren schoolhouse on the internet, an old sepia photo pops up, and there is Elsje at eight or nine years old, sitting at a wooden desk in the classroom with the other young children, looking cheerful in a plaid dress with a massive white bow in her hair. Everything in her life looks normal, for the first time in her young experience.

But of course, beneath the veneer of normalcy, the effects of the war still carry on. In Gelderland, where they live, all the NSBers are known. My grandfather has been banned from his job at the auto mechanics' school, banned from the teaching profession, and he is virtually unemployable in the area. The *Apeldoorn Courant*, the local newspaper, runs an

article on June 29, 1946, naming the NSBers from the area
who have come before the tribunal, including my grandfather. Not bothering to hide its contempt and dripping with
sarcasm, the article reads,

> *A.C. de Kock, teacher in Apeldoorn, interned at
> Wezep, was a member of the NSB until September of
> 1944, a local group leader in the movement . . . The
> accused believed that the NSB could deliver better so-
> cial benefits. He denied having spread political pro-
> paganda at the mechanics school where he worked. He
> was disappointed that the organization later devel-
> oped in "a deplorable manner." His defense witnesses
> paint the accused as someone who was regarded by
> those with opposing views during the war as a real
> mensch. Defense lawyer asked for consideration that
> the accused's four children are living in a children's
> home. His 14-year-old is forced to live with Kraut
> girls and similar "riffraff" that are causing the girl, who
> feels far removed from them, to develop an inferior-
> ity complex. Sentencing [A.C. de Kock]: Internment
> until September 15, 1946, and loss of voting rights.
> Mrs. M.C. de Kock-Barto, of Apeldoorn, was a mem-
> ber of the NSB, but never showed up actively in the
> movement. She was interned for 7 months and is now
> home. Sentencing: Internment in camp as time served,
> loss of voting rights.*

With articles like this in the local newspaper of a small
city, my grandfather and the family are marked in the community. He will not be hired anywhere near Hoog Soeren.
Even those who would consider it would be ostracized for

hiring an NSBer. With five mouths to feed, my grandfather has to find a way to earn money. Eventually, he manages to do this, getting a job at the National Aerospace Laboratory in Amsterdam, where he works on aerodynamics projects. The job requires him to be in the city, so for several years, he returns home only on the weekends to see the family. Together they bike through the woods to the train station in Apeldoorn on Saturday afternoon to pick him up, and they drop him off on Sunday evening when he takes the train back to Amsterdam. Elsje sees her father very little. He plays a very minor role in her day-to-day life in Hoog Soeren.

On one of his weekends home, he gets my grandmother pregnant for the fifth time, and nine months later, in May 1948, little Rob is born, something that brings joy and hope back into their lives. Eight-year-old Elsje is no longer the baby in the family, something she is thrilled about. In photos, she carries her baby brother around like a doll. She dresses him and feeds him his bottle and coos at him through the bars of the playpen set up in the tiny living room of The Red Pan. Uncle Rob now writes of his birth, "I believe, or like to believe if you want, that I represented an allusive sort of restart for this pair of parents. They couldn't undo history, but they could give themselves another go. Unfortunately, that was never going to be quite realistic. Babies and toddlers are very good at soaking up in considerable detail the state of mind of those around them, even if they don't have the grown-up words. All that denial. All that frigging silent denial." Rob pushes back against the narrative that my mother seems to want to adhere to: fresh start, no enemies. I understand his resentment now at having been used as the savior figure in a family unwilling or unable to reckon with the past. Certainly as he grew up, he would have known that something had happened to the family unit that was not to be spoken of, and that he was excluded from. It seems a heavy burden for a child to carry.

The family gets a dog, a German shepherd they call Bandit. They play in the garden and go to the lake in the summers. Elsje learns to swim and makes a best friend, a girl named Eva who lives a few houses away in the village, a friend she will keep for the rest of her life. In the summers, Mrs. Parqui comes to stay. My grandmother does her washing and cooks her meals, and the children play with her grandchildren, including Heidi.

But despite the relief from the immediate terror of war, the country has not healed, perhaps will never heal. Buildings haven't been rebuilt. Lives have been lost. The anti-German and NSB sentiment is everywhere. There are businesses that won't even serve people with a German accent in the decades after the war. My grandparents would have been, of course, hyperaware of this as blacklisted adults. But by and large, young Elsje is insulated from it, growing up in the forest and on the heath in rural Hoog Soeren with the occasional exciting visit to the village from the teenage Princess Beatrix, stopping by in her horse-drawn coach on weekend outings from the royal palace in Apeldoorn. Elsje becomes Else as she turns eight, nine, ten, eleven, twelve, all in the tiny cottage in the village.

Her older sister, Hannie, graduates high school in this time and moves into a small apartment in a nearby city where she works as a lab technician. Through that job, she meets a research student, Hans, and before too long, young people's impulses being what they are, she is pregnant. Little Rob, her toddler brother, is beside himself. He runs through the village of Hoog Soeren, yelling, "I'm an uncle! I'm an uncle!" Else, now thirteen years old, is excited by the prospect of being an auntie to her big sister's baby. She adores babies. She beams when she is told the news by her mother. "This is going to be so great!" she says. Her mother frowns. "No, Else. This is not so nice at all. This is not good news." Hannie will have to marry Hans. There is no other option in the 1950s for a pregnant girl. Word of Hannie's fate spreads through the village, where two other young ladies have also become pregnant. The baker, bringing loaves to the houses on his *bakfiets* cargo bicycle, raises his eyebrows when my grandmother tells him the news during their customary chit-chat on the front stoop of The Red Pan. "Goh, that stork sure be flying hard round here," he says in his heavy regional accent. "Here's your whole-grain loaf and twelve biscuits, Mrs. De Kock. Congratulations on the blessed news."

The baby comes, a little girl named Maaike, and she is beloved by the family. Hannie, who has received the most rigorous high school education among the children and is extremely smart, abandons her pursuit of a career. She marries Hans and they live with baby Maaike in the university city of Leiden, where Hannie becomes a stay-at-home mother. Later, she follows her geologist husband to Libya and Texas before settling right back into a farmhouse in the Veluwe, with three more children. This is the house where I will later live for a year and where our family will spend our summers.

When Else is fifteen and her elder siblings have already left home, she and her mother and Rob move to Amsterdam to join her father, who has finally reached the top of a waiting list and has been issued government housing, an apartment on the outskirts of the city. It marks the end of the happiest time in her life, and a move into one of the most difficult ones. Before they leave, her father uses the money he has saved up to buy a parcel of land in Kootwijk, very close to Hoog Soeren. The parcel has only an old barn and the burned remains of a house on it, and my grandfather plans to build the family a house on the site of the former house. But when he submits the application for a building permit to the county office, he is inexplicably denied the permit, despite the parcel's clear zoning for a residence. There is no explanation for the denial. Shortly thereafter, the mayor's office changes the zoning of the parcel to preclude building any new structures on it. Later, rumors filter back to the family. No NSBer is going to build a home in that county. So the family leaves for Amsterdam owning an overpriced parcel of land on which they can only camp on the weekends, sleeping on cots in the barn. They will never live in the Veluwe as a family again.

11

FOUT IN THE CITY

Amsterdam, the Netherlands, 1955

My mother hates Amsterdam, with its horizon-marring buildings and its pressing inhabitants, the thousands of unfamiliar eyes watching, scrutinizing her in the thick crowds of the Kalverstraat where they shop. The family doesn't live in one of the stately brick homes lining the canals, but rather deep in West Amsterdam, in the blocks of government housing. Else is fifteen when they move, an awkward age to transfer to a new school in this unfamiliar city. Bert is at university studying chemistry, Pim has also just started his university studies, and Hannie is living with her husband, Hans, and pregnant with her second child at twenty-three. Only little Rob and Else live in the Amsterdam apartment with their parents. Else learns to navigate on her bicycle the streets from West Amsterdam to her school in the Jordaan, one block from the house where Anne Frank hid during the war, and possibly the school Frank would have attended at my mother's age had the war not intervened.

Else is a shy, nature-loving girl who has spent very little

time in any big city. The teens in her class have heavy Amsterdam accents. They are more mature in the ways that city kids are usually more mature, discussing films and music and current fashions about which Else has no clue. She is also one of only two girls in her class, as Dutch high schools are separated into different levels and emphases, and this is the HBS B (Beta), the high school for kids studying math and science. In the 1950s, hardly any girls study math and science. Else becomes something of a ghost, silently floating in and out of her classes. She spends her free time reading and getting out of the city entirely, going on nature walks with the NJN, the Netherlands Youth League for Nature Studies. But as one of two girls in the class, she can't avoid the inevitable attention from teenage boys. The following year, when she is sixteen, she'll get a boyfriend, Dick, who will be her only friend at school. Despite this, depression is the main thing she will remember about Amsterdam.

—

Amsterdam, the Netherlands, 2014

When we are in Holland, my mother always stays with her brother Pim's wife, Bouk, at her farm in the north, and I stay in an apartment in Amsterdam. I ask her multiple times to schedule time for us to visit her former neighborhood in Amsterdam, but she resists. "Let me think about it," she says. "I've already seen it," she says. And finally, "I don't want to see it." In the end, I visit the site of her old apartment alone, which is perhaps more fitting. The place symbolizes a time of extreme isolation for my mother, and perhaps it is in isolation that I should view it.

I bike there on a rainy afternoon, my hair slicked wet to

my face and my clothes damp and cold because I don't have a raincoat. I cycle out of the center, through Westerpark, until I find myself in an industrial area. I bike under the freeway overpass, and still I keep going. It's much farther than I anticipated, twenty to thirty minutes away, and not at all the kind of neighborhood I imagined it would be in when I arrive. I get a bit lost in the maze of project buildings, all identical to one another. The streets are empty. One woman, her eyes averted, passes too quickly for me to stop her for directions. I finally spot a man entering one of the buildings. "Hello! Hi! Excuse me? Fritz Conijnstraat?" I ask him. "Sorry, I don't know," he answers in English, with a heavy Eastern European accent. He turns and vanishes inside the building.

Cycling on, I find Fritz Conijnstraat just one block over in an identical housing structure, and see that my mother's former home was in the middle of one of the large apartment blocks. I snap a photo of her former building, the brick now tagged with graffiti on the side. Laundry hangs to dry on most of the balconies, and the exterior is lined with a pipe wrapped in foil insulation. The balcony door to my mother's former apartment is open, and I can see part of a stove, a woman cooking, and a toddler looking at me through the window. A man talking on his phone on one of the balconies looks down at me as I lurk by the tree in front of the building, and I give him a half wave and a smile, lamely hoping to connect and share with someone, anyone, that my mother lived in this building sixty years ago, maybe learn something more, be invited in. But he walks inside and shuts his door.

A few weeks prior to my visit, a newborn infant was found in a public Dumpster by a passerby who heard the baby's cries echoing up from the depths next to these buildings, only steps from my mother's former front door. Had the woman not

passed the Dumpster at 4:00 a.m., the baby would have
been crushed in the garbage-compacting truck that would
have mechanically lifted the container into the compacter
that same morning. The police are unable to trace the child
back to its parents. In a newspaper article in *Het Parool*,
residents describe the neighborhood: "There are some high-
rises in this area, and who knows what goes on. In those
blocks, it's all very anonymous." The tragic story of the
discarded child only intensifies my deep sense of the isolation and depression my mother felt while living in this place.

After only a few minutes, I want to leave. So I get back
on my bike to trek back to the city center, with its pictur-
esque canals and romantic drawbridges. There is nothing
more to see here. A dark melancholy settles over me while I
ride back through the neighborhood. The difference between
this place and the cottage in Hoog Soeren is stark. It seems
an injustice to ask an introverted child who has spent the past
decade in the woods in a fairy-tale chalet to adapt to this urban environment.

I visit my mother's old school building in Amsterdam. Before it was my mother's school, in the seventeenth century it
was the home of one of the biggest slave traders in the Netherlands, the Coymans family. I think about the Coymans descendants today and whether they feel the inheritance of
shame. Ironically, today the building houses Amnesty International. Between a slave trader and a human rights organization, my mother sat within the brick walls at Keizersgracht
177, and this too, feels symbolic to me, a child on the time
line of history, existing between the extremes of human behavior and morality.

I am also struck by how close her former school is to the
Anne Frank House. My mother would have been in school
there the year that Otto Frank established the house one

block over as a museum, saving it from demolition and development. She would have been well aware of the family and
of Anne Frank's diary, which had just been published and
was a sensation in Amsterdam. She would have been aware
of the reminders everywhere in Amsterdam of the fate of the
Jews who had suffered in the city only a decade and a half
earlier.

When I ask her about this, the conversation quickly becomes uncomfortable, though illuminating. "When you saw
the Anne Frank House every day, were you reminded of your
father? I mean, did you connect it to your father's membership in the NSB?" I ask.

My mother's face goes blank, and I realize that she had
not connected the two until just this moment. "No. I didn't.
I mean, no. I knew what happened to the Jews, and I knew
it was awful, but I didn't think of that having anything to
do with my dad. I mean, now that you ask, I wonder why I
never thought about it that way, but I didn't."

"Did you think about why your parents went to jail?"

"He was a member of a bad political party."

"But you didn't connect it to the Nazis or the Holocaust?"

"My dad never betrayed any Jews. He had Jewish friends."

"Well . . . You say 'friends,' but he wrote racist articles
and was a member of an anti-Semitic organization. You really
didn't think about that when you were in Amsterdam, next
to the Anne Frank House every day?"

"No. It sounds weird now, but no."

"If it were me, and I was fifteen, sixteen years old, reading and learning about the Holocaust, I think I would start
asking questions and making connections, even if I was little
and didn't understand at the time it was happening."

My mother falls silent again.

"Maybe you didn't want to know?" I offer.

She nods. "Yes, I think there is something to that. I recall asking my mother something about the NSB when I was older, and she said she didn't want to talk about that and I knew not to ask again. And my father definitely didn't want to talk about it. It was not discussed. Ever."

—

Amsterdam, the Netherlands, 1957

When my mother graduates high school in 1957, she isn't sure what to do next. She wants to go to university to study to be a doctor, but there is no money in the family for the girls to go to university. The rest of her life, my mother will regret not having had the opportunity to become a doctor and being discouraged by her parents from pursuing a university degree while her brothers are encouraged and supported in attending university. (Pregnancy resolves the issue for Hannie, who resigns herself to her role as housewife, though later in life she will go back to school and become a psychologist.) So despite having studied math and science at the HBS B and having the qualifications for university, my mother lives at home and attends classes to become a home economics teacher. Her brother Pim studies biology at the University of Amsterdam, and Else visits him a lot in his little apartment across from the Artis zoo. When he spends a year abroad in Suriname, a colony of the Netherlands, to research marine life in Paramaribo, Else sublets his apartment and enrolls in the professional school for dietitians. There she learns to make meal plans for diabetics and people with a whole range of medical conditions. For the first time in Amsterdam, she makes real friends, including her best friend, Bouk, a tall, blond, blue-eyed woman after whom my sister will later be named.

When Pim returns from Suriname after a year, Else brings Bouk around to his apartment, and the two are smitten with each other. Else and Bouk are both accepted for an internship at a hospital in Paris, so the best friends eat croissants and practice their French for a year, a year of fun and adventure for my mother. When they return to the Netherlands, they both apply for the same job at the hospital in Leiden, and the hospital decides to create two positions, so the best friends can continue to work together, writing menu plans for patients in the hospital. Meanwhile, Pim visits his sister and his sweetheart a lot, and Else's best friend becomes her sister-in-law when Bouk becomes pregnant.

Back in Hoog Soeren, a letter arrives at The Red Pan one day. The envelope reads merely, "Else de Kock, Hoog Soeren, the Netherlands." The village is so small that the mailman knows the family has moved to Amsterdam; he forwards the letter to their address there, and the letter is forwarded from there to Leiden, where my mother works in the hospital. The letter is from my father, and it asks if she might want to correspond with him. In the United States, he has come to the conclusion that he wants to meet a nice Dutch girl, but he has found that there aren't too many of those in California.

Before Sjef's father traveled to Indonesia to work as a doctor, Sjef's parents were friends with Else's parents. The families rekindled a friendship when my father's family returned to the Netherlands from Indonesia and my mother's parents were released from prison. My parents often say that it was likely the friendship endured because my father's parents weren't in the Netherlands during the war and didn't have the perspective of those who had lived under Nazi occupation. Further, they had experienced their own imprisonment. They did not have the context and judgment of the Dutch friends who turned their backs on my mother's parents.

While she is eight years younger than he is, my father remembers meeting my mother once before he left for America, and his parents tell him she is now a young woman, and recently single. On a whim, he writes to her, and when she receives the surprise letter in Leiden, they begin corresponding. After years in Leiden, my mother, now nearly thirty, has split with the man she had been dating and feels stuck. In the 1960s, being thirty and unmarried is just about the same as being a spinster, and she is worried she will never find a partner or have a family. In Leiden, there don't seem to be many options.

Bouk and Pim, with their new infant, have moved to Curaçao, a Dutch colony in the Caribbean. Else misses them terribly and wants a change. When they tell her they would love for her to come live there and there is a job opening for a dietitian at the local hospital, she packs her summer dresses and heads across the Atlantic. On the way to Curaçao, she has to stop over in New York City, where my father's little brother, Kees, is living with his wife and child. So she and my father make a plan to meet in New York at Kees's house, where my mother has planned be a guest for a week. It's enough to ignite a romance, and they take a spontaneous trip to Montreal to visit the World's Fair, delaying their departures for an extra week. In the taxi to the airport, where my father will fly to Los Angeles and my mother to the Caribbean, Sjef asks Else to marry him. They've only been together for two weeks, officially, but my mother says yes, calling her mother in Holland with the news as soon as she arrives in Curaçao. "I have a surprise for you!" Else says through the crackling phone. "You're getting a son-in-law!" "I'm getting a sunny log?" my grandmother yells back through the fuzzy connection. "A son-in-law!" Else laughs. "Son-in-law!" They marry in the Netherlands a year later, after Sjef makes a few visits to Curaçao. My mother moves to Los Angeles, where my father builds a house on a hill overlooking the Pacific Ocean, far from Indonesia, far from the Netherlands, in a country that knows nothing about their backgrounds and offers them a clean slate.

12

LET THE RECORD SHOW

The Hague, the Netherlands, 2014

In the shadow of the International Criminal Court, where they hold war crimes tribunals for global dictators, is the National Archives of the Netherlands. It is where the sealed transcripts of the war trials for NSB members are kept. It takes me years to see the dossiers of my grandparents. A request must be filed with a statement of intent, and only family members are permitted access to a dossier. This request, if approved, prompts a reciprocal request for photocopies of birth certificates, death certificates, passports, and other documents. After these have been submitted, the government assigns a date and time for you to show up. No deviation from these rules is indulged in the years I try to obtain access. The Dutch are nothing if not committed to a bureaucratic system of fairness. Every time I had started the process in years past, I had returned to the United States before getting a date or approval. Finally, one summer, I am able to cut through the bureaucracy and get an appointment. My mother decides she wants to go with me, though we discuss the possibility that there will be information contained in her parents' records that she won't know or like. "I am past being disappointed in my father," she says. "I don't think it will upset me anymore." We have four hours on our assigned date to view my grandparents' dossiers.

On the date of our visit, we are fingerprinted and photographed. We have to put all of our possessions in a locker, except for my laptop, which is inspected, and a notepad for my mother, who doesn't have a laptop. My mother may use only an assigned pencil to transcribe what is contained in the files. She must leave her pen, eraser, and pencil sharpener in the locker with our other belongings. A guard sits with us at a long table with around fifteen other people looking at dossiers. I'm struck by the knowledge that most of these people are doing what I am doing: trying to find out the facts about their dark family histories. Hundreds of thousands of Dutch people carry this secret about their heritage. In our own quiet conference with the past, we all sit around a table, absorbing the only written record. Most of them inherited a silence about it too, the inheritance of a collective national taboo. I open my laptop to begin taking notes, and another guard walks over and places a sticker over the camera eye on my computer.

I am astounded at the volume of information the government was able to amass in their case against my grandfather as a collaborator. I can't imagine the man-hours involved or how they managed to collect it all. Letters to and from the NSB office, private notes written by neighbors and family members, receipts, real estate papers, affidavits, employment papers, magazine subscriptions, ID photos, and, of course, the trial transcripts with my grandfather's defense and the verdict finding him guilty of treason, along with his sentence:

THAT HE, CITIZEN OF THE NETHERLANDS, BORN 22 APRIL 1904

I. *During the enemy occupation of the empire in Europe until Sept 1944 remained a member of the National Socialist Movement of the Netherlands . . .*

II. *During the enemy occupation of the empire in Europe as a member of the Technical Guild and the Teacher's Guild and as an allied member of the Dutch Germanic S.S.; shall be deemed based upon foregoing facts to have acted knowingly and deliberately contrary to the interests of the Dutch people . . .*

In view of the relevant Legislative Acts: We declare the accused guilty of: acting deliberately in contravention of the interests of the Dutch people;

WE SENTENCE THE ACCUSED TO

Internment, in which the Tribunal proposes to set a period calculated from 14 May 1945 to end on 15 September 1946; B. Revocation of the right to vote. 27 June 1946.

The files fill four three-inch-thick folders. The contents are at times contradictory, and the apparent conflicts in my grandfather's character confuse me: What was his true ideology and what was born out of pressure or ulterior motives?

There is a list of his positions in the NSB party. *Committee member. Group leader. Committee Organizer. Branch Spokesperson. Inspector-in-training.* Subscriber of NSB and Nazi newspapers and magazines. The list of official affiliations runs down one page. *Member. Member. Member.* His membership in the Germanic SS specifically upsets me. Like most people I know, I have always believed that the SS was made up of hard-core Nazis, and I assume that he is a member of the *German* SS, which absolutely shocks me. I don't understand how this squares with his insistence that he was not in favor of the Nazis. Later, to some relief, I learn that the NSB had its own version of the SS, first called the Dutch SS and then changed to the Germanic SS in the Netherlands, not to be confused with the German SS or Waffen SS. The Dutch SS was a political designation established by Mussert under pressure of Hitler, and served more as a symbolic Dutch unit, as opposed to the German Waffen SS, which had Dutch recruits as well but was active in the persecution of the Jews. Further research reveals that my grandfather's membership was due to the fact that he gave members of the Dutch SS lessons in genealogy, a hobby of his. While I am relieved that he wasn't a member of the German SS, this detail rattles me. I cannot imagine what use the NSB or the Dutch SS would have had for a lesson in genealogy besides the obvious: a focus on Germanic bloodlines and racial purity and, worse, a tool to track down Jewish citizens. I have no proof of this, but to my mind, there can be no other explanation for the genealogy lessons. I can't know whether my grandfather was specifically aware of how his lessons in methodology would be applied, but it's one of the more upsetting things I find in the dossier. It is possible that he was naive about the implications of sharing his enthusiasm and knowledge of genealogy. An internet search of "SS" and "genealogy" returns several passages in a report on the Dutch SS and NSB assembled by the Netherlands Institute for War Documentation titled "The SS and the Netherlands, Documents from the SS Archives 1935–1945" that asserts that many NSB members were interested in genealogy as a hobby. It includes the following passage, which revisits a paganist theme found in the NSB philosophy and offers somewhat less sinister, if not nationalistic, motives for the high level of interest in genealogy in the NSB/Dutch SS:

The roots of the people and the unifying elements of blood and land resulted in the interest of . . . traditions, legends, folklore, old traditions, proverbs . . . and also in more concrete examples of the folk history: Saxon farms, runes, Germanic fairy mounds, Fresian folk art but also word origins, medieval art (the more primitive the more folksy), historic Dutch names, etc. etc. Knowledge of the ancestors added a new dimension to the present-day existence, also individually; one could fulfill one's interest in one's kinfolk via studying the history of tribes, or, to speak in Roman terms, genealogy (this turned out to occasionally be a rather risky hobby for race-conscious detectives).

There is also a lot of information in the dossier complicating the damning pieces of evidence about my grandfather's involvement with the NSB and Dutch SS. There are affidavits from his neighbors that they had Jewish people in hiding and were in the resistance, and that my grandfather kept their secrets to the end. Affidavits that he helped members of the resistance in concealing radios, bicycles, contraband items. In a way, this dossier is as close to putting my grandfather on the psychoanalyst's couch as I can get. Viewed together, the documents paint him as a fairly conflicted and pathetic man. Though most of my questions will remain forever unanswered, I do get a few more clues as to the "why" behind my search, the great "why" that my grandfather has taken to his grave. One of the more telling documents is my grandfather's letter to the NSB head office after the Nazi occupation regarding his years-long study of cryptology:

> *During the mobilization I offered the Dutch Department of Defense my services multiple times. I know that I am one of the few Dutch experts in cryptology. If everything had been well managed in our motherland, then they surely would have at least taken note of my offer . . . Presumably the fact that I never received a single word nor a letter back is connected to the coincidence that I, as NSBer, was seen by them as "untrustworthy." Should it come to pass, then I gladly offer myself as a consultant to the NSB in this regard.*

His words reek of bitterness. To me, they reflect the low self-esteem of a rejected man who, feeling the sting of disregard by his government, joins forces with the enemy purely out of spite.

In the end, after the smoke of war clears and the horrible truth of it comes into view, he feels betrayed and undervalued by all parties. In a letter to the judge in his own defense, he states, "I have believed that the social needs of the Dutch people could best be met by a political party that, according to its stated platform, served them. Over the course of the last few years I have been disappointed and disillusioned in many ways. I have not profited from my membership [in the NSB] in any respect."

In another letter in the dossier, one sent to the courts after his arrest, he goes into even more detail, writing,

> *I became a member of the NSB because, given the societal situation prior to 1940, the NSB's platform was the only one I saw for building a just community.*

After 1940 I also believed that only that platform could help form a good society. The mistakes of the Germans can't be projected onto the NSB members, in my opinion. I never profited from the political developments after 1940, as some would have done. I rejected a number of good opportunities that were offered to me, such that I stayed true to myself. I didn't accept a radio, as other Dutch people also weren't allowed radios. I never bought anything on the black market. Everyone could speak to me openly about their beliefs, without having to fear that I would turn them in. My students and character witnesses can attest to the fact that I consistently cursed and condemned the razzias, prosecutions, the concentration camps, etc. of the Germans. Further, I never once revealed anything; Germans never came in my house. I have never wanted to be anything but a good person. I reject the accusation of "traitor" with indignation. I think the aforementioned reasons are sufficient reason to release me immediately. Measured by my intentions and the way I conducted myself, it is my impression that I have not earned being arrested.

Another document I come across was added after my grandfather was released from prison. It regards the "Cleansing" or "Purification" Act of 1945, which was enacted after NSB members and other collaborators had served out their sentences and many were due to reenter society. The Cleansing Act Advisory Commission sought to further "cleanse" the Netherlands of these fout people, removing them from jobs and all other positions and stripping them of their right to their pensions. In effect, the Cleansing Act added a life sentence to their prison sentences. I am struck by the specific use of the word *cleansing*, because it is so close to the language the opposing side used during the Holocaust. This is uncomfortable for me, because it allows for a conflation that should not be allowed to exist.

MINISTER OF EDUCATION, ARTS, AND SCIENCES. JANUARY 1948.

Given the advice of the Advisory Commission named in article 5 of the Cleansing Act of 1945 from December 10, 1945; Whereas, the person named below . . . having been found guilty of treason, the aforementioned Commission has approved:

   a. *dismissal from his post for A.C. Kock, teacher at the "Dutch Institute of Community Education" in Arnhem;*

   b. *Expiration of all rights to current or future pension and other rights. The Hague, January 31, 1948*

2. Termination as Special Education Teacher for the Engineer and Automobile Technical School Apeldoorn per 11-2-45. "Was a member of the NSB."

Upon this decree, notes are handwritten in the space provided at the end of the document:

Not NSB profiteer. Should be regarded as an "idealist." Spread no propaganda at school. Warned some of the teachers about the [German] S.D., who wanted information from them. This man belongs to the group of "good" NSB members before the war. He disapproved openly of the Holocaust and razzias and resigned in Jan/Feb 45 as a member.

I am perplexed. Who has written these extra notes on the form? The judge? An administrator? The form has been placed in the dossier by the government officials associated with the special tribunal, so the notes will have come from the hand of the same government that sentenced my grandfather. If these are the notes of the judge, or of persons at the Cleansing Act Advisory Commission, I can't help but wonder what their advice would be for "bad" NSB members.

My mother and I leave the archives drained, with hand cramps from copying down as much as we can. We talk in the car. One thing she realized in reading the dossiers was that she didn't know her father very well. And now that her parents are gone, we cannot ask them why they made the choices that they made. We cannot ask them what happened in the internment camps for collaborators, about the lived experiences behind the typed sentences and forms in a dossier in a box in the national archives of the Netherlands. They refused to speak of it, and so the dossiers are all we now have. I discover that I have more questions than answers now, and must be content with the idea that the true character of my grandfather lies somewhere between idealist and monster.

—

Rotterdam, the Netherlands, 2016

In all of the years I visited the Netherlands, I avoided Rotterdam. In the southern part of the country, it's not where my people are from. But I also had a bias against the city. Because the center of Rotterdam was destroyed by the Germans in the war, it was rebuilt in the ensuing years, and the city became a European center for contemporary architecture.

Perhaps because I grew up in a midcentury modern house

in Los Angeles, a city of eclectic architecture that tears down and rebuilds as if it were changing socks, I have a romanticized love for the historic architecture of European cities: the cobblestoned streets, the art nouveau and stained glass art deco buildings, the red clay roof tiles and spires of churches so old that William Shakespeare could have sat in their pews. I fetishize oldness. Rotterdam, with its glass cube houses and mirrored skyscrapers, never really appealed to me. But one day I find myself there when meeting a friend for a day of pure tourism and the delight of aimless exploration, and I begin to appreciate the juxtaposition of the old and the new in this strange city, as I see how the contemporary architects respected what was left of the old landscape. Progress works in harmony with history in Rotterdam, and while the last thing on my mind on this day is my parents, I suddenly see that this is a natural stop in their narrative. Rotterdam is a city ravaged by war, but it is redefining itself with its scars laid bare.

My friend and I visit Hotel New York, which has been recommended to him as a nice place to eat in the harbor. What my friend doesn't tell me is that Hotel New York is the former terminal for the Holland America Line, which carried thousands of immigrants to America. The restaurant where we have come to eat is the former departure hall where my parents left the Netherlands together for a new life in the United States. Standing in front of it, I look at the last landmark my mother would have seen of her home country before seeing the Statue of Liberty come into view on the other end of the Atlantic. The stone building has two green patinated clock towers and *Holland Amerika Lijn* spelled out across it in art nouveau lettering. Built in 1904 by a Jugendstil architect, it somehow survived the German blitzkrieg as the rest of the city burned. When I get home, I immediately play the home movie my father shot in 1967 as they left Rotterdam, and there it is: the same building, the two green clock towers exactly as I saw them. Below it on the wharf are my father's parents and my mother's mother, and Hannie and her kids, waving goodbye.

For my father, the Netherlands was never really home. He had watched his home vanish into the horizon from a ship sailing out of the Semarang harbor two decades earlier. But for my mother, this was the home she loved, the home she deeply wanted to belong to, the home she left behind. The home where she would have preferred to stay. In grainy silent film, I see my mother standing on the deck of the SS *Nieuw Amsterdam*, newly married, waving her scarf to her family members standing on the quay below. As my father trains the camera on her, I see my mother waving and waving as they leave the harbor, her eyes full, a forced smile on her face. She hangs over the railing of the ship and waves until she cannot see them waving back anymore, and then she is watching this beautiful building with its two round clocks like goalposts recede farther and farther into the distance until it disappears for her and there is only the vastness of ocean and the things she left behind. As I stand on the same wharf in Rotterdam completely by chance, I think about how perfect this is, how it is a puzzle piece I didn't realize was missing until I could almost see the whole picture come into view. Of course, this ends with her daughter following her through history, crisscrossing the Netherlands in search of the past, and ending that journey here, at this very point where she left it all behind on a ship spewing salt water back at the shore.

PART III

COMING TOGETHER

We shall not cease from exploration
And the end of all our exploring
Will be to arrive where we started
And know the place for the first time.

—T.S. ELIOT

13

THE IMMIGRANTS

Antwerp, Belgium, September 26, 1950

The MS *Edam* is loaded up in the harbor of Antwerp, wind whipping under a clouded sky. Sjef and a group of young men and women stand on the quay, waiting to board. Sjef's parents, my grandparents, are there to see their son off. My grandfather holds his fedora from blowing off as he gives his son his last words of advice and presses an envelope of guilders into his hand. *To start you off when you get over there.* My father is now a young man of nineteen, and he shakes his father's hand. My grandmother hugs her son and kisses his cheek. *We will miss you, but I know you're going to do great out there. Make sure to write.* The gangway is lowered, and my father and the other travelers walk up to the ship.

This ship has come from Rotterdam, but Dutch maritime laws forbid passengers to travel on a freight ship. Belgium has no such laws, though, so Sjef has traveled to Antwerp for a cheap ticket as one of fifty passengers allowed to bunk in the makeshift quarters belowdecks. Destination: New York City.

He has a giant steamer trunk filled with all of his possessions, which two muscular sailors hoist onto their shoulders and carry onto the ship for him. Sjef can barely contain his excitement as he thinks of the possibilities ahead in America.

Throughout the trip, he gets to know his travel mates. They have impromptu dances on the deck and sing "Goodnight, Irene" in the dark, faces into the salty wind. Twice there are terrible storms, and the *Edam* is tossed violently in the waves. Sjef's father has given him a camera as a going-away gift, and he snaps photos of it all: the storm, his new friends on the deck, the girl he develops a crush on somewhere in the middle of the Atlantic. He has people take his photo too, at the stern of the boat, beaming in every one. You can see it on his face: Finally, his life can start.

He's been accepted to UC Berkeley. His uncle Henk in Bolivia, as the Dutch ambassador there, has connections to the university and has written a letter on his behalf. Sjef wants to study aeronautics, having become obsessed with airplanes, but his application to Caltech indicated a year and a half wait time for aeronautics majors, and UC Berkeley has an excellent engineering program. It also has a waiting list, but Uncle Henk advises Sjef to apply to the College of Letters and Sciences and transfer into the engineering program later.

After ten days, a journey twice as long as that on the big passenger liners, a speck on the horizon becomes a massive woman rising up from the sea with a torch. New York. America. The ship sails into the harbor, with dockworkers yelling, and anchor chains rattling, and ropes thrown to calloused hands that tether the *Edam* to shore. Sjef disembarks and stands dockside, waiting for his trunk. The luggage comes down a conveyor belt, and Italian men stand at the bottom, throwing the luggage onto the dock, yelling to one another with animated gestures. *Attento! Mettilo lì! Dai! Dai! Idiota! Ho detto mettilo lì! Sei sordo?!* Sjef understands nothing. He watches trunks and suitcases crash to the dock, rolling onto their sides, skidding across the planks. Everything he owns for his new life is in his trunk, and he begins to panic. He approaches one of the Italians. "*Scuzi? Hallo?* Thank you please, can you be more careful?" The Italians narrow their eyes at this goofy blond cheesehead with his white teeth and gullible eyes, quite literally FOB. They wave him away with irritation, and throw the suitcases even harder as if to make a point. Sjef looks to an immigration officer who has met the ship and stands to the side with a clipboard. The officer shrugs. "Why don't you sue them?" he says, and laughs. *Why don't you sue them* are the first words spoken to my father on American soil.

It is difficult to articulate Sjef's level of naiveté at that juncture, except to point out that four hours after leaving New York City in a Greyhound bus, my father approaches the bus driver and asks him if they're almost in California. "Only if you consider three days 'almost,'" says the driver. My father is shocked. "Three *days*?" The bus driver nods. "It's OK; you can get off at the motel stops and get back on the next bus a day later." Sjef has no money for motels. He barely has enough money for food. So he buys bologna and bread at the first stop and sleeps on the seats at the back of the bus, and spends the entire three days watching America go by his window: Illinois, Nebraska, Wyoming, Utah, Nevada. Then Lake Tahoe, and down the Donner Pass into Sacramento, California's state capital. Finally, the bus pulls in to Berkeley, where Sjef steps out onto Telegraph Avenue with his enormous trunk, wrinkled and stinking.

He drags his trunk with great effort the couple of blocks to the campus. Classes have already started; it is three weeks past the beginning of the fall semester. Asking directions, he finds his way to the International House, bumping his heavy trunk up the front steps. Breathing hard, he enters the lobby, now pushing the trunk in front of him across the Mexican clay tile. The woman at the reception desk looks up. "Hello. I am Sjef Eerkens," he says, out of breath. "But you can call me Jeff."

The woman says, "Can I help you, Jeff?"

My father, in his heavy Dutch accent, says, "I have been accepted to this university. I need a room." The woman asks him if he's applied for student housing in the International House. "Uh, no," says my father. She asks him if he's applied for student housing anywhere. "Uh, no," he says. But because my father is possibly the most perseverant man alive, somehow he finds himself sleeping in a spruced-up closet at the International House that night. A few weeks later, a Chinese student drops out and returns home, and Sjef, now reinvented in America as Jeff, has a real room.

His "coming to America" story makes me laugh because of his naiveté, but it's also inspiring. I consider my father's dogged determination no matter what the circumstances and see it as connected to his experience in the camps, where he had to learn to survive without any guidance and where giving in meant potential death. All he had was himself and his persistence. I see how this character trait carried on throughout his life. In some ways, it has been a source of tension in my relationship with him. But in other ways, his stubbornness and agathism have been an inspiration to me. I don't naturally have his persistence. So I often ask my mother to put him on the phone when I am struggling with something. It doesn't matter what the issue is or that he can't possibly know the future. I just want to hear his standard line, the only setting he has: *Everything will be OK in the end.*

Jeff has finally arrived at Berkeley, but classes have already started, so he enrolls in UC Extension math courses for the first semester to get started on his requirements. He takes English lessons to improve his English. He also gets the first of what will be many jobs, this one at Cutter Laboratories, a pharmaceutical company that produces anthrax, cholera, and polio vaccines, where he works on the assembly line recycling blood plasma supplies. Later, Cutter Laboratories will be at the center of an incident in which live polio virus is mistakenly released in a vaccine instead of inactivated virus and forty thousand people contract polio as a result. But not my father. He will also go on to work in chicken farms, nursing homes, and factories; as a cabdriver and a truck driver; and harvesting crops. He works at a pump factory with the Jacuzzi brothers, and while eating lunch out back on the railroad tracks with them one day, he tells them his idea for a submersible pump that would give you a massage in your bathtub. To this day he says it is possible that the Jacuzzi brothers used his idea and we could have been millionaires soaking in Eerkenses. He works in the Alaskan canneries and gold mines in the summer, hitchhiking there with a tent to pay for his tuition and room and board at Berkeley on his own. In subsequent years, he buys a car and makes the journey over the Alcan Highway with friends. On one occasion, this leads to his sharing a small cottage in Fairbanks with, unbeknownst to him, a dangerous fugitive from Chicago who is apprehended by the Fairbanks PD.

On holiday breaks, Jeff stays in Berkeley while others go home to visit their families. He is invited to have Thanksgiving dinner at the house of the Dutch consul, and doesn't find it at all odd when it's just him and the consul at a candlelit table, or when the consul plays jazz and pours him a brandy afterward, and sits next to him on the couch, where he asks

Jeff to tell him about himself. It isn't until the consul leans in with a hand on his knee that the pieces connect and an awkward stammering of misunderstanding occurs. This is the naiveté of Jeff Eerkens in his first years in America.

If naive, he is also determined, working doggedly through his bachelor's degree, transferring to the engineering program as planned. By then, however, he has other plans besides aeronautics. He enrolls in a master's program in chemical engineering. But while he is in that program, UC Berkeley announces a brand-new Ph.D. program: nuclear engineering. Jeff is immediately intrigued. He's thought about the nuclear bombs a lot. He wants to know everything about how they work, and how nuclear energy can be harnessed for other uses. The first year, foreign-born students are banned from the classified program. But by the second year, it is declassified. He applies and gets into Berkeley's Ph.D. program in nuclear engineering, a member of their second graduating class.

My father and I have discussed at length the fact that his interest in nuclear energy probably comes from the fact that the nuclear bomb saved his life, in a perverse way. To him, it was simply intellectual curiosity. He doesn't consider the more psychologically introspective questions, but I do. I ask if he ever dwelled on the bombs' horror, the fact that 120,000 or more innocent people died with two strikes. To learn in university that that same power could be harnessed for energy to power cities must have at least touched some personal psychological investment in using that technology for good, to know that he could in some way make up for the lives of people who involuntarily gave their lives for his. For him, the thought isn't that complex. "Well, we as a class discussed how important it was not ever to use the technology for that again. But as long as we had the technology, we wanted to find out how to use it to help society. I wrote about nonproliferation. There were a lot of nonproliferation groups and efforts established then."

The one thing that doesn't go so well for Jeff in America is love, but he keeps trying. He is lonely; he wants a wife. The American women think he's funny, and they enjoy dancing with him, but he struggles to get close to any of them. There is a cultural disconnect. Always the pragmatic problem solver who persists until he succeeds, he approaches this problem the same way. He asks his little brother, Kees, a senior in high school back in Holland, who the cutest and most outgoing girl in his class is. And in 1953, when he goes home on summer holiday, he goes on a few dates with this girl, Agnes. By the time he leaves a couple of months later, she's agreed to be his wife. They have an engagement party in Eefde, where his parents live, and they plan to marry when Jeff graduates Berkeley with his BS degree in 1954. Agnes will join him in the United States. But as the months go by and the excitement wears off, Agnes rethinks her decision. She has only just finished high school. She doesn't really want to leave her friends and family and move to America. She breaks off the engagement the following summer. He returns to Berkeley alone to start grad school, dejected.

As a graduate student, Jeff meets Martha, an American woman, and they start dating. Jeff thinks maybe the broken engagement with Agnes was for the best. He and Martha get married and Martha gets pregnant. He now has a wife, the promise of a good job in Los Angeles after graduation, and soon he will have a family. They move down to L.A., as my father finishes his dissertation for his Ph.D. But they have increasingly heated fights after their daughter, Laura, is born, and Jeff is the wrong type of person to deal with volatile relationships. When Martha gets frustrated with him, he simply leaves the house. After about a year, they divorce.

In 1960, he gets a job at Aerospace Corporation, working on rocket propulsion and space surveillance satellite systems. In order to get security clearance to work on classified projects, he has to become a naturalized American citizen, renouncing his Dutch citizenship. He does so immediately and unsentimentally, severing his last ties to the former Dutch kid Sjeffie. He lost his home long before this anyway, and considers himself a nomad. He's very happy to become American and find a new home. In 1963, he is appointed chief of the laser systems department at Northrop Space Laboratories. It is there that he begins working on the laser isotope separation process that he spends the rest of his life trying to perfect. When war once again intervenes in his life, this time in Vietnam, it costs him his project. With the end of the war and the United States struggling to pay for it, the government cuts funding to Northrop's space labs, and my father's department is eliminated. He is offered a job in another department, but he chooses instead to leave Northrop with members of his team and continue their work on laser enrichment projects as a small, independent lab. Thus begins years of working with companies and on his own, but he always stays focused on this one area of research, laser isotope separation. (In the '70s, my father brings home some early prototypes of handheld green lasers, and my siblings and I shine them onto the neighborhood patrol car in the streets below the house. Well before the laser-pointer era, the patrol officer repeatedly exits his vehicle to shine his flashlight into the shrubbery on the hillside above him while we laugh our heads off at our prank, imagining he believes that aliens have descended.)

After the divorce in 1959, Martha gains custody of my half sister and moves to Arizona, and then Texas, with my half sister flying to see my father sporadically. My father returns to the idea that he wants to meet a Dutch woman. Enter my mother.

14

FORMING A FAMILY

Pacific Palisades, California, USA, 1967

As Jeff and Else travel across the Atlantic on the SS *Nieuw Amsterdam*, in Los Angeles, workmen pour concrete and erect a frame and build a house at the top of a hill in the Santa Monica Mountains. This is where my parents will live. With his first job securing the mortgage, my father buys the lot before my mother joins him from Holland. Together, the lot and house will cost $60,000, which seems an astronomical sum to Else. The neighborhood is a new one, half empty, with lots for sale and several models to choose from, customizable. They choose a sprawling 2,500-square-foot model, a midcentury modern bungalow with wide bay windows that look out over the city and the Pacific Ocean below. From the spacious backyard, there is a nearly 360-degree view, and the house is situated such that the neighbors can't be seen. In an equally spacious front yard, my parents plant a tree that grows massive over the years, its lowest branch worn smooth by all the children who know and love it, including me. Roses line the fences, and an exuberant flowering bougainvillea bush frames the walkway to the house with a shower of fuchsia. By any account, it is a spectacular house. And in the home movies from their first years there, my mother looks happy. She is beautiful, and her body is strong. I watch movies of my parents visiting Yellowstone, camping, going to Catalina Island together, dolphins surfing the waves next to the ferry. There's a palpable optimism in the images; my parents are living a new life in a new place that isn't marred by bombs or famine, and nobody they know is identified as a traitor or an occupier. They believe they've left it all behind.

But I've learned that while you can leave places behind, you can't leave yourself behind. My father is driven to make his mark at work, and my mother finds herself at home on top of this mountain alone most days. She barely speaks English and doesn't know anyone there in her first years. She misses the Netherlands intensely, and in later years she describes her move to the United States as very lonely, something she never really got over. I grow up with an awareness of this palpable loneliness she has, living in a culture in which she always feels like an outsider. Sometimes she forgets where she is for a moment and says something to a neighbor in Dutch, shaking her head afterward like she needs to shake herself back into America. "Oh, I'm sorry, I wasn't thinking." I often think that while her parents were jailed for their war activities, lost their voting rights, and were rejected by the community, my mother exiled herself. Her brother Rob, now living in New Zealand, writes me, "Maybe it isn't coincidence that the two youngest siblings are the ones who have gone overseas. There is something in that. I can't quite speak for your mother, but as for myself, I have always had a tendency to distance myself from my origins. It was especially Hannie, who eventually became the mother hen, who was unhappy with that. But here I am, intentionally or not, at the maximum possible distance from Apeldoorn."

In 1969, my brother, Jelmer, is born, and he becomes the vessel for my mother's hopes and desire for a purpose. He occupies much of my mother's time. There are hours of film of my brother as a baby. My mother is happy to have a child, and writes effusively about him in letters back home to the Netherlands: baby's first steps, his first words, his indefatigable toddler-boy love for airplanes and trucks. But she also writes about the difficulty of the long days alone, how she tries to be content washing clothes, cooking, cleaning. For many new mothers this is true. For a new immigrant it is doubly so. Her family is an ocean away. Her mother comes to visit for a couple of weeks, but it is an expensive and long trip, and when she leaves, my mother knows she won't see her again for a long time, not until my birth three years later, and my sister Boukje's birth three years after that. Meanwhile, my father continues to spend long hours in the lab. When my parents married, my father's younger brother, Kees, warned my mother that my father would always be married to his work first and his family second, and this bears out to a large extent.

The focus on his work is evident throughout the whole marriage, such that he is still preoccupied with it today in his mideighties; and while I believe that this dogged determination to succeed and focus on his own goals is a character my father was born with, I also believe that being in an internment camp by himself in extreme conditions from ages eleven to fourteen strengthened this trait and made it very difficult for my father to learn how to focus on other people's needs. How could he know how to do that when for some of his most formative years he learned day in and day out that focusing on others instead of himself meant death? My thoughts return to his friend who died brokenhearted in the camp, whose suit-case was filled with toys. Is it any wonder that my father con-tinues to live in survival mode for the rest of his life?

The ways in which the war traumas of my parents infil-trated the lives of my siblings and me are manifold, and often quite subtle. As an adult, I often find myself connecting my parents' behaviors to their war trauma, and connecting my own behaviors and psychology to theirs.

My brother and sister and I were raised on a mountain-top in Los Angeles with odd Dutch names and speaking Dutch, while our grandparents and uncles and aunts and cousins all lived in the Netherlands. I wonder if it ever gave my parents pause to be raising their children in another cul-ture, apart from their families, if the concept of home and belonging are an illusion for them. Both of them were taken from their homes at a young age, sent to live in an intern-ment camp and a children's home, respectively, where they were treated poorly. Both of them were fiercely and angrily rejected by the communities in the places they considered home, my father fleeing Java as rebel fighters shot at him, my mother's family shunned as traitors and shouted down as fout in the streets, her home boarded up. My parents' deci-sion to raise us in the United States made us outsiders to some degree, too. To be tribeless and feel like an outsider in two cultures caused me to cling to the one home I had, a tiny na-tion of 2,500 square feet on the top of a mountain, something that could not last, of course, as we grew up. Eventually, my siblings and I would move away, the home would be sold, and I would feel perpetually homeless.

The first years of our life in Pacific Palisades are idyllic. I watch the home movies taken then with great nostalgia. I can still feel and smell every part of that home in Los Angeles. The sandbox; the birthday parties on the back patio; the kiddie pool; our dog, Eva; pedaling in the driveway on a Big Wheel; the camper with its vinyl glitter seats and musty scent. Sunlight filters through the bougainvillea onto the paved walkway in our garden. I lie there on a hot Los Angeles day, the smell of the concrete steaming up through my nostrils, mixing with the specific smell of tar and volcanic pebbles from the roof. We have hosed down the roof to cool the house, and the water streams off the sides like a shower. My siblings and I put on our bathing suits and stand under the stream, then lie on the wet pavement in the sun to dry. I trace the lines running across the concrete, poke roly-poly pillbugs, those tiny armadillos that roll into balls when my chubby fingers touch them. Blue-bellied lizards do push-ups on the brick retaining wall. There is a patch of grass worn away where we have created home base for baseball games. The neighbor's dog, Skipper, barks. It's all there in the home movies—the bottlebrush, the rabbit hutch my father built with the sign that says "Bunny Hilton," the creased mountains and blue ocean backdrop, locked in forever.

In 1979, my father gets a contract in Iran, then an ally of the United States, to develop a laser isotope separation process for its nuclear program. We are going to leave behind the mountaintop home and move to Iran. I'm in kindergarten. I will be raised in Tehran. My brother and I are taken out of school. Our home is packed up. And we fly to the Netherlands to spend two weeks with my mother's sister, Hannie, before flying on to Tehran. On the two-week stopover, however, two things happen. First, my father's father dies, and I attend my first funeral. Second, the Iranian Revolution breaks out. The pro-West shah is overthrown, and the Ayatollah Khomeini, an anti-West theocrat, is installed as Supreme Leader. Once again in my parents' lives, war intervenes. My father's lasers, already having been shipped to Iran in advance of our arrival, are quarantined at the Tehran airport by the ayatollah's regime, and years of lawsuits against the new Iranian government to be compensated for them will ensue, as the ayatollah refuses to return the lasers. This results in my father's being forever linked with the Iranian nuclear program, leading to years of reporters calling the house and surveillance by American intelligence agencies. My father is under suspicion from the country to which he pledges his loyalty. Only days away from having emigrated to Iran, we are now stuck between countries, so we stay in the Netherlands for a year until we can get back into our home on top of the mountain in Los Angeles. This is the year I will go to school in Hoog Soeren and we will all live together in my aunt Hannie's farmhouse, and I will begin to think of that as a version of home too. When we return to the house in Pacific Palisades, I have to make friends all over again, and I miss the Netherlands.

While it's solidly upper-middle-class when my father has our house built there, Pacific Palisades quickly becomes one of the wealthiest areas in the country after a flurry of development in the 1970s, its coastal location and village vibe within the city of Los Angeles appealing to actors, lawyers, doctors, and other moneyed people. Their children become my peers in school, but I feel miles away from them in experience, because despite living in a beautiful home overlooking the sea, my parents behave as though we are on the verge of losing everything at all times. And in their respective experiences, maybe we are. Maybe trucks will pull up to our doors tomorrow and march us off at gunpoint. Maybe we'll

be invaded by another country and be living in a camp tomorrow. Maybe the shelves of the supermarket will be empty
next week. This is their lived experience of the world. However, for my siblings and me, as children experiencing life in
a place with the most obscene displays of abundance, the
messages we get at home are confusing. Our friends live in
homes where they have their own wings and housekeepers.
They have expense accounts at beach clubs and wear designer
labels to school after shopping sprees with their mothers. I
get sturdy leather European shoes, my brother's hand-me-
down jeans, the neighbor girl's castoffs. After a post–swim
practice pizza dinner with my girlfriends during which I order only a salad because my allowance is running thin, they
want to split the bill evenly and look at me skeptically when
I question this idea, one thirteen-year-old girl saying, "What's
the issue? Stop being so cheap. Just put it on your credit
card!"

My siblings and I spend weekends with these friends on
their yachts, at their ski cabins, driving around in their
BMWs. Some of my friends' parents are movie stars or musicians, and I envy the gifts and vacations they get from fans
and sponsors. My mother, by contrast, thinks fruit roll-ups
are an extravagant indulgence. Before I am exposed to the
real world outside of the Palisades–Malibu–Santa Monica
area, I am convinced we are poor, which, given our actual
circumstances, is outrageously offensive to people who really
live in poverty.

Pacific Palisades has a large Jewish community, and many of
my friends growing up are Jewish. Every Hanukkah, I play
dreidel at their parties, and at age thirteen, I attend a lot of
bar and bat mitzvahs. One of my friends' grandmother, a

woman my mother also knows quite well, has a number tattooed on her arm. My mother tells me that means she was in a concentration camp during the Holocaust. One afternoon, my friend's grandmother speaks at our school about her experiences in Auschwitz, about the dangers of groupthink and judging people for things beyond their control. At the time, I am too young to know anything about my mother's war history, but I have an intense awareness of the horror of the Holocaust. It isn't until high school that I really become aware of my grandfather's collaboration. I believe for many years that it is an enormous family secret I should never reveal. I feel the shame deeply and am certain that if I tell any of my Jewish friends about it, they won't want to be my friend anymore. In drama class in high school, after someone does a monologue from *The Diary of Anne Frank*, one of my Jewish peers, a young man who is always quite emotional, turns to me and says, "Any person who ever had anything to do with the Nazis in any way should have been shot." I wonder if he can see it on me, if his declaration is directed at me, and in the back of my mind, I wonder if my mother is included in that group by proxy—or worse, if I am. Of course I reveal nothing and nod. "Yeah, I know, totally." I always feel shame when it comes to my family history. It is something I hide. I wish I were a normal kid born to normal American parents.

In the years following high school, I wander, trying to find out where I belong, and end up in very different circumstances from life in Pacific Palisades. I wander to Athens, Greece, sleeping in subways and on rooftops, earning seven dollars a day from an abusive hotel owner who locks me out if I don't recruit enough guests and holds my passport hostage in a safe. Later, I join a circus as an usher and live on the road in trailers with bunk beds stacked three high next to addicts and racist, violent roustabouts, and when I see how the rest of the world lives, I learn, maybe through some self-exile of my own, that my family was never poor, and that lack is just a learned mentality that would exist in my family no matter what our circumstances might be. Tilting at windmills like Don Quixote, always fighting an imagined devastation about to happen. Even now, we are perpetually waiting for the knock, the bomb, the rejection.

15

THINGS

Pacific Palisades, California, 1981

My father tumbles in from the cold, his hair blown every which way. He is carrying a fractured lamp. "Look at this! This is a perfectly good lamp someone's just throwing away," he states incredulously, ignoring my mother's objections as he begins to apply silver duct tape over the fissures in the lamp's bright orange base. "I don't want that broken lamp in here," my mother complains, and we all watch the word land like a flaming paper bag on my father's doorstep.

Broken.

Of course he steps on it. The word is too loaded for him to accept. "It's not *broken*." He spits the word at her. "It has a small crack. It's not *broken*. This lamp still works. You guys think everything is *broken* if it has a little crack." Admitting that something is broken is an indefensible resignation, to his mind. Indeed, there isn't much that cannot be repaired with duct tape, in my father's estimation, and he routinely rescues the most tattered items from curbsides all over town to render them whole again. He is egalitarian and unbiased in his approach. When the leg breaks off the eighteenth-century carved wedding chest, it too is wrapped back into place with duct tape. Our garage is packed floor to ceiling with things. Things like boxes he hasn't looked at for decades. Things like a massive, inoperable, rusted iron drill press from the 1940s. Things like cracked lawn chairs and carpet remnants from other people's houses and gray institutional metal desks missing drawers and nonfunctioning coffeemakers.

"Look at that. You see? Perfectly good," my father says, regarding his duct-tape resurrection of the lamp. *Perfectly good* is one of my father's most used phrases. The lamp goes on his nightstand, right beside another duct-taped lamp. It stays there for the next twenty years and is never turned on.

It's just one example of how my siblings and I learn in myriad unspoken ways growing up that we are perpetually balanced on the precipice of loss, and to hold on white-knuckled to every object that crosses our paths. We learn to transfer our fears onto the things we can see and hold, because there is so much we have no control over losing.

Despite my best efforts, despite growing up surrounded by wealth, the anxiety creeps into my own behavior. I don't seem to be able to discern what's normal or neurotic as I age. I see more and more schisms erupting each day. With irritation and surprise, I recognize my father in me when I start to recycle my dental floss, rinsing it and setting it next to my toothbrush for a second use. But I also cannot stop doing it. Without being aware of it, I seem to have appropriated the "poverty mentality" my sister, a psychologist, describes us as having. At Christmas in our family, we all unwrap our gifts carefully so that we don't rip the paper, and we fold it up to use again, winding the ribbons around saved paper towel rolls. Sometimes there is another person's name crossed out on the packages we open, the paper passed down from a prior year. I never questioned this practice until later in life; I thought it was what everybody did. It is so ingrained in me that it is still always a slight shock to watch somebody open a gift I've given them by tearing into it and throwing the paper aside or stuffing it into a garbage bag. When I buy a jar of expensive face cream on sale, I always start to use smaller and smaller dabs as it begins to dwindle. Unable to let it go, I save the last little bit at the bottom of the jar in my medicine cabinet for a "special occasion" that never comes, until it dries out and becomes unusable. When I move out of my apartment, I reluctantly discard a whole graveyard of cream jars and shampoo bottles under my sink, each with a centimeter of product left in the bottom. My sense of loss is significant.

My whole life, my mother has had an almost fetishistic interest in small, insignificant gifts, trinkets and baubles. Better still are found items—stones, feathers, pennies, an earring. Large gifts don't have the same effect on her. A new car, a fancy dress, or a new piece of furniture won't hold her interest for long. But a chipped egg cup or a tarnished teaspoon will have her cooing. I grow up learning this feeling, though I can't quite put a name to it. It's almost as though the tinier the item, the more honored I can feel that it has been bestowed on me. I learn that there is a romance in re-enacting lack.

As adults, my siblings and I each receive four pieces of fine silverware from a set that has been divvied up. I ask my mother what we should do with silverware that cannot be used formally for more than one person, why she chose to do this. "It's pretty," she says, as though she can't imagine why we would think it strange that she would break up a set and render it useless as a table setting. "I just like to take the spoons out and look at them." For a few years, my mother created miniatures for a boutique as a side business, and some of her creations ended up in museums. I don't believe that this job making miniatures is just coincidental. Being small and taking up little space is her specialty. In a curio cabinet at my parents' house, she has a collection of tiny stuffed teddy bears, some as small as a thimble. The root of that particular teddy bear interest, however, lies in a more obvious place, on that street in Apeldoorn during the liberation.

I think I know what it is that underlies the desire to re-create the feeling of receiving a small token for which one feels a disproportionate gratitude. It is a deep feeling of shame, a feeling of unworthiness. In the Netherlands, the families of NSB members are still called fout to this day. People say, "Your family was fout during the war." It's a laden word that plagues the children of NSBers throughout their lives. *Fout*. Documentaries and books have been written about this label in the Netherlands. I believe this word has seeped into my mother's soul, into her very identity, and then, in some ways, into mine. Fawning over tiny things—trinkets and pebbles, in our case—feels familiar and right. It feels like the appropriate manner in which to express our gratitude for being worthy.

Certainly many other people who survived the Depression and World War II have these tendencies, regardless of what side they are on. But the specific way it is exhibited in my mother and her older siblings indicates a deeper reflection of personal identity. Before she died, my mother's sister, Hannie, came the closest to actually articulating the mentality to me. I remember a particular day when we were in a thrift store and my aunt was looking at a coffeepot.

"What a rip-off," I said, checking the price. "You can buy this same coffeepot brand-new for only a few euros more.

Why would you get a used one of inferior quality for basically the same price? That seems foolish."

She shook her head, became irritated with me. "Maybe we aren't always supposed to have things of superior quality in life, even if we can get them," she said. "We aren't just automatically entitled to nice things."

While I questioned her choice to accept inferior things for herself, it is difficult to think of an instance in which I have ever paid full price without looking for a cheaper alternative. It was drilled into my head to search for bargains. When all the children were wearing Dolphin shorts as a child, I was wearing "Doves." When all the other kids were turning up the collars on their Izod and Polo shirts, I was wearing a "Fox" shirt. When Guess jeans came into fashion, I became obsessed along with the rest of my classmates. But my mother refused to pay for expensive jeans for a growing twelve-year-old. While shopping with my mother at a discount overstock clothing store in downtown Los Angeles, I came across a purple acid-washed jean vest. It was absolutely god-awful. But it was Guess, and that red triangle logo is all I saw. I begged my mother for it, and because the price was so low, she bought it for me. In a place like Pacific Palisades, my bargain clothing provoked a great deal of teasing that I might not have experienced in another community. Of course it is shallow and snobby, and now I also see the gift in it; these experiences gave me an understanding of privilege that many of my peers never got. I'm grateful that I had a different perspective than they did. But I am slightly concerned about my extreme internal dogma to buy only what is on sale or inexpensive, the chipped and defective, the fixer-upper, the leftovers from last season, rather than the quality things I really want. Or rather, I am concerned about the emotional source of it. I want to break these patterns. I had a conversation with my mother about this once, when I noted that she had purchased a cheap cheese slicer that wouldn't slice cheese. She then purchased another cheap cheese slicer that also would not slice cheese. "This makes no sense, Mom. If we bought better things," I said, "maybe we'd spend less money than we do having to replace things when they fall apart."

At home when I was growing up, our kitchen drawers were filled with hundreds of rubber bands from the daily newspaper, stacks of rinsed plastic yogurt containers, wads of plastic bags. Today, my drawers are filled with rubber bands, plastic yogurt containers, and plastic bags. I don't know how that happened. I recall visiting my father when he relocated to Missouri for a brief period, before my mother could join him. I opened the cupboards and they were filled with stacks of plastic and Styrofoam containers he had saved from take-out meals, straws, and flimsy pie tins. At the time, I chastised him and could not understand his compulsion to keep everything. Now, after mining his war experiences, I know that this is a testament to an unrelenting drive to triumph over the unpredictable circumstances in life. It's spectacular, his will to survive, even when the rest of us don't see any perceived danger. It's in his bones to prepare for what he can.

When I encounter his hoarding tendencies now, accompanied by his insistence that everything could be useful "someday," my exasperation is tempered by a realization that this is precisely what got him through a war that killed his friends. With thousands of miles between us, and the liberty of reflection gained by being removed from the day-to-day frustrations of living with the mess, I have gratitude for that quality. Now I think that the "camp syndrome" doesn't need to be an apology or an excuse for his behavior. Maybe it doesn't need to be a detriment at all. Maybe when the deluge comes, my father will fashion an ark out of lawn chairs, rubber bands, and duct tape, and he will show the rest of us how to float.

16

FOOD

On my father's birthday, my mother always makes fried bananas. I love them too: the sticky caramelized edges, the sweet warm center. My father makes *ketimun* snacks— crackers with peanut butter, cucumber slices, and spicy sambal. We eat *kroepoek*, the crunchy prawn crackers we kids love. We eat satay with peanut-coconut sauce and nasi and bami goreng, rice and noodles. As a child, I don't know that these things aren't Dutch, and that I am getting Indonesian culture mixed in with my already muddled identity growing up in the United States with Dutch parents. Some days we eat *pannekoeken*, thick Dutch crepes rolled up with bacon and Gouda cheese or *stroop*, a thick, dark sugarcane syrup. My mother is an expert pannekoeken chef. She fries them in butter until they are perfectly browned and bubbled on one side, then flips them over to brown the other side before sliding them out of the pan onto the stack that she keeps warm under a tea towel. For me, pannekoeken are the ultimate comfort food, greasy and crisp at the edges, breathing the familiar breath of Holland into my face. Food is part of my cultural identity and inheritance. The power of food in my life is learned, as much as my tortured interaction with it is learned. More than perhaps anything else, the influence of my parents' war trauma on my family's behavior around food seems clear. In the camps and during the Hunger Winter, food was a constant focus and source of anxiety for both my parents. War robbed them of this most basic necessity for life at one time; now food would become imbued with all sorts of power in our home.

My relationship with food is and has always been fraught. This is predictable, I think, given both my gender and the cards my family was dealt. With the exception of my brother, I think every member of my family has a dysfunctional relationship with food. As a three-year-old, my little sister goes into a full-scale meltdown when any food on the table is nearly finished. *"Niet opmaken!"* she yells in her tiny voice, panicking whenever someone reaches for a half-empty jar of jam or the last piece of bread. "Don't finish it!" If the food item is indeed finished, she dissolves into an inconsolable, sobbing mess. It's amazing to me now how early we learn nonverbal cues, absorb invisible anxieties, inherit the traumas of our parents, even when none of us realize that it is happening. How does a three-year-old learn such extreme anxiety over the prospect of running out of food in a house where there are two refrigerators stuffed full of it, one in the kitchen and one in the garage? Perhaps it's from seeing the urgency with which those refrigerators are stuffed. When I am seven, I tell my mother that I love ketchup, and she tells me about the time she got a little tube of mayonnaise all for herself, and how she loved to go into a corner and squeeze a small dollop onto her finger, rationing the mayonnaise out over weeks. She buys me a bottle of ketchup for my birthday and I do the same as my mother, sitting in a corner of the kitchen with a tiny egg cup filled with ketchup, feeling special and bonded with her. As when she remembers the soft-boiled egg she ate on weekends away from the orphanage, or when she emphasizes how special getting *real butter* is, she fetishizes the lack of food. "The best treat in the world is getting the leftover rice after dinner and putting butter and brown sugar on it," she says. "We never had dessert in my family, and butter was so rare. I loved that so much." Later, when I am eight years old, she tapes a diet to my bedroom wall because I have grown a bit chubby. "If you get hungry, drink a glass of water," she says. We aren't allowed any fancy snacks. For years, I fantasize about getting a fruit roll-up or a cookie in my lunch like my friends, but I get only half a sandwich and a piece of fruit.

My father always wolfs down his food at the table, then hiccups for several minutes. I imagine this is the way he learned to eat in the camp—the kind of eating that starved animals do. After dinner, he puts the leftovers into Tupperware, and I see him scoop hasty spoonfuls of macaroni or mashed potatoes into his mouth when he thinks we aren't looking, hunched over the counter protectively. I know this stance, because I've learned it too. Eating like we're shoplifting. When food has spoiled, my mother has to flush it down the toilet to stop my father from pulling it back out of the garbage to inspect it. His standards are significantly lower than ours. I watch him cutting blue fuzz off of crusty bits of cheese that he fishes out of the garbage while chastising us. "You guys are so wasteful. If you cut this little bit of mold off, it's totally edible. Look at this. This is still perfectly good!" *Perfectly good.* He eats the hard pieces of post-surgery cheese just to show us how *perfectly good* it is, even though he just ate a meal and doesn't particularly like the cheese. This is how I learned to live with food, day in and day out.

—

Pacific Palisades, California, 1983

We have rabbits growing up in Pacific Palisades. First we have two rabbits. Then my little sister lets them out of their cages at the same time, and soon we have eight rabbits, then twelve. We can't give the rabbits away fast enough. My sister likes to watch the male rabbit run around the yard after the females, and she keeps opening our painted "Bunny Hilton" hutch before my mother can stop her. So we have a lot of rabbits. At some point, my mother discovers that the supermarket in the center of our small community throws away boxes full of produce every day. So after doing our grocery shopping inside the store, she starts pulling our green Volvo station wagon around the back to their giant Dumpsters. I always slump down low, beneath the window, when she walks brazenly up the ramp to grab crates of wilted lettuce or carrots off the top of the Dumpster, certain one of my school friends will pass by in their movie-star parents' Mercedes-Benz and spot us, and that will be the end of my social life. But it gets more embarrassing than that. One day, my mother spots a box of canned peaches in the Dumpster. The labels are torn, but the cans are intact, so she takes those home too. Then a box of twelve ketchup bottles with only one broken bottle makes its way home with us. And that's how it becomes routine for my mom to climb into the Dumpsters behind the grocery store in one of the most upper-crust neighborhoods in America to root around for several minutes while I hide, knowing it is futile to try to be inconspicuous in our very distinctive mint-green car.

I am half embarrassed but, oddly, also proud sharing this anecdote now. I want to see this aspect of my parents' war trauma as not all bad. On the one hand, I am certain that this hoarding relationship to food contributed to some complex issues and the inherited "Don't finish it!" anxiety my sister and I both have. On the other hand, as a grown woman removed from the privileged community in which I was raised, I am grateful for the lessons in humility that I might have otherwise missed. After all, my irrational fear of there "not being enough" comes from a real fear my parents once felt, a fear based in experiences. And while this fear is the source of some of my dysfunction, I don't want to forget my gratitude that there is enough, and that it isn't something to take for granted.

Some studies have shown that there is a prevalence of eating disorders in the offspring of concentration camp survivors, and I am intrigued by these studies. In one 2004 study in the *European Eating Disorders Review*, out of eleven adult offspring of concentration camp survivors who were interviewed in the admittedly narrow study, ten had eating disorders, and they reported eating disorders in twelve of their seventeen siblings. While that's admittedly a very small study group, I am both alarmed and soothed by that astounding ratio if it can be extrapolated to the broader population. I wonder why more studies have not been conducted on this subject, and whether any behavior can be attributed to nature or nurture. Is disordered eating in my siblings and me a result of my parents' behavior around food, is it a result of societal pressures, or could it have to do with epigenetics, a fairly new, controversial, and inconclusive area of study? I find that I want some sort of scientific explanation for why I struggle against my damaging relationship with food.

Per epigenetic researchers, it is theoretically possible that my father's starvation literally stays in his body and is imprinted on my genes, according to their studies of offspring of concentration camp victims and survivors of the Dutch Hunger Winter. If that turns out to be the case, it would mean I am set up to be susceptible to these issues by a toxic mix of history, physiology, and psychology, but to my mind, it also means there is a physical explanation for some of my problems. My sister and I both struggled with eating disorders in our teenage years and into young adulthood, and have a conflicted relationship with food to this day. As a teen, my sister restricts her food, counting fat grams in everything that passes her lips. I binge and purge, food soothing my anxiety momentarily, then filling me with guilt, causing me to vomit it up for absolution. When I am in my twenties, I can't bear for people to see me eat. I don't feel I deserve to eat and believe people will judge me if they see me eating. I buy a yogurt on the way to class because I haven't eaten lunch and I am running late. As I open it, I see people I know approaching, and I panic, dumping the uneaten container, completely full, in the garbage. The yogurt sits there, taunting me from afar as my stomach growls during class.

Now I can eat in front of people, but it is still with a sense of shame. I imagine that people think I don't deserve to eat anything. Only when I am alone do I feel relaxed when I eat. I no longer purge, but I cannot have large quantities of food in my house when I am alone. An open bag of chips, for example, causes intense anxiety. I spend hours with therapists trying to figure out the source of this anxiety. There is a voice inside of me that tells me that a bag of chips—or any opened package of food in my cupboard or fridge—needs to be eaten immediately because it might be gone later. In an irrational paradox, it's a mirror emotion to my three-year-old sister's "Don't finish it," something along the lines of "Finish it now" so I don't have to live with the building anxiety about finishing it. Is there any proof that my food issues exist solely because of our parents' war trauma? No. There are millions of girls with eating disorders whose parents do not have war trauma, especially in the wealthy suburbs of Los Angeles, where I made extra cash swimming as a background extra on episodes of *Baywatch* as a teen and watched famous supermodels and actresses walk around the grocery store. But I know the charge around food in our household has something to do with my relationship to eating and self-worth, and I know that charge is strongly influenced by my parents' experiences during the war.

In the end, I am left with more questions than answers as I go down the rabbit hole of epigenetics, psychological studies, and the evergreen debate about nature vs. nurture, but I do seize upon a few lines in an article about a 2015 *Biological Psychology* study on Holocaust survivors' children that demonstrates "an association of preconception parental trauma with epigenetic alterations that is evident in both exposed parent and offspring, providing potential insight into how severe psychophysiological trauma can have intergenerational effects." The journal's editor, John Krystal, states, "Holocaust survivors had 10 percent higher methylation than the control parents, while the Holocaust offspring had 7.7 percent lower methylation than the control offspring. The observation that the changes in parent and child are in opposing directions suggests that children of traumatized parents are not simply born with a PTSD-like biology. They may inherit traits that promote resilience as well as vulnerability." I hold on to this last possibility, as I do to another epigenetic study I hear about on the radio, in which grandchildren of starvation victims actually have *more* resilient genes in some areas. Maybe trauma is like a vaccine, and the bodies of the future generations can learn to protect themselves.

17

HOME

Pacific Palisades, California, 1978

As a little girl, I share a bedroom with my sister. When we grow older, my parents build an addition onto the house, a new living room. I am told I can move into the old living room, which will be converted into a bedroom. I am excited to have my own room, a bedroom with a stone fireplace and a sliding glass door to the garden. "We'll go shopping for furniture and make it yours," my mother says. In the meantime, a metal industrial desk, a castoff my father brought home from work, is placed in the room. Temporarily, my brother's old toddler bed, a bed built by my father, is dragged into the room. It has both a headboard and a footboard and is a few inches too short for my body, so I have to sleep on my side with my knees bent to fit in it. My room is a temporary room, but it turns out to be permanently temporary. I should have known. This is how it is for so many things with my parents. After I complain for several years about the bed and the fact that I still don't have a closet for my clothes, my father glues foam cushions to the top of a huge wooden crate that a massive laser had been shipped in, turning the bottom of it into a closet and the top into a bed. An old blanket is hung in front of the windows to keep out the light until curtains can be made. At some point my parents are given an old couch by some friends, so they move the couch into my room—temporarily, of course. There are two things I absorb spending my adolescent years in that room. One is that we will always live with repurposed discards in my family. The other is the perpetual unsettled feeling of transience and transition, a hovering sense of impermanence in the place I call home. I yearn to land, but I don't know how.

I believe that if a person doesn't trust in the permanence of home, then they live in permanent transition. I believe that my parents live in perpetual readiness to leave and never fully settle into a place because that's what they learned from war. And I believe that I learned to live that way too.

—

Pacific Palisades, California, 2000

In 2000, because my father has the opportunity to continue his research at the University of Missouri, my parents move to a rural community just outside of Columbia, and they sell the Pacific Palisades home.

When my parents sell my childhood home, I am absolutely devastated. I count it among the greatest heartbreaks of my life. My mother, on the other hand, is delighted. She has spent thirty years in L.A., a city she never liked in a country to which she feels no sense of membership. I beg them to reconsider, tell them if they can just hold on, maybe I can figure out how to buy the house. I'm in my late twenties, but I regress completely, sobbing and having a full-blown meltdown.

"It's just a house," my mother says in response to my tears, because for her, that's what it is. Her home will always be in Holland, with her brothers and sisters, on their farms. For me, this home, perched on a pinnacle above the city and the sea, is all I have. My grief stems from the fact that I know my immediate family will scatter to different corners of the country once the house is sold, and that will be the end of home for me. We will never come back to this town, this house, this cupped palm that I curled up in for twenty-seven years of my life whenever I needed it. As the boxes are packed and the trips to the Salvation Army with loads of our collective lives become more frequent, I become increasingly despondent, until two nights before they move, my mother stands in the kitchen yelling in response to my tears, "You have to pull yourself up by your bootstraps and get over it!" and I tell her she doesn't understand a thing about not having a single place in the world where you belong completely, and I go outside and throw up in the roses and lay heavy in my melodrama on the driveway, staring up at the stars.

But that is a lie. Of course she understands. It's what makes her carry the memory of things falling from the windows before her home was sealed off from her forever. In a way, I think understanding my hysterical, childlike grief is what makes her so cold about it. There seems to be a bitter kinship in it for her to watch me get the same blow she has gotten in life. It makes her less alone if I feel homeless too. So her impassive "It's just a house" is disingenuous and she knows it. If anyone would know the significance of my loss, it would be her, but she keeps her face stony and tells me to pull myself up by my bootstraps, that life is about adapting to change. I mean, it's easier to be a nomad when you have a tribe to travel with you, right? I am the last person to sleep in the house after my parents' U-Haul drives away. With only a desk lamp and a blanket, I sleep in the hollowed-out skeleton of my former home, until in the twilight a cab pulls up to take me to the airport, where I will fly to Europe with a backpack. In later years, when I move to the Netherlands, I mention in passing to an elderly neighbor how crowded the city is with tourists that day. "What are you complaining about?" he says. "You're a tourist here too. Look at you. Here for a few months and you think you belong." "I'm not a tourist!" I say, stung. "I've been coming here my whole life. I speak the language. I have dual citizenship." He sniffs. "Oh-ho. Dual citizenship. Even worse!"

Since my parents' home was sold, I have had an unhealthy obsession with real estate. I search real estate listings every day. I search them for the places I've lived and the places I've never lived and the places I imagine living. I spend several hours a week looking at photographs and reading descriptions, imagining planting gardens or restoring fireplaces or baking cookies or escorting a friend to the guest bedroom in home after home. I know you can buy a house for $100 in Detroit, $5,000 in Baltimore, $20,000 in Youngstown, $100,000 in Spokane, $1,000,000 in San Francisco. I know where you can buy an old abbey or castle (with moat and turrets) in France, a cottage in the hills of Liguria in Italy, or an apartment on the "Bulgarian Riviera." I have emailed real estate agents from the fields of Maine, from the banks of lakes in Massachusetts, and from the Oregon woods. I go to auctions of foreclosed properties. I compulsively calculate and recalculate mortgage payments and building costs for various home plans I find online. I look at tiny homes on wheels, modern modular homes, old barns, straw bale homes, shipping container homes, pedestal homes for building in floodplains. I learn that there is a loophole in building codes and order a stack of books about underground homes. I send away for brochures on cabin kits and the kit for a saltbox house "that a couple can build in approximately fifteen weekends." "Build yourself a solid future!" the website says.

When I pass abandoned houses, I often stop and walk around them, pulling vines from cracked and rotting windows to peer in at the decaying guts of the structure, imagining myself making a home there. While on a drive in upstate New York, where I live for half a year, I see the massive abandoned brick buildings of a crumbling psychiatric hospital, its ward for the criminally insane surrounded by loops of razor wire. I tell the guy I am dating to pull off the highway to have a closer look. "Let's go. This place is creeping me out," he says as I high-step through the tall grass and under "No Trespassing" signs hanging on chains around the buildings. "This would make an amazing condominium complex!" I answer. I sometimes make appointments to tour homes and squint my eyes as I envision the potential. I look at the broker with my hands on my hips and a pensive look on my face. "Now, tell me, Janet, is this a load-bearing wall? It would be really great to put French doors out to the garden here. Where exactly is the property line? How far down does my land go? All the way to those woods?" I have never actually owned a single piece of real estate.

I do know how ridiculous this is. I know it stems from something more than a casual interest in real estate. Home is not just the place we refer to when we say "It will be nice to sleep in my own bed again." When I talk about home, when I say that losing my home was a real trauma to me, I don't really mean the physical home. I mean home in the sense of citizenship, in every sense of that word. Home as a community. Home as a family. Home as identity. I think the psychological concept of home was the biggest loss for both my parents in the war, so they didn't have it to give me.

—

Pacific Palisades, California, 2011

I stand in front of a ten-foot concrete wall. Behind the wall is my former home. Behind the wall is my tree. I can see the tree's branches peeking above the wall. I have driven here while in Los Angeles for a reunion. The tree is the only thing left that reminds me that this compound was once my house. I know every ridge on that tree's bark, the knot gnarled in the middle of its gray trunk. It's the same tree worn smooth from years of being sat on and hung from by my very own knees. The house is once again for sale, and in the photos on the Multiple Listing Service, the grass is gone, and the tree is now surrounded by a neat square of white pebbles and an uplight to illuminate its branches. It is now merely a tree for looking at. "Views forever from Downtown to the ocean," the listing says. Always there was that. Did I take the forever-views for granted? The current owners have added a bedroom. "Perched on a 17,300 sq ft lot, this 5 bedroom home is a private sanctuary," the listing continues. It makes no reference to the way that children emerged from the hills into each other's backyards in the home's younger days in this neighborhood, whether we knew each other or not. It makes no reference to the way we'd stand on the front lawn, chatting with the neighbors, dog and neighbor dog wrestling at our feet. The house was not a private sanctuary then at all. Now the neighbors would need rappelling equipment to make it inside.

My home has traded up. It is not for my kind anymore.

The freshly planted palm trees communicate this. I would not know how to live in the cavernous spaces created when the current owners knocked down walls, how to actually converse in the stark white "conversation areas." I want the creaky wooden breakfast table. I want the purple chair and the old wooden radio. I want the green player piano with one broken key. But that home has vanished, those relics vanished in yard sales. Months later, I see that the house has sold. My father bought the house in 1965 for $60,000. It sold on July 21, 2011, for $3.5 million. It is now valued at $4.7 million, according to the internet. I think about the people I imagined might have bought it, successful actors or producers, people who paid $3.5 million to show off their giant backyard Buddha and conversation areas to important people. They will eventually sell it, because for them it's just a house.

—

Rocheport, Missouri, 1998

In Missouri, the neighbors have guns and mow acres of lawn on riding mowers, and the sound of cicadas is like a permanent tinnitus. My parents buy a massive ranch-style house in the countryside on a dirt road where the air conditioner has to be on all summer and the heater on all winter. It's just a house. My mother calls me every time the tornado sirens wail. She never heard tornado sirens in California. "It reminds me of the air raid sirens when I was a kid," she tells me, voice shaking, as she sits in the basement under the stairs with the dog. As always, my father spends most of his hours at work in a nondescript brick building on the university campus, and my mother makes the best of it. She rescues a litter of possum babies from a roadkill mother and keeps the one with a physical deformity in its front legs that can't be released back to the wild, holding it on her lap like a cat in the evenings as they watch television. Always rescuing and trying to stitch up life's wounds. She makes baby blankets for strangers she meets in internet groups. She joins a quilting group and makes some friends, but Missouri is not home. This is not home to her children either, and she knows it. We are halfway across the country and can't visit often. When we do, it's like being in a strange land, and we look forward to getting back to California. I feel for my mother, who is simply swept along in my father's choices. And then my brother has a baby, and for the first time ever in my parents' relationship, she insists on having things her way. She is moving back to California with or without him, she says. She is going to be a grandmother. So eventually, my father, whose research project never is fully funded by the university despite his initial optimism, agrees to return to California with my mother.

—

Woodland, California, 2005

My brother lives in Davis, California, but my parents settle in a town called Woodland near Sacramento. It's a generic suburban neighborhood with very little to do. They move there instead of to Davis because my father will not compromise on downsizing. He brings seventy years' worth of things that were dragged from Los Angeles to Missouri and back to California, and he fills all four of the house's bedrooms, a two-car garage, a storage shed in the backyard, and three rented storage units with his things, things he never looks at or uses. The same rusted iron drill press. The same broken lawn chairs. The same carpet remnants and institutional desks and broken coffeemakers. All of the same things that lived in our garage when my siblings and I were growing up live in the garage in my parents' home in Woodland. But the collection keeps growing. Four coffeemakers become five become six. It is here, as I visit my parents and see that they are drowning in things, that I really feel the tragedy of their unresolved war traumas. All of these things my father neither uses nor needs have prevented them from living in Davis, a nicer community closer to their grandchildren, a place where my mother could walk to the store and make friends more easily. People don't visit them often. For many years now, their living room has consisted of an awkward formation of an old couch I gave them when I moved and some wooden banker's chairs, which makes hosting company uncomfortable. They are always planning to get a better couch, but it never happens. The few times I have suggested helping them to organize and sort through the mess, create a more permanent décor in their home, my father flies into a panic, forbidding me to touch his things. My mother gives up. And this is part of her war trauma too. Never be the bad guy. Never go against the grain. So they are two people stuck in a four-bedroom, three-bathroom house filled with things and not people. "There's no place to put anything away, is the trouble," says my father when I say that it's hard for us to come stay there because there are boxes and clutter everywhere. "You need to get rid of a lot of this stuff," I say. "No," says my father. "We need a bigger house."

Meanwhile, I drift from Amsterdam to Massachusetts to the San Francisco Bay Area to Iowa City for four years to get a master's degree and teach, before moving back to Los Angeles and then back to Amsterdam. I'm trying to find home, in every sense of that word, but I know that no one place can be that for me. I know my parents wish I would come back to California more. I know it's a catch-22, that the more I stay away, the more estranged I become, and the more I feel the urge to stay away. I know I should cherish the time with them. But it's difficult to be there at Thanksgiving or Christmas in a strange, half-unpacked house. It doesn't feel like home.

My brother has dealt with our sense of homelessness by focusing on his own family and home, and he is an avowed minimalist, rejecting consumerism and clutter in rebellion against the pack-rat behavior of my parents. My sister is a psychologist, trying to understand our family's trauma that way. She and I talk about our continued wish for roots. She has a husband and a child now, but still we dream about buying a house in the Netherlands, and reminisce about our house in Los Angeles.

Unlike my married siblings, with lost love in my past but no partner and no child, I am untethered. I keep drifting like an old balloon that is leaking its helium, occasionally attempting to touch down with people who feel like they could be my kin, but it doesn't stick. I seek out local woods wherever I go so I can walk the trails; I feel most at home there. After my nature walks, I emerge into neighborhoods, and as I stroll home in the dimming evening, I peer into the windows of families sitting down to dinner, doing homework with their children, playing piano, watering their houseplants, lives framed in window after window like paintings in a museum. Every morning, compulsively, I check the real estate listings and take copious notes, searching. *Amsterdam studio near tram! Petaluma cottage needs TLC. Goosetown charmer just ten blocks from downtown. Perfect for a family! Won't last. Priced to sell! This home has so much potential!*

18

WORDS

Woodland, California, 2013

It's in my parents' current home in Woodland that I find the Dutch-English dictionary my father still has from Indonesia, one of the only surviving items from the camp. I pull it off the shelf. My father comes over and takes the dictionary from me. The title page has been torn out.

"I stole this in the camp," he says. "I was pushing the cart around the camp, collecting the contraband books for the Japanese officers, and I saw this dictionary lying on top. I got it in my head that I needed to learn English, that it was urgent." He laughs, embarrassed. "So I stuffed the dictionary down my pants and hid it. It's so ridiculous," he says. "I thought that when the American soldiers came, they wouldn't know we needed help unless we told them. And I was afraid they would leave us there because we wouldn't be able to speak their language." He laughs again and shakes his head.

My father dismisses the theft of the dictionary as *ridiculous*, but here is the dictionary, in his bookcase in California seventy years later. I am struck by what that actually means.

It means that when his camp was finally liberated by the Americans in September 1945, my father carried that dictionary with him out of the opened gates and to his mother's camp. He carried it while fleeing rebels with guns out of Semarang. He carried it on a Red Cross ship to Ceylon and on to the Netherlands after the war. He carried it across the Atlantic to New York. He carried it on that Greyhound bus for three days straight from New York City to Berkeley, California. He carried it through dozens of boardinghouses as he put himself through UC Berkeley to earn a BS and then an MS and then a Ph.D. in physics, working the Alaska gold mines in the summer and Petaluma chicken farms in the winter. My father is terrible at articulating for me the details of the war or how exactly it still moves inside him, but he carried this little Dutch-English dictionary all of that way, and then through two marriages, four children, and five houses. My father carried this dictionary the way others carry the Bible.

I'm unbelievably moved, especially as a writer, holding this dictionary and knowing its journey and the salvation it represented to a child, and then to the man who carried it with him. I return to the microscopic penciled diaries of the boys in my father's camp that I read in the archives. I return to the privilege of communication. And then I return to this moment:

My father hoards corks. He has done so my entire life. I open the drawer in Woodland, and they are there, dozens of them, as surely as there is toilet paper in the bathroom and food in the fridge. Once, fed up with the clutter in my parents' home, I became irritated and began to empty the corks into the garbage, snapping at my father.

"Come on, Dad, this is madness. You don't need all these

corks. Why are you wasting a drawer with these? This place is a mess."

But he flew into a rage, scooping the corks back out of the garbage. "Don't you throw these away!" he fumed. "You wait. One day you might need these!"

Irked by the complete illogic of such a statement, I responded, "What the hell are you talking about?! What on earth would I need an entire drawerful of corks for?"

"To burn the ends to make charcoal to write with!" he blurted out.

The shouted phrase hung there between us for a moment, pregnant with its absurdity. I was confused by his statement, and I think he felt embarrassed. He turned away and muttered, "Just stop meddling in my business."

"Fine, but that's ridiculous, Dad. You have an entire drawerful of pens, too," I said, shaking my head. His thinking seemed so obviously to have come from a place of deep trauma, not easily combated with reason. But I remembered the camp diaries I read.

13 Sept. Boys fr Lampersari arrived. 19 Sept. J Kramer died. 28 Sept. Won't lend my pencil anymore. Getting too nubby. 1 Oct. Can't think straight. Have the runs. 29 Oct. Have malaria. Pencil just nub now.

When the prisoners' pencils were gone, they burned the ends of corks and wrote with them. I recalled the burning of books, the forced propaganda postcards, the drawings on cigarette papers, the forbidden school lessons in the camp and ABC's written in the dirt with sticks. So I closed the drawer with the corks, and the corks remain part of our daily lives, even if we never use them.

That clear moment of regression into a prisoner's mentality comes full circle and connects to this moment when I stand in a living room in Woodland, holding a dictionary. It's another puzzle piece filling out the big picture for me. Words. Communication. Expression. Things also to be hoarded and guarded in case someone tries to take them away. Corks and dictionaries are part of my father's survival kit.

I am a collector of old books, and I hold the dictionary to my nose to breathe in that particular scent of aged paper. I marvel at the fact that I am holding it in the present day. It's not a small object to travel with. It has substantial weight. Its endurance is remarkable. My hand smoothes over the pages. "Why is there a page missing, Dad?" I say, referring to the dictionary's absent title page. Again, he laughs sheepishly, and takes the dictionary out of my hands. "It had the previous owner's name on that page, so I tore it out." I wait for him to tell me more, but he doesn't elaborate. He flips through the brittle pages slowly, then hands the dictionary back to me. I notice that on the inside cover, next to the torn-out title page, is my father's name. Resolute. Defiant. Handwritten in ink.

I often think about how my own choice to be a writer might have stemmed from the repressed silence of my parents' respective wars, because I knew that we were different and that there was a sadness that ran through my heritage, but it was never articulated. I want to examine everything about my parents' experiences, to try to understand things, and to communicate them. I feel myself intensely connected to a complicated lineage that I want to do my best to put into words. I also feel some sense of duty to tell the narratives of people who are so close to their trauma or their shame that they aren't able to articulate it themselves. I am the generation that can dig through the muck and give them a voice after so many years of silence. My writing is a form of reparation, for myself and for them. While interviewing my parents and their siblings for this book, I watched as the other shoe dropped for my mother, as feelings of anger and grief and recognition of what had been muzzled by shame rose in her and were finally allowed to be explored. Her brother Rob wrote to me, "My mother emphatically and repeatedly told me, when I was not yet ten years old, to keep to myself any political opinion I might have or come to develop, and keep shtum, because [sharing] it was a dangerous thing to do." The silencing was both implicit and explicit for them. I can fight to prevent the same mistakes and trauma of the generation that came before us, and tell the stories they can't to the generations who come after us to remind them to pay attention. And if we believe in fighting for better, then we need to look at the past. By that I mean to communicate to those who feel they have been abandoned in their losses: We're right behind you. All ships.

19

THE SURVIVORS

Though my mother was the child of an Axis power collaborator, and my father an Axis power victim during World War
II, this is only a surface difference. Their war experiences
have more commonalities than differences. And hundreds of
thousands of people like them went through similar traumas.
But despite these hundreds of thousands of victims, the
children of war, their stories aren't often told. The fact that
the Japanese government had POW camps for military prisoners is fairly well known. But the fact that they had brutal
labor camps for *civilian* prisoners including women and
children, where thousands of innocent people were starved
to death, is something that seems to have slipped through the
cracks of common knowledge. Likewise, the internment of
collaborators and sympathizers of the Nazis at even the most
minor levels of involvement after the war ended has also
historically been left out of the main narrative. What happened to the innocent children of these collaborators, the
trauma that many of them underwent after the war, was

never even considered for decades, and they were often too ashamed to call attention to the fact that they were struggling. While the direct victims of the Nazis had government-sponsored therapy and organizations to help them attempt to recover from their trauma beginning immediately after the war, for a long time it was not acknowledged that the children of collaborators were indirect victims of the Nazis too.

I think it's important to make public my parents' narratives for that reason. There are so many victims of war. They don't always look the way we think they look, just as perpetrators don't always look the way we expect them to look. It's controversial to say so, and I've grappled with conflicted feelings for years, but I believe that my mother's parents, while collaborators (at least with regard to her father), can be seen as victims too, a mixture of both. Hitler didn't arise out of a vacuum overnight. A large percentage of his followers, the ordinary members of the public, were victims of lies and propaganda fed to them by his regime, as well as enormous pressure and intimidation if they tried to leave. Later, they were victims of inhumane treatment as prisoners, before they'd even been sentenced for anything. This is one way in which war isn't a zero-sum game where there are no shades of gray. The vast majority of people aren't all good or all bad. Likewise, while I think colonialism was wrong and independence was right, I can sympathize with the individual colonial residents in Indonesia and recognize their loss in being ejected from the only home that generations of their families had known. Again, there is no black-and-white for me here, only a profound sense of sadness, the acknowledgment of which doesn't minimize the victim status of others.

Most of all, recognizing these simultaneous realities

underscores for me my absolute truth that war destroys everybody, regardless of sides. Refusing to see the vulnerabilities and human flaws of perpetrators—at least at the level of those who don't directly carry out torture or murder—refusing to see them as human beings rather than cartoon villains, begs for a repeat of war. I write that with the full knowledge of how difficult it is to do that and how my words may be misinterpreted and cause pain. Even at the conclusion of researching this book, there is no clear moral resolution for me regarding my family history, and perhaps it's fitting that I learn to live in the shades of gray in the middle. As I write this book, political situations are developing across the globe that challenge my own beliefs. There is a rise in white nationalism, and there are increasing attacks on immigrants and minorities in both the United States and other countries. People I know and care about have endorsed candidates and political positions that I find unconscionable, and I struggle to find any understanding of their points of view. At the same time, though it's incredibly challenging for me, I know that simply writing them off as evil, instead of trying to understand why they believe what they believe and then pushing back against the ideology instead of the person, means I will never be able to reach them to change their minds. I recently watched a program that focused on the Adverse Childhood Experiences test as a measure of how likely people were to have future behavioral issues. The test results reflect the level of childhood trauma of a subject. This is then used to provide "trauma-informed care" to address the behavioral issues. What stood out to me was the notion that as a society, we can better fix behavioral problems when we stop asking "What's wrong with you?" and start asking "What happened to you?" It clarifies a cycle of perpetrator and victim, illustrates clearly the overlap that can exist between these labels. When looking at my mother's father, it helps me to view his behavior through this lens. Likewise, it helps me to view those whom I see supporting dangerous ideology in today's political environment through this lens.

—

NSB Children Today

Perhaps of all my mother's siblings, my aunt Hannie, who was like a second mother to me, suffered the most from the war. As the eldest, she understood the most and felt the greatest responsibility. I hadn't realized how much it plagued her life until her death. After her death, her children gave me stacks of articles she had clipped out about the children of NSB members, stacks of newsletters of support groups for the children of collaborators called "Recognition Workgroup" and "Child of Wrong Parents," and special issues of other magazines with titles like *What Did You Do During the War, Mother?* These all were resources for her that became available only when she was well into adulthood, decades after the war.

I also learned that long before I visited the National Archives to see my grandparents' NSB dossiers, my aunt Hannie and uncle Pim, both deceased in the past decade, paid a similar visit and took notes, including of their thoughts on what they viewed. Their notes speak to the complicated pain of having parents who were on the wrong political side in World War II and show how this affected the psyches of that generation of NSB children. Some two hundred thousand children of NSB members never received any psychological care after the war, nor were they considered victims at that time. But my uncle's and aunt's written notes give us another perspective as my uncle recounts their discussion in a café after reading the dossiers of their parents:

> The first feeling that came up in us was: Glad that we no longer live in that period; it was an incomprehensible morass in which it was hard to make the right choice—and our parents didn't succeed in doing so. Naiveté played a role in their choices in the political arena . . .
>
> We think the punishment was quite severe for their offenses. On the other hand, we have to remember that in 1945 the situation was chaotic and internment may have saved political delinquents from lynch parties.
>
> The second generation is made up of the children who have been handed the bill. First, through the fact that our family was torn apart. In addition, we suffered from the fact that on the one hand we felt loyal to our parents, but on the other hand to the victims of the political system that they chose.
>
> As far as we are concerned, the bond with our parents remained, even as we, retrospectively, don't endorse their political views. The aggression that prevailed towards the occupier and the NSB partially came to lay on our shoulders. As siblings we had to support one another more than normal, which actually strengthened the underlying bond: Home, inside the family, was our only safe harbor; outside of that it was a jungle.
>
> Altogether, the subsequent psychological effects on the family De Kock could have been worse. From recent documentaries on NSB children we learned that others suffered even worse than we did.
>
> It seems as though this visit to look at our family history was a final step in integrating our past into our present lives. From this point forward we can continue down the track without Gordian knots, and with some life lessons.

In the Netherlands, there has been a new movement in the last couple of decades to speak openly about what was done to the families of NSB members after the war. Dutch books such as *Wrong and No Good* (2010) by Koos Groen, along with documentary films featuring interviews with children of NSB party members and allies of the German occupiers who tell shocking stories of deplorable treatment, have only recently started to appear as the country finally seems ready to talk in a more nuanced way about a deeply painful and traumatic period in their history.

In an article for the *Historisch Nieuwsblad* titled "The Last Taboo in the Netherlands: NSB Children," Bas Kromhout wrote, "Many children of parents who were 'wrong' during World War II feel themselves as outsiders in Dutch society. Even in the extensively documented history of the occupation years and their aftermath, they still come in last place." Kromhout's observations are based on the first real study done, in 2002, on the effects the war had on children of NSB members. He wrote, "For the first time, children of 'wrong' parents have been systematically surveyed on such a large scale. The results don't lie: a large group of children of NSBers have serious struggles to date due to their parents' pasts and the social rejection they experienced after 1945. Even though they are not guilty of the crimes committed in the name of the NSB, they still feel tainted." The study concluded, among other things, that among the 229 now-adult children of NSB members surveyed, almost all had been "bullied and cursed at by classmates and neighborhood children" during the war, and:

- 75% had difficulty developing and maintaining relationships

- 16% were interned behind barbed-wire fences, while 24% were put into children's homes or foster care
- 42% made a traumatic escape to Germany [during and immediately after the country's liberation] and 10% went into hiding
- 75% of their parents did not reintegrate into Dutch society, causing the children to withdraw from society as well
- 59% felt their educations had been stifled as a result of their parents' affiliation and 49% their career opportunities
- 85% suffered from psychological and psychiatric problems, including extreme fear of failure, social phobias, depression, and/or suicidal ideation and attempts
- 57% experience the national day of remembrance for the victims of the Nazi occupation on May 4 as an extremely difficult day
- 92% felt they had paid a high price for the pasts of their parents

Kromhout further shared some of the specific difficulties that those who were surveyed added, and the stories all have the same thread running through them. One man called May 4, the Day of Remembrance in the Netherlands, when the city observes a minute of silence and lays wreaths for the victims of the Holocaust, "the most terrible day of the year." He felt he must show his respect by going to Dam Square in Amsterdam, where a ceremony is held. "To show that I feel awful about what happened. I felt all alone between the people; I thought they could see it by looking at me." This man was an infant when the war ended. This year, I found myself in Amsterdam on May 4, and I too walked to Dam Square alone to stand among hundreds of people, tears welling during the minute of silence. Afterward, I laid a flower on the monument for the dead, and astonished myself with the level of guilt that I, generations removed, felt about the past. In Kromhout's study, a woman who has lived in the same village in the Netherlands her whole life and was the teenage daughter of NSB members during the war speaks of her struggles with the Day of Remembrance too. "On that day, [the congregation] won't let me sing along with the choir in my church." More than half a century later, she is still being punished for her parents' sins.

The study goes into depth about how the NSB children have been specifically traumatized, identifying common issues caused by a number of mutual triggers. The first is the shared sense of duty to keep the family secret, and I realize that this too is a trauma that is passed down to subsequent generations. I am breaking the taboo by publicly acknowledging our family history, but for decades I didn't dare talk about it. I remember the classmate who said all people who had anything to do with the Holocaust should have been killed, and recall my secret shame. When I began working on this book and submitted my application to an artists' residency, I wrote that if chosen, I would be working on a book "about my father's internment in a Japanese concentration camp and my mother's experiences in Nazi-occupied Holland." I deleted the last half of that line and inserted: ". . . experiences as the daughter of Nazi sympathizers in WW II Holland." The cursor blinked. My stomach knotted. I deleted that line. Inserted: ". . . experiences in an orphanage after her parents were arrested as Nazi sympathizers in

WW II Holland." I deleted that line. Inserted: ". . . experiences in Nazi-occupied Holland." My cursor blinked at me. *Liar. Liar. Liar.* Why couldn't I just write it?

The second common trauma among the children of NSB members is the often inadequate warehousing of these children while their parents were interned. Many, like my mother, went to children's homes or foster care, but a number of them were also interned in camps. The separation from their families, as well as mistreatment and hunger after the war, affected many NSB children.

In addition, most families experienced financial ruin. Like my mother's home, their homes were sometimes looted before they returned from internment. If they had rental homes, their possessions were sold or taken by landlords. They struggled to find work, as people were reluctant to hire former NSB members. Many families were homeless because landlords would not rent to them, and ended up in government-appointed housing. The ensuing poverty resulted in a tangible trauma for many of the children. My mother's family was comparatively lucky to get to live in the summer cottage in Hoog Soeren, and my grandfather very lucky to get a job in Amsterdam, though he would not be allowed to teach again.

The fourth common traumatic experience identified in the study is an institutional rejection. Children of NSB parents experienced bullying but report that their teachers and the other children's parents did little to stop it, and in a few cases actually joined in. Church congregations and groups could also be very harsh toward NSB families. One of the respondents reported that in his Sunday school, "NSB children had to sit apart from the rest and at Christmas they got nothing." Generally, the understandable anger in the community after the occupation simmered for years, and this was made evident in the open hostility an NSB family could expect in stores, schools, churches, places of employment. The nuclear family often became the only place of security, and society outside, as my uncle articulated it, a "jungle" they should fear.

Internally, families also became volatile as parents dealt with the stresses. Parents fought, placing blame on each other for their political choices. Parents sometimes emerged from the internment camps for political delinquents with PTSD symptoms if they had been tortured, and the children were also the victims of this if the parents who returned after serving their sentences were not the same parents they remembered.

Today, we still see the shame and guilt of family members of those on the "wrong side of history," for whom the war is still very present. In the past couple of decades, they are occasionally interviewed for news programs in the Netherlands, something that would not have been done even forty years ago. NSB children, now elderly, dissolve into tears as they recall their childhoods as the objects of loathing, being teased by both children and adults alike, and not having any way to reconcile their love for and dependence on parents who were deemed evil by their communities.

In 1981, the first support group for the children of NSB members was established, Werkgroep Herkenning, "Recognition Workshop," though it would not be acknowledged as legitimate until the mid-1990s, according to their website. I know my aunt got great comfort from her membership in the group. In 1988, more than forty years after the end of the war, the first child of an NSB member was interviewed on national television without concealing her identity, and thus began a serious conversation about the real war trauma this overlooked group of people had experienced. To this day, there is still debate in the Netherlands, with some people expressing outrage over the notion that the NSB families could be labeled as victims, but in general, the public has begun to take a more nuanced look at the events of the war and the mistakes made in the postwar quest for justice.

FORMER POWs OF WORLD WAR II JAPAN TODAY

The survivors of World War II are thinning as the generation that experienced it firsthand enters old age. The newsletter for the survivors of my father's camp has faltered as the president and members pass away. Years ago, when I began researching my father's war experiences, I attended a reunion of survivors and got excellent information from them. They all told me how surprised they were to see a young person there. Survivor after survivor told me, "My kids don't really want to know about it." They wrote about my visit in the newsletter, *The Bangkonger*, and the president of the group occasionally sent me memories from the camp. He told me how touched he was that somebody was going to tell their stories. He died before his story could be shared, as did a number of the men I met at that reunion. I can only hope that the promise of sharing my father's story, and by proxy theirs, gave them some comfort, because for most of the years following their internment, the world didn't seem to know or care.

A 2008 report of the Global Law Research Center for the U.S. Law Library of Congress on Japan's World War II forced-labor compensation cases states, "Japanese courts have been dealing with post-WWII compensation cases from foreigners since approximately 1990. In the cases of POWs, forced laborers, and comfort women, some lower courts have awarded compensation, but most of them have not." In 2007, the U.S. Supreme Court decided the outcome of most of these cases when they ruled that victims of the Japanese war crimes during World War II have no recourse to restitution because of the San Francisco Peace Treaty signed by forty-eight Allied nations on September 8, 1951. The treaty officially brought hostilities with Japan to an end. But with it, the Allied nations signed away their rights to legal justice for their citizens who had been affected by Japan's war crimes. Further, Japan maintains that reparations were already made, per the treaty.

Japan had paid £4,500,000 to the Red Cross, it claimed, to compensate civilian POWs. This money, a paltry sum to cover all the global victims, never made it to the individual POWs, as it was used by the Red Cross for its operations, including repatriating the POWs. Furthermore, according to historian Linda Goetz Holmes, these funds "were not Japanese government funds, but several million dollars of relief funds contributed by the governments of the United States, United Kingdom, and Netherlands . . . and sequestered in the Yokohama Specie Bank . . . by the Japanese government during the final year of the war." Article 14 of the treaty further states that Japan acknowledges that it should pay "for the damage and suffering caused by it during the war," but that it is unable to pay and maintain its economic stability. It states that Japan will enter negotiations with countries affected by its occupation to compensate for the "cost of repairing the damage done."

Again, no money from these actions made its way to POWs like my father, but Japan considered its obligations met with the San Francisco Peace Treaty. And yet, beginning in 1994, the first cases were filed against Japan for restitution to the people it had harmed. Per the Congressional report, "The first western POW case was filed in 1994 in Japan. In this case, Dutch POWs and civilian internees sued the Japanese government, seeking damages for their suffering while they were detained by the Japanese military in East Indochina during WWII." My father was part of this class of plaintiffs. This began many years of debating semantics. The Japanese government had destroyed the records of its war crimes, and if an official record did not exist, the government could not be responsible for reparations. Further, the San Francisco Peace Treaty was used repeatedly to block further action. It also asserted that "claims of nationals of the Allied Powers were 'abandoned' by the Allied Powers." In other words, Japan claims that the failure of Allied nations to pursue the restitution further on behalf of its citizens over the years meant that they were no longer liable and any claims "ceased to exist." Other cases have been brought by individuals and classes, and emails have been exchanged with lawyers representing class action suits, but ultimately, the United States, like other Allied nations, halted further lawsuits against Japan in order to keep the peace, citing sovereign immunity. Aside from a little over one thousand dollars distributed in 1991 to each survivor of the camps, which was paid out by the Dutch government in lieu of Japanese reparations, my father will never see any compensation for the loss of his home, possessions, and childhood, or for the abuse and starvation committed against him in violation of international law. In 2016, Prime Minister Shinzō Abe of Japan finally formally apologized to the hundreds of thousands of "comfort women" who were systematically selected and raped by Japanese forces during the Japanese occupation. The Japanese government

gave $8.5 million to an advocacy group as a symbolic ges-
ture. The hope for further financial or legal restitution for
the victims of Japan's war crimes is now unlikely.

My father and the men I spoke to from his camp are less
interested in legal or financial reparations than they are in
recognition. Like all human beings, they seek the healing that
comes only from the simple words we all long to hear after
being wounded: *I'm sorry I hurt you.* But getting this apology without a list of caveats undermining the official apology has been a long and bumpy road for survivors. The
Japanese government has been extremely reluctant to acknowledge its war crimes officially or as part of its national
history. Seventy years after the end of World War II, controversy and conflict regarding the Japanese government's re-
luctance to fully come to terms with the past have only
intensified.

Debate continues over whether or not the Japanese government, the Allied governments, and the media have done
enough to acknowledge what many in former occupied nations dub the "Asian Holocaust." Perhaps because of this lack
of similar attention to what Nazi Germany received after
World War II, most Westerners remain unaware that as many
civilians died at the hand of Japan as at the hand of the
Nazis, with estimates ranging from a low of 6 million civilians (by political scientist and war historian R. J. Rummel)
to a high of 20.3 million (by Werner Gruhl, author of *Imperial Japan's World War II*).

While the Holocaust has rightfully gotten worldwide attention and the survivors and victims have been memorial-
ized in popular culture so that we may never forget, Japan's
crimes during the war have managed to avoid similar wide-
spread attention from the general public. It is only in the past
decade that its government has considered removing the

names of over a thousand convicted war criminals from its
Yasukuni Shrine honoring its war dead. Japan has also had
controversy surrounding its history textbooks, which have
tended to whitewash the Japanese government's actions in
World War II, with the Ministry of Education rejecting textbooks with references to internment camps, comfort
women, and the Rape of Nanking.

The minimization of Japanese war crimes is being addressed within Japan, however, and past decades have seen
leaders take increasing accountability, offering official con-
dolences for its war crimes. But these apologies are often interpreted as half apologies by victims, the "I'm sorry you
were hurt by the unfortunate thing that occurred when you
offended me" so many people are familiar with, rather
than the "I'm sorry I hurt you" they long to hear. Over the
years, the apologies have referred to the "unfortunate events,"
"regretful error," or "unfortunate past" of the war. Emperor
Hirohito's 1984 statement—"It is indeed regrettable that
there was an unfortunate past between us for a period in this
century"—has turned into Abe's apology in 2015, which begins by stating that Japan "lost sight of overall trends in the
world" after World War I, and apologizes for the "countless
losses" "in countries that fought against Japan" such as
China.

I'm struck by that phrase in particular. "Countries *that
fought against Japan*" seems an odd way to describe countries in which Japan was the occupier. I can understand why
victims may feel that the apologies contain asterisks and fine
print. The language is overtly passive, and Abe describes the
countries Japan invaded as "the battlefields [where] numerous innocent citizens suffered and fell victim to battles as well
as hardships such as severe deprivation of food," avoiding using the active voice, as though these countries spontaneously

became battlefields on their own. In the speech, he offers his sincere apologies, but only couched within descriptions of the atomic bomb victims and the former POWs of Japan who have come to Japan to pray for the war dead on both sides.

Of course, the United States is guilty of similar resistance over the decades, with Barack Obama being the first American president to officially pay his respects to Japan's atomic bomb victims with a visit to Hiroshima. Paying respect is not about assigning heroes and villains or creating two sides, but about acknowledging the losses of innocent people caused by war. I still remember the time a Japanese colleague of my father's visited us in Los Angeles. My father spoke some Japanese to him, and the man asked how he knew the language. When my father told him he had learned it in a Japanese internment camp, the man became very emotional. "I am sorry for what my country did to you," the man said. My father told him he didn't need to be sorry for something he had played no part in, but just hearing those words spoken genuinely and with empathy made a big impression on him. I think the mere recognition that something happened to him that deeply altered his life was immensely healing.

I myself would like to see more explicit attention paid to the losses experienced due to the Japanese occupation in the Pacific during World War II, and for this history to be as much in dialogue with Western culture as the war in Europe and the Holocaust has been, both in film and art, as well as in classrooms and literature. Not only do I think it is important for the Western survivors of the internment camps like my father to be acknowledged and their trauma addressed, but the vast majority of the Japanese forces' victims in World War II were millions of Asians, and with the singular focus on the Nazi occupation, I think there is a great deal of Eurocentrism in our Western understanding of the Second World War. It's important that we address this, because an attitude in the West of dismissal toward regions we deem as less important can lead to events such as the Rwandan genocide of 1994, during which the Western world turned a blind eye and the United Nations refused to send aid as an estimated 800,000 people were slaughtered. As long as we continue to divide the world according to our "us and them" mentality, I believe these tragedies will continue. This is not just about politics. Because when we talk about politics we are talking about people.

In a clearing of his internment camp many years ago stood a boy with his arms raised to the plane above. On a ship to the United States a woman thought about a new life ahead in a place where she was not fout. As I write this, quite coincidentally, it is my parents' fiftieth wedding anniversary, a date I know they have reached despite challenges and conflicts along the way from which others might have turned away. It has been fifty years since the flickering home movies were filmed in the port of Rotterdam, my mother waving her silk scarf at her family below and my father zooming in on his bride. I'm now in Amsterdam and call her in California. "Mom, how does it feel, being married for fifty years?" "Old!" she says, laughing, and the digital phone line warbles her voice in transmission. "I hear you," I say. My mother's voice settles. "Oh, sweetheart. We've come through a lot."

EPILOGUE

As there are neuroses and dysfunctions I have inherited from my parents' war, there are also gifts. I grew up in the United States, a country that has seen very few wars on home soil, and none since the Civil War. The wars we tend to be most aware of in this country—World War II, Korea, Vietnam, Iraq, Afghanistan—live mainly as secondhand knowledge if we are not in the active military, shaped by our history books and media and imaginations. Americans tend to prefer clean, categorical narratives about war. They prefer conflicts with clear victims and perpetrators, examples of good and evil. Having grown up with my parents, I understand that narratives don't often fall neatly into that formula.

My father was a colonist, part of a system of colonialism that his father and his father's father were part of. Those in academia and elsewhere tell me that as a colonist, he is the oppressor, and that therefore, his claims to victimhood are null and void, because they defy the conventional dichotomy.

Critiques by peers of my past writing that mentioned my father's war experiences as a Dutch colonist invariably included several notes in this vein, and I am often forced to justify his entitlement to a voice at all, pushing me back into the dichotomy I want to avoid. When I say that my father's Indonesian babu cared about him and that he cared about her, it is problematic because of the colonial relationship. But still, inconvenient as it is to acknowledge, this is a true thing; we are talking about real people and their relationships, not simply the dynamics of systemic power structures. It was also true that my father's djongos, Suwardjo, was upset when the family was taken away by the Japanese, and that he followed them to Semarang and lived outside of their internment camp, waiting for their release. "In the history books, when the war ended, the Indonesian people revolted and won independence," my father says now. "But all Indonesians weren't the same. There were Indonesians who weren't happy at all when the Japanese invaded during World War II and took power from the Dutch. It wasn't a simple question of good and bad. It was a mixture." When Sukarno took power in Indonesia, ending Dutch colonial rule, Dutch families like my father's had to leave the country they had called home for centuries. A necessary moment in history, true. A painful moment for many of the people in the system, also true. My grandmother gave Suwardjo all of the money she had left when he appeared in the camp at the end of the war, hoping to get his old job back. Injured by bombs in the Semarang harbor where he had worked in the shipyards after their internment, he was crushed to learn there was no place for him with the family anymore.

I certainly am not trying to justify colonialism. But to place humans into a predictable narrative is simplistic and reductive. All Americans besides those who are indigenous or descended from slaves are also part of an oppressive colonialist system, regardless of our personal politics, though I suspect many of us don't consider that context of America as a continued colonial occupation or think of ourselves as colonists in our daily lives. Informal surveys on social media suggest that most Americans in my circle do not, which is interesting to me considering that most of them are also academics with knowledge and strong opinions about historic colonialism in other parts of the world. Part of what I want to illuminate is the ease with which we grasp for simple narratives that elide the complexity of history. I'm susceptible to this myself, and am reminded of it when I hear my parents' stories. I am surprised when my father talks about colonial Indonesia in the 1940s and refers to the neighbor whose father is German and whose mother is a black woman from Suriname, a medical doctor and the breadwinner in the family. I am surprised when he talks about the indigenous Indonesian doctors his father worked with who lived in mansions and had servants too. I'm surprised when I learn of my grandmother's deep friendships and my great-aunt's business ventures with local Indonesian women in their communities during the colonial era, including "Aunt Soer," who was considered part of my father's family. On the ground, Dutch colonialism looked different than we imagine it.

It is difficult to write about personal human struggle when saddled with a rigid view of history. I find it frustrating that I must always grapple with the evils of colonialism first when writing about my father's war experience at the hands of the Japanese. How we would be burdened when telling the stories of personal suffering of Americans if we had to preface them all with the fact that the United States is itself a product

of violent oppression of the native people. We should be able
to hold two truths at once.

Even if we could cleanly divide the world into "good guys"
and "bad guys," we'd still have difficulty keeping the players
straight. Because what do we do with life's tangled and shifting narrative? The Dutch as colonialists oppress the Indonesians. The Japanese arrive with Koreans they have oppressed
and imprison and brutalize the Dutch. The Japanese are initially seen as liberators of the Indonesians, but soon the
Indonesians realize that they are being oppressed by the
Japanese as well and turn against them. The Allied forces of
Dutch, Americans, and British liberate the Dutch and defeat
the Japanese. The Indonesians revolt against the Dutch and
begin attacking innocent civilians. And the former Japanese
and Korean occupiers, who haven't even had a chance to
leave the country after their defeat, are now enlisted by the
Allied troops to defend their former Dutch prisoners against
the attacks of the Indonesians. The roles of villain and victim change places so often, it's dizzying.

War lives in the human experience, in the personal. Where
in the collective narrative do I place German soldiers hiding
their enemies beneath their train seats and feeding them their
own lunch? Where do I place a Korean officer dragging a piano out of hiding on Christmas and allowing his prisoners
to play it? A Japanese officer crouching next to a homesick
child in a prison camp and telling him that he's homesick too,
and that they both need to stay strong to get through the
war? Nazi sympathizers being beaten, tortured, shaved bald,
and their children left on the street by the people supposedly
on the "right side" of the conflict? Dutch citizens condemn-
ing the Holocaust but snatching up their Jewish neighbors'

possessions and homes for a bargain price when they are taken away to the concentration camps?

My grandfather was a Nazi sympathizer, the great shame of the family. My cousin cannot share this fact with his wife's family because they'd hold it against him. For decades after the war, her parents refused to serve Germans in their bakery.

For a long time, I internalized the monolithic narrative fed to us, and believed that there was some kind of rottenness I had inherited from my grandfather, as if Nazism were something that could be detected in the blood. After all, people are proud of their successful ancestors. Wouldn't it follow that we would feel shame about the ancestors who did bad things? I spend a lot of time thinking about the children of SS officers in Germany, about the children of terrorists or serial killers. I want to know how they reconcile their parents' acts with the love they feel for them.

I search online for information about Hitler's family. I want to know if he had children, and what happened to them. There are no offspring, it turns out. In fact, the Hitler bloodline ended in 1987. There are claims that this was a deliberate choice on the part of the descendants. If it was, I can understand this impulse. When you grow up with the unspoken fear that your legacy is shame, that your identity is tainted, then, like my mother, you want to call as little attention to yourself as possible, to be as small as possible. And if your last name is Hitler, what could make you smaller than disappearing? Several of the descendants of the most famous Nazis, including those in the Göring, Himmler, and Höss families, have intentionally ended the bloodlines with themselves, as told in the documentary *Hitler's Children*. Their grief, shame, and sense of culpability run that deep.

The fact that a person can feel conflicted about their

feelings toward the people they love is what keeps the thousands of children and grandchildren of Nazi sympathizers silent. Even racist, alcoholic abusers sometimes tuck their children into bed at night with sweet kisses or take in a hungry stray cat. I don't like to think about those things. It upsets a social code of safe, identifiable characters to contend with. But the children of our villains don't have that luxury. They actually have to contend with the Nazi who takes them fishing and sings lullabies, the one who is flesh and blood and not just a one-sided concept.

My family went to the screening of a documentary in which the filmmaker discovered that his grandparents had been Nazis. The filmmaker was there, and there was a lengthy, heated discussion afterward with the audience about complicity during and guilt about World War II. Our family sat in absolute silence as people all around us, Americans with no direct ties to the Holocaust, offered their opinions. Because how could my mother tell a roomful of Americans that she was fout, that her father was fout, but that she loved him anyway? How can she tell people she suffered during the war because her parents were allied with the Nazis and ask for their empathy? Like those who say my father's suffering in a concentration camp is problematic because of his membership in a colonialist system, my mother's family's suffering is canceled out because of their affiliation with the Nazis. So she submits to the accepted narrative. She holds her tongue.

My father never admits he's fallible. When we play board games in my family, we always refer to my father as the straight man. He invariably bumbles the rules, and as we tease him, he looks perplexed, protesting in mock outrage.

"What? That's how you're supposed to do it!" We correct him, and during his next turn, he makes the same mistake, and we all laugh at the idiocy of it. He's good-natured about the ribbing, but then I am pretty sure he knows he's playing the straight man and does it on purpose. This refusal to admit to weakness is fun in that circumstance, but often it's infuriating. When he loses something, he accuses others of stealing it. When he drives into a pole, it's the fault of the people who put the pole there and the car manufacturer for making the brake pedal too far from the gas pedal and the glare of the sun for blinding him.

This is extremely annoying to those of us who have been living with it for decades. On the other hand, this is the same quality that makes my father "unbreakable," as my mother calls it. Not being willing to show weakness or defeat under any circumstance is what keeps my father persevering long after others would give up. He keeps moving forward no matter what. *All ships follow me.* Once, hopelessly lost on a family vacation in France, all of us frustrated and near tears, I said, "Forget staying in Paris. Let's just get off here and find a hotel. We are miles off course." And my father replied, "We are not off course. There are many ways into a city." He kept going, and we did eventually get to see Paris. So while my friends and I have made a joke out of the phrase "There are many ways into a city," I find myself saying it to myself when I meet an obstacle. "There are many ways into a city," I say when a friend and I arrive at a restaurant to find it closed, when I get turned down for a research grant, when somebody tells me no.

I try to be the ship that will follow my father in going forward against the odds, because it's not my own nature to shake these things off and keep moving. That's just my survivor father speaking in me, a positive inheritance of his war. I'm ashamed to admit that there has been more than one occasion on which my father has helped me move that features me standing in tears in a half-packed apartment the day before a moving truck has been reserved, saying, "Forget it. I can't do this. Let's cancel the truck." And my father has gotten me through, because surrendering is simply not an option for him. I can't say whether my father brought that quality into the war or whether he learned it during the war or a little bit of both, but I know that it's what got him through the war, and that his maddening refusal to admit his short-comings comes from a relentless will to survive.

I have thought a great deal about the irony of victimhood. We think that acknowledged victims are the most damaged and suffer the most, but when I look at my parents, I see the reverse effect. I see the power my father derived from sur-viving abuse, and the weakness my mother learned from her family's perpetrator status. Victims are by default survivors. Victimhood goes hand in hand with the concepts of triumph and overcoming. We have survivors' groups and resources and fund-raisers, and we openly champion the strength of victims. Victims are permitted and encouraged to be resil-ient and to speak their pain. But perpetrators and their children? Perpetrators are given no survivor status. We have programs for reconciliation, and increasingly, with time, we have more open dialogue to heal the scars of conflict. But society doesn't really allow you to overcome being fout emotionally. It's a perpetrator's burden to carry being fout with them until the day they die. For many children of per-petrators, the emotional burden is extremely painful for them, too. The grandchild of Auschwitz commander Ru-dolf Höss, in an interview with *The Telegraph*, commented,

"I can't forgive the burden he brought into our lives. We had to carry a very heavy cross."

When I think about the trauma I have inherited from my parents' war experiences, I acknowledge the neurosis, anxiety, and compulsions I learned from my father. But I believe that the trauma my grandfather passed down to me through my mother is far more damaging on an existential level. It is the trauma of an eternal and unchangeable identity of being somehow inherently fout by blood, of not having the right to survive and succeed. I know, of course, that I didn't make the choices, and that my grandfather's actions are not my mother's or mine. But much as a person feels connected and special for having a notable ancestor, I feel connected to a legacy of shame and the most notable mass murder of the modern era. And my mother feels it more so, because she experienced the wrath firsthand. And so she passed on to me *be selfless, don't rock the boat, let the rest go first, don't be greedy, don't disagree with others, tell people what they want to hear, live frugally, sacrifice.*

My father hoards corks, my mother has an inferiority complex, and we all have trouble expressing ourselves without showing our damage. But we are doing our best with this ghost in our midst. There's no way to undo the psychological effects of war completely, but at some point in the chain of that multigenerational pileup, the last car will absorb the remaining energy and come slowly to rest. Then we will all climb out of our dented vehicles and peer back into the fog, our hands on our hips, and get to the business of calling a tow truck or helping the injured. I'm trying to overcome my tendency to sacrifice myself. I'm trying to use up the last inch of shampoo instead of saving it out of a feeling of lack, and to let the potato chips remain uneaten in the cupboard because they will still be there tomorrow. I'm trying to see the universe as abundant and benevolent. I'm working to create a sense of home.

One of the great frustrations of writing this book has been the discovery that the narrative, as I come to understand it, keeps shifting. My parents correct me about things I misinterpreted, new information comes to light that challenges my previous assumptions, and I learn that my understanding of the past is wholly subjective, no matter how much I research. However, the more the ghost takes shape for me, the more I can see its movements, and being able to see it has always been the main problem for me. *So that's where that comes from,* I think when I hear the stories, and some dark part of me that I don't understand begins to fill in with pictures and color. I may not have the memories of my parents' wars, and I will never know exactly how it all really happened, but when I see the source of my learned habits and fears, I can at least reclaim them from a battle that was never mine. I am doing my best with the neuroses, just like my parents, like we all do with our myriad traumas. I am finding my way forward, as are they.

Wars don't emerge out of understanding, compassion, or reason, and they are rarely simple, much as we would like to entrench ourselves in clearly delineated ideology. As I write this, Syrian men, women, and children flood into Western nations to escape a tyranny based on "us and them" thinking in their home countries, only to find themselves on the other side of "us and them" discrimination in the countries of their refuge. Neofascism is on the rise globally, with far-right political parties gaining power in multiple countries. Huge segments of the population are poised to enter into another violent global battle based on simplistic dichotomous thinking. Racial tensions, religious tensions, and class tensions all are increasing again. Already, a whole new generation of children are suffering the wounds of war and persecution that they will pass on to their children in turn. Some of them, when their families try to flee violence to other countries, are separated and placed in youth detention centers while their parents are prosecuted as undocumented immigrants, causing further trauma. This is why it matters that we lay bare the whole complicated, conflicted snarl of the past, examine our preconceptions, and try to do better. My family is just one family with transgenerational trauma. There are millions. It's time to talk.

ACKNOWLEDGMENTS

This book was many years in the making, from conception to realization. I had a great deal of help along the way, for which I am immensely grateful. Thank you first and foremost to my parents, Else and Sjef, and my siblings, Boukje and Jelmer, as well as to the extended Eerkens and de Kock families, who allowed me to expose them on the page and gave so freely and generously of themselves when I had questions. In particular, thank you to Rob and Orselien de Kock, Bouk de Kock, Jozien Verschoof, Liesbeth Verschoof, Joost Verschoof, Petra Verschoof, Cees and Metty Eerkens, Willemien de Kock, Hanke de Kock, Sjoeke van der Meulen, Aris van Hoeflaken, Maaike van Hoeflaken, and Frans van Hoeflaken, as well as the late Hannie de Kock, Pim de Kock, and Fieneke Verschoof, for their contribution to my family research. Thank you to the kind employees of the Netherlands Institute for War Documentation (NIOD) and the Dutch National Archives for the hours of research in their libraries. For their gift of time, space, and/or financial support, I'd like to express my gratitude to the Virginia Center for the Creative Arts, the James Merrill House, Hambidge Center for the Arts, Foundation Obras, the Stanley Foundation, and the John Anson Kittredge Fund. This book would never have found its way to print without my supportive and hardworking agent, Sarah Levitt, and my amazing editor, Anna deVries, whom I appreciate immensely. Thank you to Sibylle Kazeroid for her copyediting, and to my publicist, Brianna Scharfinberg. Thank you also to all my former colleagues, professors, and workshop cohorts at the University of Iowa's Nonfiction MFA program who read various parts of this in its earliest fragments, and in particular Robin Hemley, Patricia Foster, John D'Agata, Geoff Dyer, and Matthew Clark Davison for their guidance. Thank you (in no particular order) to Amy Butcher, Kerry Howley, Kristen Radtke, Inara Verzemnieks, Zaina Arafat, Rachel Yoder, Ariel Lewiton, Jen Percy, Lina Maria Ferreira Cabeza-Vanegas, Matt Siegel, Cheryl Strayed, Rachel Pearson, Julie Rae Mitchell, Shana Ting Lipton, Bryan Castille, Dorothianne Carr and all "Camp Dot" residents, Huan Hsu, Alice Elliott Dark, Diederik van Vleuten, Franca Treur, and Kyle Minor, for their various words of book-related encouragement, input, and/or inspiration over the years when I needed each of those things to keep going in my writing.

If I included all the people I love in this list, there wouldn't be room, but know that you are acknowledged and thanked too, for all the things you do to support and nourish me.